D0260545

Questions & Answers

Cost
Accounting

Questions & Answers

Cost Accounting

Second Edition

Richard Jenkins

First published in Great Britain 1983 by Financial Training Publications
Limited, Avenue House, 131 Holland Park Avenue, London W11 4UT.

© Financial Training Publications Ltd, 1983
   Second Edition, 1986

ISBN: 1 85185 017 1

Typeset by LKM Typesetting Ltd, Paddock Wood, Nr Tonbridge
Printed by The Garden City Press Ltd, Letchworth, Herts

Contents

Introduction

All of the questions in this book are of examination standard, though they range from questions that are a simple test of knowledge to those which require a more complex and analytical approach. The questions give relevant and comprehensive examination practice to all students of accountancy, and in particular those who are studying for degree courses and professional examinations.

The book is divided into 23 chapters, each of which contains up to 10 questions. Each chapter is prefaced by an explanation of the type of question and subject area covered and also suggests specific study requirements necessary before tackling the questions.

Each chapter starts with the more simple questions and concludes with the more difficult. In general, the simpler questions in Chapters 1 to 17 represent the sort of problems likely to be encountered by a student preparing for the Institute of Cost and Management Accountants examination in Cost Accounting 1; whilst the more difficult questions would correspond to the requirements of Cost Accounting 2.

Any of the types of question illustrated could be relevant to the Chartered Association of Certified Accountants Level 1 paper in Costing, the Association of Accounting Technicians final examination paper in Cost Accounting and Budgeting or the Institute of Chartered Accountants in England and Wales Professional Examination I costing questions in the paper Accounting Techniques.

The 2nd edition of this book incorporates a number of recent examination questions from the various professional bodies, so that students will gain familiarity with the type of question currently encountered in Cost Accounting papers.

Marks have been allocated to each question as an indication both of its relative importance for examination purposes and also of the time within which a candidate should be capable of answering it under examination conditions.

The answers provided illustrate the clear and logical approach which a student should aim to develop. Commentaries have been added where necessary to explain why a particular approach has been adopted or to draw attention to points of difficulty. It is hoped that this will help students in improving their understanding of the subjects covered.

At the end of the book there is a comprehensive index of the topics covered, relating them to the questions and answers in which they appear.

Acknowledgements

The author and publishers wish to thank the following professional bodies for their kind permission to include selected past examination questions in this publication:

The Chartered Association of Certified Accountants
The Institute of Chartered Accountants in England and Wales
The Institute of Cost and Management Accountants

About the author

Richard Jenkins, BA, ACA is a director of Financial Training (Manchester) Ltd. He qualified in 1978 and joined the company in 1980. He specialises in Management Accounting, Financial Accounting and Taxation.

1 Introduction to cost and management accounting

Sometimes, though not frequently, questions are set specifically on the nature of cost accounting or on the tasks undertaken or the techniques used by the cost accountant. You may be required to contrast the purposes of cost accounting with those of financial accounting, or to explain the wider concept of 'management accounting' and the place of the cost accounting system within the overall plan for the provision of management information. The understanding of these interrelationships is fundamental to a right approach to all cost accounting problems.

Answers to such questions may sometimes be required in narrative form; but you are advised wherever possible to use a tabulated presentation. This has the three advantages that it helps to clarify your thoughts, prevents waste of time and is easier for the examiner to mark.

STUDY REQUIREMENTS

(a) Financial accounting: preparation and purpose of final accounts.
(b) Relationship between financial and cost accounts.
(c) Role of the accountant in providing information for management.

QUESTIONS

1 Tabulate the distinctions between cost and management accounting and financial accounting information.

(10 marks)

2

    (a)   Set out the factors that will influence the decision whether or not to set up a cost accounting function separate from the financial accounting function.

    (b)   List the typical tasks undertaken by the costing department.

(12 marks)

3 'The generation of costing information is important, but the clear presentation and communication of such information is vital to decision-making.'

With this quotation in mind, what are the essential features of reports to management?

(14 marks)

4 A small business with 50 employees and three main sections, cutting, machining and finishing, manufactures four products. The management has relied on a financial accounting system created and developed to meet statutory obligations but it is now considering the installation of a costing system.

You are required to prepare a report for management listing nine benefits you would expect to follow from the introduction of a cost accounting system.

(20 marks)

ANSWERS

1

Cost and management accounting	Financial accounting
Primarily for internal purposes	Primarily for external reporting
Information is used to take decisions about the future	Records what has happened (in a true and fair manner)
Tailored to suit the needs of the user	Must comply with statute and standard accounting practice
Emphasis is on products, processes and departments	Emphasis is on the type of expense
Gives a detailed analysis of all aspects of the organisation	Provides an overall view of the organisation

2

(a) Factors that will influence the decision are:

    (i) The size of the organisation. The provision of information becomes more formal as the organisation grows, necessitating employees who specialise in this information dissemination.

    (ii) The complexity of analysis required. For many organisations, the financial information prepared is not detailed enough.

    (iii) The structure of the organisation. The financial accounting function may be centralised while the information prepared to help run local divisions is decentralised.

(b) Tasks undertaken by the costing department:

    (i) Preparation of reports to management.

    (ii) Coding and classification of costs.

    (iii) Collection and analysis of cost information.

    (iv) Assistance with the preparation of budgets.

    (v) Recording of labour time.

    (vi) Recording of stock.

    (vii) Special studies, such as contract pricing.

3 The essential features of reports to management are:

(a) Clarity and conciseness. Both these features make for easier understanding of the report.

(b) Information. This should be relevant for the decision to be taken on the strength of the report.

(c) Timing. Action is usually taken, so speed is of the essence in the presentation of a report.

(d) Distribution. The report should be distributed only to people who need the information.

(e) Technicality of content. The report writer should be aware of the technical knowledge of the reader, and write accordingly.

(f) Standard layout. This saves time for the writer, and presents the reader with information presented in a familiar manner.

(g) Exceptions. These should be highlighted, so that the reader's attention is focused on them.

(h) Recommendations, assumptions, bases chosen. These should all be made clear.

(i) Accuracy. The report should be accurate enough for its intended purpose.

4   REPORT TO THE MANAGING DIRECTOR: INTRODUCTION OF A COST ACCOUNTING SYSTEM

The expected benefits from the introduction of a cost accounting system are listed below.

(a) The preparation of budgets and the setting of standards will be aided by the information generated by the system.

(b) Greater awareness of costs will lead to better control of waste and inefficiency.

(c) Stock valuation will be simplified.

(d) Decisions concerning selling prices will be assisted by information on product costs.

(e) Decisions whether to make or buy components can be made.

(f) Decisions concerning methods of production will be helped by knowledge of machine and labour costs.

(g) Strategies for the mix and quantity of products can be based on product contributions.

(h) Information will be most up-to-date.

(i) Overhead allocation will be eased by the cost accumulation process.

Comment

The question asks for nine benefits only. Several more could be suggested, for instance:

(a) The financial accounts will be prepared more quickly.

(b) Resources will be utilised more efficiently.

(c) Employees will have a greater understanding of cost accumulation.

2 Cost accounting fundamentals

Narrative questions may be set at an elementary level on the classification of costs between, for example, manufacturing, selling and distribution costs; direct and indirect costs; or fixed and variable costs.

In some cases you will be asked to apply your classification to a simple numerical example.

At more advanced levels these basic classifications will be implicit in the solution of a complex problem.

In dealing with such questions, always bear in mind that the way an item of cost is classified will depend on the cost unit or cost centre to which it is to be related; the purpose of the classification and the practicability of achieving the desired analysis. If alternative classifications appear to be possible, then select the one you prefer, but point out to the examiner the alternatives that might be used.

STUDY REQUIREMENTS

- (a) Nature and classification of costs.
- (b) Elements of cost.
- (c) Cost centres and cost units.
- (d) Theory of cost behaviour.

QUESTIONS

1

  (a) Explain briefly the difference between a direct cost and an indirect cost, giving an example of each type. *(5 marks)*

  (b) For each of the following items, state whether they are direct or indirect costs:

      (i)   Sheet steel for a motor-car manufacturer.
      (ii) Machine operators' wages for a golf-ball manufacturer.
      (iii) Supervisors' wages for a golf-ball manufacturer.
      (iv) Chargeable time in an accountancy practice.
      (v) Factory rates for an oven manufacturer.
      (vi) Production royalties for a mining company.
      (vii) Electricity for a brewery.
     (viii) Hire plant for a building contractor in a long-term contract.
      (ix) The audit fee of an oil company.
      (x) Glue for a furniture maker. *(10 marks)*

(Total 15 marks)

2 Mike has overheard the following conversation whilst being measured for a suit: 'There are different costs for different purposes — you can classify costs in a number of ways.'

Mike is baffled by this, and asks you for your opinion as a cost accountant.

You are required to suggest six different bases under which costs may be classified, and for each basis, suggest the different classifications of costs contained therein.

(15 marks)

3

  (a) 'Fixed costs are really variable: the more you produce the less they become.'

Explain the above statement and state whether or not you agree with it.

  (b) You are required to *sketch* a separate graph for each of the items listed below in order to indicate the behaviour of the expense. Graph paper need not be used but your axes must be labelled.

      (i)   Supervisory labour.
      (ii) Depreciation of plant on a machine-hour basis.
      (iii) Planned preventive maintenance plus unexpected maintenance.
      (iv) Monthly pay of a salesman who receives a salary of £3,000 per annum plus a commission of 1% paid on his previous month's sales when they exceed £20,000; assume that his previous month's sales totalled £30,000.

(15 marks)

4

(a) Define:

    (i)   prime cost;
    (ii) factory overhead.   *(4 marks)*

(b) Give three examples of each of the following:

    (i)   Fixed factory overhead;
    (ii)   Variable factory overhead;
    (iii) Partly-variable factory overhead.   *(9 marks)*

(Total 13 marks)

5   The BATE company makes art prints. The following details are available for the year ended 30 June 19X2:

	£ thousands
Opening stocks: Direct materials	13
Work-in-process	37
Finished goods	60
Direct materials purchased	218
Direct labour	60
Indirect labour and supervision	22
Administrative expenses	80
Factory rent, rates and insurance	47
Depreciation of factory equipment	35
Selling expenses	70
Factory power, heat and light	10
Sundry factory overheads	6
Financial charges	60
Sales	730
Closing stocks: Direct materials	21
Work-in-process	27
Finished goods	40

The company values work-in-process at factory cost.

You are required to prepare:

(a) A schedule of cost of goods manufactured for the year ended 30 June 19X2.
(b) A profit statement for the year ended 30 June 19X2.

(15 marks)

6

(a) Describe the role of the cost accountant in a manufacturing organisation.   *(8 marks)*
(b) Explain whether you agree with each of the following statements:

    (i)   'All direct costs are variable.'
    (ii)   'Variable costs are controllable and fixed costs are not.'
    (iii) 'Sunk costs are irrelevant when providing decision making information.'   *(9 marks)*

(Total 17 marks)

ANSWERS

1

(a) A direct cost is an item of cost that is physically traceable to a cost unit in an economically feasible manner. A good example would be the cost of a bought-in component (e.g., an engine) for a motor car.

An indirect cost is a cost that either cannot be identified with any one finished unit, or is not traced to individual cost units because of the insignificance of the cost. An example of the former would be rent; of the latter, nails.

(b)
- (i) Direct.
- (ii) Direct.
- (iii) Indirect.
- (iv) Direct.
- (v) Indirect.
- (vi) Direct.
- (vii) Indirect.
- (viii) Direct.
- (ix) Indirect.
- (x) Indirect.

2

Basis for classification of costs	**Types of costs**
1 Ease of traceability	Direct, indirect
2 Function	Manufacturing, administrative, selling
3 Behaviour in relation to changes in activity	Fixed, variable, semi-variable
4 Time when computed	Historical, budgeted or standard
5 Time when charged against revenue	Product, period
6 Degree of averaging	Total, unit

Other possibilities include:

1 Natural characteristics	Material, labour, etc.
2 Responsibility	Cost centre, process, department, plant, company
3 Decision-making	Relevant, non-relevant

3

(a) Fixed costs are those costs which remain unchanged in total, despite wide fluctuations in activity (output or turnover), for a certain range of activity and for a limited period of time.

For instance, factory rent may be £90,000 in total whether 5,000, 10,000, or 15,000 units are produced. The cost per unit is, respectively, £18, £9, and £6.

The statement in the question intends to explain this idea, but unfortunately does not distinguish between total and unit costs. The rent is fixed in total at £90,000, but varies per unit, and decreases as more units are produced.

Hence the statement is not correct, since it fails to convey the idea of a unit cost.

(b)

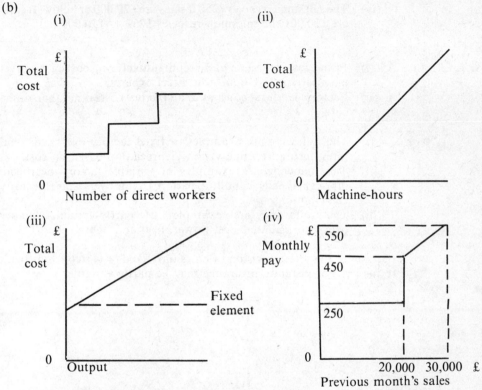

(i)

Total cost (£) vs Number of direct workers

(ii)

Total cost (£) vs Machine-hours

(iii)

Total cost (£) vs Output — Fixed element

(iv)

Monthly pay (£): 550, 450, 250 — Previous month's sales: 20,000 30,000 £

An alternative graph for preventive maintenance may be drawn as follows:

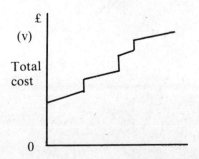

(v)

Total cost (£)

This shows the unexpected maintenance portrayed as random jumps.

9

Comment on graphs

(i) The cost of supervisory labour is fixed until an extra supervisor is required. This supervisor can oversee (say) 20 direct workers, when another supervisor is required. This is an example of a stepped fixed cost.

(ii) This is a variable cost.

(iii) The cost has two elements — one fixed and one variable. Some maintenance is required whatever the output, but as output rises unexpected maintenance also increases.

(iv) The salesman receives £250 if sales are £20,000 or below. If sales are £20,001 the salesman receives £250 + (£20,001 × 1%).

4

(a)

(i) Prime cost is the sum of direct manufacturing costs, i.e., direct material, direct labour and direct expenses.

(ii) Factory overhead consists of all factory costs other than direct costs.

(b)

(i) The following are examples of fixed factory overhead: rent, rates, insurance, supervision, depreciation based on cost.

(ii) The following are examples of variable factory overhead: lubricants, nails, handling, patterns, employers' social security contributions.

(iii) The following are examples of partly-variable factory overhead: maintenance, power, heat and light.

In practice this sharp division of costs into fixed or variable is difficult to justify. For instance, insurance may be partly variable.

5

(a) Schedule of cost of goods manufactured for the year ended 30 June 19X2:

	£ thousands	£ thousands
Direct materials:		
Opening stocks	13	
Purchases	218	
	231	
Less: Closing stocks	(21)	210
Direct labour		60
Factory overhead:		
Indirect labour and supervision	22	
Rent, rates and insurance	47	
Depreciation of equipment	35	
Power, heat and light	10	
Sundry	6	
Manufacturing costs incurred		120
		390
Add: Work-in-process, opening stocks		37
		427
Less: Work-in-process, closing stocks		(27)
Cost of goods manufactured		400

(b) Profit statement for the year ended 30 June 19X2:

	£ thousands	£ thousands
Sales		730
Less: Cost of goods sold:		
Opening stocks of finished goods	60	
Cost of goods manufactured	400	
	460	
Less: Closing stocks of finished goods	(40)	(420)
Gross profit		310
Less:		
Administrative expenses	80	
Selling expenses	70	
Financial charges	60	(210)
Net profit		100

(a)   The role of the cost accountant in a manufacturing organisation is to provide management with information about costs and revenues. The information is then used for three broad purposes: planning, control and decision-making.

In order to fulfil his or her role, the cost accountant will generate the necessary information through cost accumulation procedures. Costs are collected, classified and analysed, first by department and then by product. In some cases decisions concerning the allocation of costs to different departments will be taken by the cost accountant.

Costing information generated by these procedures would normally include:

   (i)   monthly accounts;
   (ii)   stock valuations;
   (iii) departmental analyses;
   (iv)   budgets;
   (v)   product contributions;
   (vi)   variance analysis.

The cost accountant may also be involved in other areas such as the setting of standard costs, the investigation of variances and the pricing of long-term contracts.

(b)   (i)   This statement is not true. Direct costs are those which can be traced to a cost unit; variable costs are those which in total increase proportionately as activity increases.

While many direct costs are variable, for instance materials, a fixed cost may be direct. Examples would include a supervisor's wage if the cost unit were a department, or a fixed annual royalty if the cost unit were a product.

   (ii)   Controllable costs are those costs under the control of an individual, thus the incurrence of the cost is at the discretion of that individual.

While it may be true that more variable than fixed costs are controllable by a particular member of an organisation, the statement is too generalised. In the long term all costs are controllable, for instance, decisions may be made to cancel or increase fixed costs such as rent and advertising. In the short term many variable costs are uncontrollable, for instance, the price of materials may be governed by a fixed contract.

   (iii) This statement is true. A sunk cost is one which has already been incurred; such a cost is not affected by the decision under consideration, and so should be ignored.

3 Accounting for materials

Questions on this subject will cover one or more of three topics:

(a) Recording and documentation of materials transactions. You may be asked to describe, or to illustrate, various documents used in procuring materials, receiving them into store, issuing them from store and keeping a running record of stock being held. When dealing with stock records, read the question carefully to discover whether you are asked for a record of quantities only or one with money values, which will normally be a stock ledger.

(b) Valuing stores issues and closing stock holdings, using one or more of the conventional bases. In some cases you will be asked to calculate product profits using the selected basis.

(c) Control of stocks, which may involve alternative methods of setting reorder levels and quantities including, at an advanced level, determination of an economic order quantity.

Whenever you have to produce an illustration, with or without money values, do take time to prepare a rough draft so that your final answer is well spaced and clearly set out. If the examiner can see quickly that you have used a correct approach, he may not be too worried about minor inaccuracies.

STUDY REQUIREMENTS

(a) Documentation for purchasing and stores recording.
(b) Stores accounting and pricing materials issues.
(c) Stock control.

QUESTIONS

1

(a) State briefly the distinction between a purchase requisition and a purchase order. .   *(3 marks)*

(b) List six details that might appear on a purchase order.   *(6 marks)*

(c) List six details that might appear on a goods received note.

(6 marks)

(Total 15 marks)

2 X Limited, a manufacturing company with several stores, has a materials control system which includes perpetual inventory records, re-order levels and continuous stocktaking.

(a) Draw a diagram or flow chart to show how materials would be issued, replenished and paid for. The cycle should indicate the departments involved, the procedures used and documents raised.

(b) (i) Draft a form for use by the stock checkers and include on it the following information of stock checks made in store Z on 15 May 19X8.

	Balances, in units		Physical stock, in units	Cost per unit £
Item	Stock card	Stores ledger		
A	200	200	180	20.00
B	170	170	172	5.00
C	740	760	700	0.60

(ii) State action to be taken and documents to be raised to adjust discrepancies recorded in (b) (i) above.

(iii) State a possible reason for the shortages and recommend a possible course of action by management to prevent future losses.

(25 marks)

3 Peter is confused. He imports and distributes a brand of electrical plug called 'The Mayfair' and the cost varies because of exchange rate fluctuations. His accountant, Sandra, has told him: 'Your profit depends on your closing stock, and there are so many different ways of valuing stock in your business that you can choose how much profit you want.'

(a) Name six possible methods of costing individual issues of stock where several identical items have been purchased at different times.

(6 marks)

(b) State briefly how each method determines the cost of an issue.

(6 marks)

(c)   Tabulate for each method one advantage and one disadvantage.

(12 marks)
(Total 24 marks)

4   As cost accountant responsible for the stores ledger at Pamina Ltd, you are presented with the following information relating to raw material commodity stock movements, for the three months ended 30 June 1983:

(1)	Stock at 1 April 1983	7,240 units at £11 per unit
(2)	Purchases:	
	3 April 1983	4,240 units at £12 per unit
	15 May 1983	9,217 units at £13 per unit
	17 June 1983	2,490 units at £10 per unit
(3)	Transferred to work in progress:	units
	2 April 1983	4,170
	12 April 1983	6,716
	12 May 1983	494
	1 June 1983	7,460

You are required:

(a)   to prepare statements in value and quantity terms for stock movements for the three months ended 30 June 1983 on the basis of:

    (i)   weighted average price, and
    (ii)   first in first out, and   *(11 marks)*

(b)   to suggest two other methods which could be used to record the receipt and issue of raw materials.

(3 marks)
(Total 14 marks)

5   Based on the information shown below for the liquid 'Flyte' you are required:

(a)   to calculate the amounts to be charged to cost of production; and
(b)   to show the value of closing stock,

under each of the following methods of stock accounting:

    (i)   FIFO,
    (ii)   LIFO,
    (iii)   weighted average,
    (iv)   standard cost,
    (v)   replacement cost;

and

(c) For b(iv) and b(v) calculate any differences arising, and indicate how these differences would be treated.

1 March Received 1,000 litres at £5.50 per litre
2 March Received 500 litres at £7.00 per litre
3 March Issued 800 litres
4 March Received 700 litres at £8.00 per litre
5 March Issued 1,000 litres
Current standard price: £6.00 per litre.
Current market price per litre:
1 March £5.50
2 March £7.00
3 March £7.00
4 March £8.00
5 March £8.50

(20 marks)

6 MacGowan commences the manufacture of model railway engines on 1 January. His trading account for the first year is as follows:

	Units	£	£	£
Sales	50,000			500,000
Cost of sales:				
Raw materials:				
Opening stock		—		
Purchases		500,000		
		500,000		
Less: Closing stock		(50,000)	450,000	
Labour			160,000	
Production overheads			80,000	
Cost of production	80,000		690,000	
Less: Closing stock	(30,000)		(240,000)	
	50,000			(450,000)
Gross profit				50,000

Notes

(1) Stocks of both raw materials and finished goods have increased uniformly over the year.
(2) The raw materials content of finished goods is £5.00 per unit.
(3) MacGowan was ill during August, when he received orders for 6,000 units which were held up by stock shortages and subsequently cancelled. He had a further 4,000 orders on his books at the year end.

(a) Calculate the following ratios:

    (i)   Inventory turnover for raw materials.
    (ii) Inventory turnover for finished goods.
    (iii) Input-output ratio for raw materials.
    (iv) Stock-out ratio.   *(8 marks)*

(b) Comment briefly on these four ratios.   *(4 marks)*
                                             (Total 12 marks)

7 B Limited, a young, fast-growing company, is planning to develop a new factory. The managing director of the company has discussed various aspects of the plan with functional heads and has now asked you, as management accountant, to provide him with a report on certain aspects of inventory control. He is interested particularly in the contribution which the following could make to the stock control of raw materials.

(a)   ABC inventory analysis;
(b)   setting of stock levels;
(c)   economic order quantity.

Prepare a report to your managing director, discussing briefly the important points of each of the above.

                                               (20 marks)

ANSWERS

1

(a) A purchase requisition is a request to the buying department to obtain a particular quantity of materials to a given specification for a stated purpose.

A purchase order is an order for materials by the buying department through an outside supplier.

(b) Any six from:

    (i) The order number.
    (ii) The date of the order.
    (iii) The name and address of the company ordering.
    (iv) The name and address of the supplier.
    (v) A description of the materials required.
    (vi) The quantity ordered.
    (vii) The price and any discounts deductible.
    (viii) The means of delivery.
    (ix) The required date of delivery.
    (x) The name of the person making the order.

(c) Any six from:

    (i) The goods received number.
    (ii) The date of receipt.
    (iii) The name of the supplier.
    (iv) The serial number of the supplier's delivery note.
    (v) A description of the goods.
    (vi) The quantity received.
    (vii) The purchase order number.
    (viii) A signature of receipt.
    (ix) The name of the carrier.
    (x) An inspection report.

2

(a) **Diagram to show how materials would be issued, replenished and paid for**

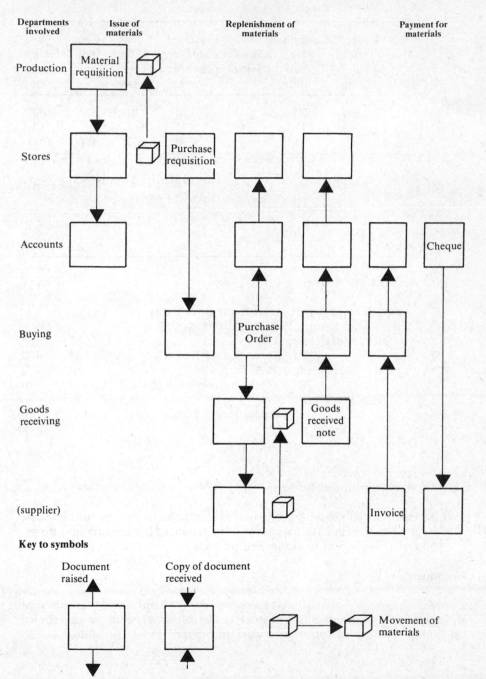

(b)

(i) PAGE NUMBER   STOCK CHECK FORM   STORE Z   DATE

Item	Recorded balances Stores ledger units	Stock card units	Checker's initials	Actual balances per check units	Gain (Loss) units	Cost per unit £	Gain/ (Loss) £
A	200	200		180	(20)	20	(400)
B	170	170		172	2	5	10
C	760	740		700	(60)	0.60	(36)

COMMENTS   RECOMMENDATIONS

(ii) Action to be taken:

    (a)   Record correct balance on stock cards.
    (b)   Adjust stores ledger accounts, as follows:

DR: Stock losses A/C	400	
CR: Stores ledger A A/C		400
DR: Stores ledger B A/C	10	
CR: Work-in-progress A/C		10
DR: Stock losses A/C	36	
CR: Stores ledger C A/C		36

Documents to be raised:

Journal vouchers as above
Stock adjustment forms

(iii) One possible reason for the shortages is theft. To prevent future losses, it is recommended that a pass must be produced before entry into stores, restricting access to authorised persons.

Comment

For b(ii) it has been assumed that the losses shown for items A and C are physical shortages (and not transposition of stock or clerical error), while the gain shown for item B results from an issue to work-in-progress being two short.

3

(a) FIFO (first in, first out).
LIFO (last in, first out).
Weighted average.
Base stock.
Replacement cost.
Standard cost.

Other possible methods include simple average, inflated price, and discounted selling price.

(b) *FIFO.* Materials are assumed to be used in the order in which they are received. Issues are related back to the earliest purchases still in stock.

LIFO. The opposite of FIFO. Issues are related to the most recent acquisitions.

Weighted average. The total cost of items in stock is divided by the number of items in stock to compute an average price, which is then applied to the items issued.

Base stock. A predetermined quantity of stock is valued at a constant price; this base stock is considered to be an essential ingredient of the particular process. Issues are assumed to be from the excess units of stock, valued under one of the other methods.

Replacement cost. Issues are priced at the cost at which an identical asset could be purchased or manufactured.

Standard cost. A periodically predetermined price is used for purchases, issues and stock balances.

(c)

Method	Advantage	Disadvantage
FIFO	Portrays typical stock movement	Issues may require two prices
LIFO	Brings in up-to-date costs for profit purposes	Stock is valued at out-of-date costs
Weighted average	Shows the flow of units for many organisations	All prices, regardless of purchase date, influence the average price
Base stock	Accurately portrays certain processes	Stock valuation does not resemble actual cost
Replacement cost	Reflects current market prices	Book-keeping is complicated
Standard cost	Simple to operate	Difficult to prepare

4

(a) (i) **Weighted average**

Date	Receipts Quantity	Price £	Value £	Issues Quantity	Price £	Value £	Balance Quantity	Price £	Value £
1 April							7,240	11.00	79,640
2 April				4,170	11.00	45,870	3,070	11.00	33,770
3 April	4,240	12.00	50,880				7,310	11.58	84,650
12 April				6,716	11.58	77,771	594	11.58	6,879
12 May				494	11.58	5,721	100	11.58	1,158
15 May	9,217	13.00	119,821				9,317	12.98	120,979
1 June				7,460	12.98	96,831	1,857	12.98	24,113
17 June	2,490	10.00	24,900				4,347	11.28	49,013

(ii) **First in first out**

Date	Receipts Quantity	Price £	Value £	Issues Quantity	Price £	Value £	Balance Quantity	Price £	Value £
1 April							7,240	11.00	79,640
2 April				4,170	11.00	45,870	3,070	11.00	33,770
3 April	4,240	12.00	50,880				7,310		84,650
12 April				3,070	11.00	33,770			
				3,646	12.00	43,752			
				6,716		77,522	594	12.00	7,128
12 May				494	12.00	5,928	100	12.00	1,200
15 May	9,217	13.00	119,821				9,317		121,021
1 June				100	12.00	1,200			
				7,360	13.00	95,680			
				7,460		96,880	1,857	13.00	24,141
17 June	2,490	10.00	24,900				4,347		49,041

(b) Two other methods which could be used to record the receipt and issue of raw materials are:

(i) last in first out;
(ii) standard cost.

Comment

Other methods could also be suggested such as replacement cost, base stock, next in first out and even highest in first out.

(i) **FIFO**

		litres		£	£	£
(a)	3 March	800	at £5.50		4,400	
	5 March	200	at £5.50 ✓	1,100		
		500	at £7.00	3,500		
		300	at £8.00	2,400	7,000	11,400
		1,000				
(b)	Closing stock	400	at £8.00			3,200
						14,600

(ii) **LIFO**

		litres		£	£	£
(a)	3 March	500	at £7.00	3,500		
		300	at £5.50	1,650	5,150	
		800				
	5 March	700	at £8.00	5,600		
		300	at £5.50	1,650	7,250	12,400
		1,000				
(b)	Closing stock	400	at £5.50			2,200
						14,600

(iii) **Weighted average**

		litres		£	£
(a)	3 March	800	at £6.00	4,800	
	5 March	1,000	at £7.00	7,000	11,800
(b)	Closing stock	400	at £7.00		2,800
					14,600

Workings

			£
Received	1,000	at £5.50	5,500
Received	500	at £7.00	3,500
	1,500	at £6.00	9,000
Issued	(800)	at £6.00	(4,800)
	700	at £6.00	4,200
Received	700	at £8.00	5,600
	1,400	at £7.00	9,800
Issued	(1,000)	at £7.00	(7,000)
Balance	400	at £7.00	2,800

(iv) **Standard cost**

		litres		£	£
(a)	3 March	800 at £6.00		4,800	
	5 March	1,000 at £6.00		6,000	10,800
(b)	Closing stock	400 at £6.00			2,400
					13,200

(v) **Replacement cost**

		litres		£	£
(a)	3 March	800 at £7.00		5,600	
	5 March	1,000 at £8.50		8,500	14,100
(b)	Closing stock	400 at £8.50			3,400
					17,500

(c) **Standard cost**

Material price variance

			£
1 March	1,000 litres × (£5.50 – £6.00)		500F
2 March	500 litres × (£7.00 – £6.00)		500U
4 March	700 litres × (£8.00 – £6.00)		1,400U
	Taken to profit and loss account		1,400U

Replacement cost

			£
3 March	800 litres × (£6.00 – £7.00)		800
5 March	1,000 litres × (£7.00 – £8.50)		1,500
Closing stock	400 litres × (£7.00 – £8.50)		600
	Taken to stock revaluation reserve		2,900

Comment

The price differences for replacement cost have been computed using weighted average price as a yardstick. The figure of £2,900 would still arise if either FIFO or LIFO were used instead (but not standard cost).

6

(a) (i) Inventory turnover for raw materials

$$= \frac{\text{value of materials consumed}}{\text{average value of inventory}} = \frac{£450,000}{\frac{1}{2} \times £50,000} = 18:1$$

(ii)   Inventory turnover for finished goods

$$= \frac{\text{sales}}{\text{average value of inventory}} = \frac{£500,000}{{}^{1}/_{2} \times £240,000} = \underline{4.17:1}$$

Comment

This might be better expressed as

$$\frac{\text{cost of sales}}{\text{average value of inventory}} = \frac{£450,000}{{}^{1}/_{2} \times £240,000} = \underline{3.75:1}$$

(iii)   Input-output ratio for raw materials

$$= \frac{\text{input}}{\text{content of finished product}} = \frac{£450,000}{£5 \times 80,000} = \underline{1.125:1}$$

(iv)   Stock-out ratio

$$= \frac{\substack{\text{orders held up by}\\\text{stock shortages}}}{\text{orders received}} = \frac{6,000}{(50,000 + 6,000 + 4,000)} = \underline{1:10}$$

(b)   Ratio (i) shows a very rapid turnover of raw materials.

Ratio (ii) shows fairly slow-moving turnover of finished goods.

Ratio (iii) indicates an inefficiency of usage of materials (11% of input has been wasted).

Ratio (iv) indicates a certain lack of stock control delegated by MacGowan.

7

REPORT TO THE MANAGING DIRECTOR: ASPECTS OF INVENTORY CONTROL

(a)   **ABC inventory analysis**

It is not necessary to use the same control technique for every item of raw materials. ABC inventory analysis is a way of determining the control techniques appropriate for various items of inventory.

Firstly, for each item, the total annual consumption cost is calculated by multiplying average usage by unit price. Then items are listed in decreasing order of annual consumption cost and grouped into three classes, A, B and C.

A typical ABC classification could look like this:

Class	Number of items	Percentage of total	Total cost	Percentage of total
A	5,000	10	355,000	71
B	10,000	20	100,000	20
C	35,000	70	45,000	9
	50,000	100	£500,000	100

The class A items (10% of the items representing 71% of the total cost) require the greatest degree of continuous control — frequent ordering and low stocks — whereas for class C items clerical work would be kept to a minimum by less frequent ordering, high stocks and less paperwork.

(b) **Setting of stock levels**

Two of the main objectives of a stock control system are:

(i) To maintain sufficient stocks in order to avoid shortages, which can disrupt production and sales.
(ii) To avoid the high costs of holding excessive stock levels — finance charges, storage costs and deterioration.

A stock level which strikes a balance between these two objectives should result in inventory costs being minimised.

There are various factors to consider in the setting of stock levels. They include:

(i) Holding costs.
(ii) Reorder costs.
(iii) Maximum stock level — limited by physical constraints.
(iv) Minimum stock level — below which shortages may occur.
(v) Reorder level and quantity.

(c) **Economic order quantity**

If annual usage of raw materials is 2,400 units, it is possible to buy 200 units monthly, 600 units quarterly, 2,400 units annually, or any other combination of order quantity and frequency of ordering.

The economic order quantity (EOQ) is the size of order that will result in minimum total annual costs for the item. This total cost consists of two parts — carrying costs and purchasing costs. The EOQ may be calculated by a mathematical formula, or may be shown graphically as follows:

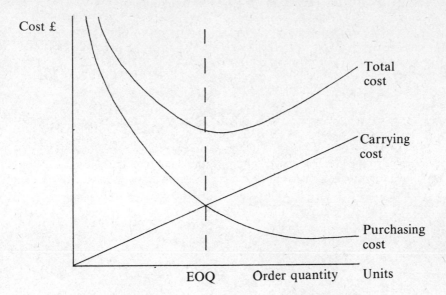

A few large orders result in high carrying costs, but low purchasing costs, whereas frequent small orders cause the reverse.

4 Accounting for labour costs

The three main topics on which questions may be set are:

(a) Methods of remuneration. Questions involving the calculation of remuneration under an incentive bonus scheme have been popular in past examinations. You must read the question carefully to identify the precise formula to be used; or if the name of a scheme is given then you must have the appropriate formula firmly in mind. Show each stage of calculation clearly. Alternatively you may be asked to compare alternative methods of remuneration. A tabulated presentation is to be preferred.

(b) The accounting treatment of various types of wage costs, including overtime and idle time. Alternative treatments may be possible and should be specified.

(c) Control of labour costs. Remember that the object is to link pay with performance. Ratio calculations, work study, time recording and internal controls on payroll routines can all be relevant, depending on the terms of the question.

STUDY REQUIREMENTS

(a) Remuneration systems.
(b) Payroll routines.
(c) Wages control.

QUESTIONS

1 'Labour turnover should be low whereas stores turnover should be high.' Analyse critically this statement, and discuss the problems inherent in calculating turnover rates for labour and stores, and the importance of these in controlling costs.

(20 marks)

2

(a) Tabulate the advantages and disadvantages of remunerating employees by using piecework rates.
(6 marks)

(b) Explain briefly the idea of a premium bonus scheme, giving three examples.
(5 marks)

(Total 11 marks)

3

(a) Discuss the general principles which should be applied to incentive schemes.

(b) Certain organisations, for example car manufacturers, have abandoned premium bonus schemes and piecework schemes and substituted a 'high day rate' system. List the advantages and disadvantages expected from following such a policy.

(20 marks)

4 Elaine and Julie work for a bicycle company making brake pedals. Details for the week ending 30 June are as follows:

	Number of pedals made	Time allowed	Time taken
Elaine	100	100	40
Julie	50	50	40

Basic hourly rate for both: £2.00.

Calculate both Elaine and Julie's remuneration for the week, and their effective hourly rate, under:

(a) The Halsey 50/50 premium bonus scheme.
(b) The Rowan premium bonus scheme.

(10 marks)

5 You have been approached for your advice on the proposed introduction of an incentive scheme for the direct operatives in the final production department of a factory producing one standard product. This department, the Finishing Shop, employs 30 direct operatives all of whom are paid £3 per hour for a basic 40-hour week, with a guaranteed wage of £120 per week. When necessary, overtime is worked up to a maximum of 15 hours per week per

operative and is paid at time rate plus one half. It is the opinion of the personnel manager that no more direct operatives could be recruited for this department.

An analysis of recent production returns from the Finishing Shop indicate that the current average output is approximately 6 units of the standard product per productive man hour. The work study manager has conducted an appraisal of the working methods in the Finishing Shop and suggests that it would be reasonable to expect operatives to process 8 units of the product per man hour and that a piece work scheme be introduced in which the direct operatives are paid 55p for each unit processed. It is anticipated that, when necessary, operatives would continue to work overtime up to the previously specified limit, although as the operatives would be on piece work no premium would be paid.

Next year's budgeted production for the factory varies from a minimum of 7,000 units per week to a maximum of 12,000 units per week, with the most frequent budgeted weekly output being 9,600 units. The expected selling price of the product next year is £10 per unit and the budgeted variable production cost of the incomplete product passed into the Finishing Shop amounts to £8 per unit. Variable production overheads in the Finishing Shop, excluding the overtime premium of the direct operatives, are budgeted to be £0.48 per direct labour hour worked and it is considered that variable overheads do vary directly with productive hours worked. Direct material costs are not incurred by the Finishing Shop. The fixed overheads incurred by the factory amount in total to £9,000 per week.

Stocks of work in progress and finished goods are not carried.

Required:

(a) Calculate the effect on the company's budgeted weekly profits of the proposed incentive scheme in the Finishing Shop. Calculations should be to the nearest £. *(15 marks)*
(b) Explain the reasons for the changes in the weekly budgeted profits caused by the proposed incentive scheme. *(7 marks)*
(Total 22 marks)

6   For each of the payroll costs given below, state the accounting treatment that you would recommend, giving your reason:

(a) Idle time caused by an explosion in the factory.
(b) Idle time in the finishing department because the assembly department delayed its production.
(c) Holiday pay.
(d) Overtime in the lubricating department, caused by general pressure of work.
(e) Overtime in the lubricating department due to a mix-up in holiday allocations by the departmental manager.
(f) Overtime resulting from a customer saying, 'I want this job done in a week, and if you have to work overtime, I don't mind.'
(g) Supervisors' wages.

(h)   Labour time involved in reworking 5 units out of a batch of 50, on a process where 10% of completed units are expected to be defective.

(16 marks)

7   It is common cost accounting practice to treat direct wages as an item of variable cost. In certain circumstances however, such as when production plants are highly mechanised or automated, operators' wages are regarded as a fixed cost.

Discuss the factors which should be considered in the cost accounting treatment of operators' wages in different circumstances.

(15 marks)

ANSWERS

1 Labour turnover is usually expressed as the following ratio:

$$\frac{\text{number of employees replaced in a period}}{\text{average number of employees in this period}}$$

A high labour turnover indicates that, on average, people leave after a short time. Typical reasons for replacement might be:

(a) Dissatisfaction with conditions, pay, etc.
(b) Lack of training.
(c) Lack of career structure.
(d) Discharge.
(e) Retirement.
(f) Pregnancy, or any change in domestic circumstances.
(g) Personal advancement.

Some, but not all, of these circumstances for leaving may be altered by the organisation.

The consequences of a high labour turnover are:

(a) Disturbance of the flow of production, which reduces productivity.
(b) New employees have to spend time learning the job, which reduces productivity.
(c) Leaving, replacement and training costs.
(d) Lowering of morale.

Hence, in general, the first half of the statement is true, in that a low labour turnover usually means a stable and contented workforce.

Stores turnover is also usually expressed as a ratio:

$$\frac{\text{average value of materials consumed in a period}}{\text{average value of materials held in this period}}$$

The second half of the statement has some merit, in that a high stores turnover avoids the following:

(a) Danger of deterioration or obsolescence.
(b) Excessive holding costs, e.g. interest on capital.
(c) Excessive storage space.

However, there are good reasons for holding high stocks, namely:

(a) Large forward purchases at cheap prices.
(b) Uncertainty of supply.
(c) Costs of stock-outs.
(d) High reordering costs.

(e) Tax purposes.

No general rule for stores turnover can be laid down; the desired turnover depends on individual circumstances.

The difficulties of calculating turnover rates include:

(a) Length of period to choose.
(b) 'Average' can be misleading.
(c) Definition of 'replacement' in labour turnover; how, for example, should internal promotion be treated?
(d) Number of ratios to calculate. One overall ratio does not isolate problem departments, whereas several ratios rely on small figures which are statistically unsound.
(e) The problem of defining 'value' in stores turnover as unit costs change.

Labour turnover may be controlled:

(a) By eliminating controllable factors which induce people to leave, such as lack of career structure.
(b) By building into budgeted costs the uncontrollable reasons for leaving, such as retirement, and the associated costs.

The stores turnover ratio is one of many techniques available for stock control, and is probably not as important as techniques for determining the optimum order size and stock level.

2

(a)

	Advantages		Disadvantages
(a)	The employee's reward is closely related to effort, giving a strong incentive.	(a)	Piecework payment can only be used in limited circumstances, e.g. where output is easily identified.
(b)	Piecework rates are easily understood and applied.	(b)	Quality may be sacrificed for quantity.
(c)	It is usual to introduce a guaranteed minimum wage to safeguard against uncontrollable factors.	(c)	Supervision and inspection costs are high.

(b) A premium bonus scheme is a combination of remuneration based on time worked, and piecework pay. The earnings consist of:

(i) Basic pay: rate × hours worked.
(ii) Bonus for reaching a target output level.

Examples:

   (i)   Halsey (bonus: time saved $\times \frac{1}{2}$ hourly day rate)

  (ii)   Halsey-Weir (bonus: time saved $\times \frac{1}{3}$ hourly day rate)

 (iii)   Rowan (bonus: $\dfrac{\text{time saved}}{\text{time allowed}} \times$ time taken $\times$ hourly day rate)

3

(a)   The general principles which should be applied to incentive schemes are as follows.

For the employer:

   (i)   An incentive scheme should increase productivity and thus reduce unit costs.

  (ii)   It should help to establish sensible standards for labour.

 (iii)   It should create a better and more efficient working environment.

For the employee:

   (i)   It should be easily understood.

  (ii)   Reward should be closely related to effort.

 (iii)   Reward should be received with the minimum of delay.

 (iv)   It should be relatively permanent.

  (v)   Bonuses should not be affected by factors outside the employee's control.

For both:

   (i)   It should be seen to be fair to both parties.

  (ii)   It should be agreed upon by both parties.

 (iii)   It should not contravene trade union agreements or legislation.

(b)   Under a high day rate system, a higher than normal hourly rate is offered to employees who are prepared to work at an above-average pace.

Advantages:

   (i)   Simple to understand.

  (ii)   Simple to administer.

 (iii)   Encourages group rather than individual effort.

 (iv)   Avoids fluctuating earnings.

Disadvantages:

   (i)   Targets may not be met.

  (ii)   Reward is at a slight distance from effort.

 (iii)   High rate may become established as the standard rate.

4

(a) **Halsey scheme**

		£
Elaine:		
Basic pay	40 hours × £2.00	80
Bonus:		
$1/_2$ rate × time saved: $1/_2$ × £2 × 60		60
Remuneration		140
Effective hourly rate		3.50
Julie:		
Basic pay		80
Bonus:	$1/_2$ × £2 × 10	10
		90
Effective hourly rate		2.25

(b) **Rowan scheme**

		£
Elaine:		
Basic pay		80
Bonus:		
$\text{rate} \times \dfrac{\text{time saved} \times \text{time taken}}{\text{time allowed}} = £2 \times \dfrac{60 \times 40}{100}$		48
		128
Effective hourly rate		3.20
Julie:		
Basic pay		80
Bonus:		
$£2 \times \dfrac{10 \times 40}{50}$		16
		96
Effective hourly rate		2.40

5

(a) **Budgeted weekly profits: Finishing Shop**

Activity level (units)	7,000	9,600	9,900	12,000
Existing scheme				Not possible
	£	£	£	£
Contribution (before labour costs)	13,440	18,432	19,008	
Labour costs: guaranteed	3,600	—	—	
basic	—	4,800	4,950	
overtime	—	600	675	
Fixed overheads	9,000	9,000	9,000	
Profit	840	4,032	4,383	

Proposed scheme

Contribution (after labour costs)	9,730	13,344	13,761	16,680
Fixed overheads	9,000	9,000	9,000	9,000
Profit	730	4,344	4,761	7,680
Increase	(110)	312	378	

Workings

Existing scheme

1 Level of output where overtime starts
   $30 \times 40 \times 6$ units = 7,200 units

2 Labour costs per unit
   (a) basic $\dfrac{£3}{6}$ = 50p
   (b) overtime 25p (for units in excess of 7,200)

3 Contribution per unit (*before* labour costs)

		£
Selling price		10.00
Less: brought-in cost	8.00	
variable overheads $\dfrac{0.48}{6}$ = 0.08		
	8.08	
	1.92	

4 Maximum output
     $30 \times 55 \times 6$ units = 9,900 units

Proposed scheme

1 Contribution per unit (*after* labour costs)

		£
Selling price		10.00
Less: brought-in cost	8.00	
labour	0.55	
variable overheads $\dfrac{0.48}{8} = 0.06$		
		8.61
		1.39

2 Maximum output
     $30 \times 55 \times 8$ units = 13,200 units

(b)   Reasons for the changes in the weekly budgeted profits caused by the proposed incentive scheme are:

    (i)   Variable overheads are lower
            Existing scheme   8p per unit
            Proposed scheme   6p per unit
        This saves £192 at a level of 9,600 units.
    (ii)   Basic labour rate per unit is higher
            Existing scheme   50p per unit
            Proposed scheme   55p per unit
    (iii)   Overtime premium is avoided
            Existing scheme   25p per unit for production in excess of 7,200
            Proposed scheme   nil

At low activity levels the Finishing Shop costs per unit will be 3p more expensive under the proposed scheme. However, at activity levels above 7,200 units the new scheme shows a saving of 22p per unit. Furthermore, the maximum activity level of 12,000 units becomes possible under the proposed scheme, avoiding possible shortfalls of output.

6

(a)   An explosion may be regarded as uncontrollable, and should be charged directly to profit and loss account.

(b)　This idle time is the responsibility of the assembly department, and so the cost should be charged there, in order that this department is aware of the cost of the delay.

(c)　Two alternatives are available for holiday pay:
   (i)　Charged to production overhead for the whole year.
   (ii)　Charged to wages, thus inflating the wage rate to include holiday pay.

(d)　Overtime arising from general pressure of work is not the responsibility of any department or individual, and so should be charged to production overhead.

(e)　This overtime has arisen from a fault in the lubricating department; the overtime should, therefore, be charged to this department.

(f)　Overtime worked on a customer's specific instructions should be charged to the customer's job.

(g)　Supervisors' wages should be treated as part of departmental overhead, unless they can be charged in their entirety to one particular job.

(h)　These costs of reworking are expected, and can be charged as direct wages to the batch of completed units.

Comment

This question is designed to illustrate some ideas of costs, controllability and responsibility for labour.

7　The following factors need to be considered in the cost accounting treatment of operators' wages in different circumstances:

(a)　The time period involved: in the short term, wages costs cannot be altered, and may be considered fixed. In the long term, as costs can be varied more and more, cost behaviour changes.

(b)　The economic state of the organisation: if the business is expanding, more operators will be taken on, making this a variable cost. If the business is contracting, the costs will assume more of a fixed nature.

(c)　The size of the cost centre: for a process, operators' wages are variable, in that the process manager can choose the number of workers needed from a 'pool'. For the company itself, this 'pool' is a fixed cost.

(d)　The range of activity: over a small range, the costs will tend to be fixed.

(e)　The type of labour: highly skilled labour will be a fixed nucleus, whereas casual labour is variable.

(f)　The method of production: highly mechanised or automated plants will have fairly fixed operators, whereas for labour-intensive manufacture labour costs will be more variable.

(g)　The treatment of ancillary payroll costs: the accounting treatment for idle time, overtime, bonuses and social security contributions can vary.

(h)　The accuracy required: variable labour costs do not rise smoothly, but in steps.

(i)　Physical observation and past cost-behaviour analysis within the organisation.

5 Overhead allocation, apportionment and absorption

This is a popular field for numerical questions, usually involving a considerable amount of basic data. Such questions necessarily carry high marks, which can be earned very easily provided you use a logical step-by-step approach and set out your answer clearly. This may involve a preliminary rough tabulation. In most cases it is recommended that the cost centres to which you are apportioning, or the cost units to which you are absorbing, should be column headings across the page, and the various items of cost should be listed down the page. The bases for apportionment are usually given in the question; but you may have discretion as to the method of absorption to be used.

At an advanced level you may be asked for cross-apportionment of service department costs; and you should have clearly in mind the alternative methods available.

STUDY REQUIREMENTS

(a) Overhead classification and analysis.
(b) Principles and methods of overhead apportionment to cost centres and absorption into cost units.

QUESTIONS

1 Norma Ltd is a retail organisation which operates three sales departments and an administration department in a large supermarket complex. Each sales department has a manager and its own prescribed gross margin related to selling price.

Exceptionally, the general manager permits the departmental managers to reduce the selling price of a product by giving a quantity discount, a special price for a large order or for an item of out-dated stock.

The following data are given:

	Audio and video equipment £	Electrical appliances £	Furniture £
Stock at 1 November:			
Cost	120,000	80,000	200,000
At full sales value	200,000	110,000	280,000
Transactions during November:			
Purchases	150,000	40,000	160,000
Net sales	215,000	63,000	224,000
Price reductions approved	5,000	3,000	7,000

Expenditure incurred during November was:

Item	Amount £	Basis of apportionment to sales and administration departments
Rates	4,000 ⎱	Area occupied
Light and heat	2,000 ⎰	
Advertising	35,250 ⎫	
Transport	25,850 ⎪	Sales value for month
Insurance	3,525 ⎬	before any reductions
Miscellaneous	1,175 ⎭	
Canteen	4,125	Number of employees
Salaries and wages	24,910 ⎱	⎱ See detailed information
Depreciation	3,750 ⎰	⎰ given below
Administration	2,500	Direct

Other detailed information for November was:

	Salaries and wages £	Depreciation £	Number of employees	Area occupied (square metres)
Audio and video equipment	11,900	500	27	600
Electrical appliances	2,000	750	4	200
Furniture	6,000	1,000	15	500
Administration	5,010	1,500	9	300
Total	24,910	3,750	55	1,600

Each month the total costs of the administration department are apportioned to the three sales departments on the basis of the sales values for the month before any reductions.

Using the data given:

(a) Calculate the value of stock at 30 November for balance sheet purposes.
(7 marks)

(b) Prepare a tabulated profit and loss statement for each sales department for November. *(15 marks)*
(Total 22 marks)

2 Porthos Ltd has decided to change its costing system, which previously operated on a marginal costing principle, to one operating on total absorption costing lines. They need therefore to calculate a fixed overhead cost per unit for their three products, foils, sabres and Épées. The weapons are produced in three manufacturing departments: forming, assembling and finishing. Fixed overhead costs have been identified as shown below with the budget for the coming year.

	£
Rent and rates	11,700
Light and heat	5,400
Insurance and maintenance of building	8,100
Depreciation of building	18,000
Plant repairs and maintenance	11,200
Plant depreciation	49,000
Supervisory staff	30,000
Personnel department expenses	11,400
Canteen expenses	17,100
Warehouse expenses	13,200
Accounts, sales and other administration departmental costs	104,500
	279,600

The following information may be of relevance:

(a) Forming, assembling and finishing departments occupy 2,000, 1,500 and 1,000 square metres; employ 20, 40 and 30 men who should each work 1,680 hours in the coming year and contain plant with current net book values of £280,000, £140,000 and £70,000 respectively.

(b) There are five supervisory staff in addition to the 90 strong workforce each earning £6,000 p.a.; the forming department employes two, the assembling department two, and the finishing department one.

(c) Materials consumed by the three departments are expected to amount to £350,000, £150,000 and £50,000 respectively in the coming year.

(d) It is felt that 20% of the accounts, sales and other administration department costs should be apportioned according to number of staff in each department, 20% according to materials consumed, 30% split evenly across the departments and 30% allotted to the finishing department.

(e) The time spent in each department on each product is shown below:

	Forming (hours)	Assembling (hours)	Finishing (hours)
Foil	0.4	2.0	1.0
Sabre	0.4	1.0	1.0
Épée	1.0	0.5	0.5

Calculate a fixed overhead cost per unit for each of the three products.

(20 marks)

3 As cost accountant of Oberon Ltd you have produced budgets for sales quantity, production, materials and labour utilisation and a variable overhead budget for the year ended 31 December 19X2. Information from the labour utilisation budget is shown below.

Department	Workforce	Labour hours	Hourly rate
North	20	35,000	£2.80
East	25	45,000	£2.60
West	30	55,000	£2.50

You have produced various estimates for the year's fixed costs, some of which can be easily allocated direct to the three departments and some of which need to be apportioned between the three departments. The work so far is shown below:

Fixed cost	£	Allocation or proposed basis of apportionment		
		North	East	West
Factory rent, rates and insurance	70,000	Floor area		
Plant depreciation	40,000	20,000	15,000	5,000
Repairs and maintenance	20,000	Net book value of assets weighted according to average age		
Works canteen	22,500	Number of employees		
Departmental office staff	59,000	15,000	18,000	26,000
Light and heat	10,500	Floor area		
Warehousing costs	21,000	Materials consumed		
Selling and administration	145,000	50,000	40,000	55,000

Your apportionment of fixed costs will be based on the following information:

	Floor area (m²)	Net book value of assets (£)	Average age of assets (years)	Materials consumed (£)
North	1,200	100,000	3	260,000
East	1,000	50,000	2	120,000
West	600	20,000	5	40,000

(a) Produce a schedule showing the allocation or apportionment of the £388,000 of fixed costs to the three production departments.

(5 marks)

(b) Calculate hourly fixed overhead absorption rates for the three departments. *(3 marks)*

(c) Produce a standard cost card showing how the selling price of a Weber PM2 is arrived at if the following variable costs are incurred:

Materials	£28.50
Labour: Department North	2 hours
East	4 hours
West	3 hours
Variable overheads	£19.85

Oberon Ltd aims for a profit of 35% on sales. *(7 marks)*

(Total 15 marks)

4 A factory with three departments uses a single production overhead absorption rate expressed as a percentage of direct wages cost. It has been suggested that departmental overhead absorption rates would result in more accurate job costs. Set out below are the budgeted and actual data for the previous period, together with information relating to job No. 657.

	Direct wages £ thousands	Direct labour thousands of hours	Machine time thousands of hours	Production overhead £ thousands
Budget:				
Department: A	25	10	40	120
B	100	50	10	30
C	25	25	—	75
Total	150	85	50	225
Actual:				
Department: A	30	12	45	130
B	80	45	14	28
C	30	30	—	80
Total	140	87	59	238

During this period job No. 657 incurred the actual costs and actual times in the departments shown below:

	Direct material £	Direct wages £	Direct labour hours	Machine time hours
Department: A	120	100	20	40
B	60	60	40	10
C	10	10	10	—

After adding production overhead to prime cost, one-third is added to production cost for gross profit. This assumes that a reasonable profit is earned after deducting administration, selling and distribution costs.

(a) Calculate the current overhead absorption rate.
(b) Using the rate obtained in (a) above, calculate the production overhead charged to job No. 657 and state the production cost and expected gross profit on this job.
(c) (i) Comment on the suggestion that departmental overhead absorption rates would result in more accurate job costs; and
(ii) Compute such rates, briefly explaining your reason for each rate.
(d) Using the rates calculated in (c) (ii) above, show the overhead, by department and in total, that would apply to job No. 657.
(e) Show the over/under absorption, by department and in total, for the period using:
(i) the current rate in your answer to (a) above; and
(ii) your suggested rates in your answer to (c) (ii) above.

(20 marks)

5 AC Engineering Company Ltd manufactures a wide variety of products. You have recently been appointed management accountant of the company and are concerned with the current method of absorbing production overhead.

You are required to prepare for the next board meeting of the company a report in which you should discuss briefly five methods of overhead absorption, and in respect of each, you should suggest, with reasons, why you would or would not advocate its adoption by the company.

(20 marks)

6 Shown below is an extract from next year's budget for a company manufacturing three different products in three production departments.

Product	A	B	C
Production	4,000 units	3,000 units	6,000 units
Direct material cost	£7 per unit	£4 per unit	£9 per unit
Direct labour requirements:	hours per	hours per	hours per
Cutting department:	unit	unit	unit
Skilled operatives	3	5	2
Unskilled operatives	6	1	3
Machining department	½	¼	⅓
Pressing department	2	3	4
Machine hour requirements:			
Machining department	2	1½	2½

The skilled operatives employed in the cutting department are paid £4 per hour and the unskilled operatives are paid £2.50 per hour. All the operatives in the machining and pressing departments are paid £3 per hour.

	Production departments			Service departments	
	Cutting	Machining	Pressing	Engineering	Personnel
Budgeted total overheads	£154,482	£64,316	£58,452	£56,000	£34,000
Service department costs are incurred for the benefit of other departments as follows:					
Engineering services	20%	45%	25%	—	10%
Personnel services	55%	10%	20%	15%	—

The company operates a full absorption costing system.

Required:

(a) Calculate, as equitably as possible, the total budgeted manufacturing cost of:
  (i) one completed unit of Product A, and
  (ii) one incomplete unit of Product B, which has been processed by the cutting and machining departments but which has not yet been passed into the pressing department. *(15 marks)*

(b) At the end of the first month of the year for which the above budget was prepared the production overhead control account for the machining department showed a credit balance. Explain the possible reasons for that credit balance. *(7 marks)*

(Total 22 marks)

7 The chairman of your company has been studying the budgets for the next accounting period and has shown particular interest in the production cost budget. In this the production overhead will increase from the current absorption rate of 200% of direct wages cost to 300%. The production manager protests that this increase is unacceptable.

As company cost accountant prepare a brief report for the chairman, explaining:

    (a)   how the overhead absorption rate is calculated and used;
    (b)   which factors may have contributed to the increase in the rate;
    (c)   the circumstances in which such an increase can be acceptable.

(20 marks)

8 A manufacturing company has two production cost centres, A and B, and one general services cost centre, GS, to which all common costs are charged.

The following data concerning the standard costs of its four products and its annual budgets are available:

Product	W	X	Y	Z
Per unit:	£	£	£	£
Prime cost	40	70	50	60
Selling price:				
first-quality products	148	218	117	148
second-quality products	30	36	35	30
Direct labour:	hours	hours	hours	hours
Production cost centre: A	12	14	6	8
B	16	24	8	8
Sales and production, per annum	units	units	units	units
	300	200	600	400

Fixed overhead, per annum:

	£
Production cost centre: A	26,400
B	52,800
General services cost centre GS	15,400*

*excludes any loss from second-quality products.

Overhead of cost centre GS is apportioned to production cost centres according to their direct labour hours. Overhead is absorbed into product costs by a direct labour hour rate.

The company budgets for 10% of its production as second-quality products, which are sold at the prices shown above.

You are required:

- (a) on the assumption that there were no second-quality products, to calculate:
  - (i) the cost per unit of each product;
  - (ii) the total profit budgeted to be earned in the year;
- (b) on the assumption that second-quality products are as budgeted and that loss on these is charged entirely to cost centre GS, to calculate:
  - (i) the cost per unit of each product;
  - (ii) the total profit budgeted to be earned in the year;
- (c) on the assumption that second-quality products are as budgeted but that the income from these is treated entirely as an addition to sales income, to calculate the total profit budgeted to be earned in the year;
- (d) on the assumption that second-quality products were as budgeted but that sales were only 85% of production in the year, to state whether you would charge against sales for the year the cost of:
  - (i) all second-quality products manufactured in the year; or
  - (ii) only those second-quality products that had been sold in the year;
  and to give very briefly reasons for your choice.

(30 marks)

ANSWERS

1

(a) **Stock valuation at 30 November**

	Audio and video £000	Electrical £000	Furniture £000	Total £000
Opening stock	120	80	200	400
Purchases	150	40	160	350
	270	120	360	750
Sales (at cost)				
$(215 + 5) \times \dfrac{120}{200}$	(132)			(132)
$(63 + 3) \times \dfrac{80}{110}$		(48)		(48)
$(224 + 7) \times \dfrac{200}{280}$			(165)	(165)
	138	72	195	405

(b) **Profit and loss statement for November**

	Audio and video £	Electrical £	Furniture £	Total £
Sales (net)	215,000	63,000	224,000	502,000
Less: Cost of sales	(132,000)	(48,000)	(165,000)	(345,000)
Gross profit	83,000	15,000	59,000	157,000
Less: Expenses	(49,275)	(13,580)	(44,230)	(107,085)
Net profit	33,725	1,420	14,770	49,915

Workings

Overhead apportionment schedules

Item	Basis	Total £	Audio £	Electrical £	Furniture £	Administration £
Rates	Area	4,000	1,500	500	1,250	750
Light and heat	Area	2,000	750	250	625	375
Advertising	Gross sales value	35,250	15,000	4,500	15,750	
Transport	Gross sales value	25,850	11,000	3,300	11,550	
Insurance	Gross sales value	3,525	1,500	450	1,575	
Miscellaneous	Gross sales value	1,175	500	150	525	
Canteen	Number of employees	4,125	2,025	300	1,125	675
Salaries and wages	Allocated	24,910	11,900	2,000	6,000	5,010
Depreciation	Allocated	3,750	500	750	1,000	1,500
Administration	Allocated	2,500				2,500
Administration	Gross sales value	—	4,600	1,380	4,830	(10,810)
		107,085	49,275	13,580	44,230	—

Comments

In part (a), closing stock is the balancing figure in the equation:

opening stock + purchases = cost of goods sold + closing stock

In part (b), the apportionment of costs is better shown as a working, leaving the answer as a brief table. Costs are apportioned amongst all four departments, and then the accumulated administration costs are apportioned amongst the three sales departments.

(a) **Cost apportionment**

	Total £	Forming £	Assembling £	Finishing £
Rent and rates	11,700 (1)	5,200	3,900	2,600
Light and heat	5,400 (1)	2,400	1,800	1,200
Insurance and maintenance	8,100 (1)	3,600	2,700	1,800
Building depreciation	18,000 (1)	8,000	6,000	4,000
Plant repairs	11,200 (2)	6,400	3,200	1,600
Plant depreciation	49,000 (2)	28,000	14,000	7,000
Supervisory staff	30,000 (3)	12,000	12,000	6,000
Personnel	11,400 (4)	2,640	5,040	3,720
Canteen	17,100 (4)	3,960	7,560	5,580
Warehouse	13,200 (5)	8,400	3,600	1,200
Administration	104,500 (6)	28,590	25,390	50,520
	279,600	109,190	85,190	85,220

Note: Costs have been apportioned according to (1) area; (2) value of plant; (3) size of workforce; (4) total staff; (5) materials consumed; (6) the basis stated in the question.

(b) **Overhead absorption rates**

Department	Forming	Assembling	Finishing
Apportioned overheads	£109,190	£85,190	£85,220
Workforce	20	40	30
Productive hours per man	1,680	1,680	1,680
Total productive hours	33,600	67,200	50,400
Hourly rate	$\dfrac{£109,190}{33,600}$	$\dfrac{£85,190}{67,200}$	$\dfrac{£85,200}{50,400}$
	£3.25	£1.27	£1.69

Fixed overhead cost per unit:

Foils: (£3.25 × 0.4) + (£1.27 × 2.0) + (£1.69 × 1.0) = £5.53
Sabres: (£3.25 × 0.4) + (£1.27 × 1.0) + (£1.69 × 1.0) = £4.26
Épées: (£3.25 × 1.0) + (£1.27 × 0.5) + (£1.69 × 0.5) = £4.73

Comment

These figures for fixed overhead cost per unit include, as the apportionment table shows, both fixed production overheads and fixed selling and administration overheads. Whereas both of these are included in the total absorption cost of sales, when valuing stock, fixed *production* overheads only should be included. This will mean that, if budgeted production differs from budgeted sales separate absorption rates will need to be worked out for fixed production overheads and fixed selling and administration overheads.

3

(a) **Allocation and apportionment schedule**

	Total £ thousands	North £ thousands	East £ thousands	West £ thousands
Rent, rates and insurance	70	30	25	15
Plant depreciation	40	20	15	5
Repairs and maintenance	20	12	4	4
Works canteen	22.5	6	7.5	9
Departmental office staff	59	15	18	26
Light and heat	10.5	4.5	3.75	2.25
Warehousing costs	21	13	6	2
Selling and administration	145	50	40	55
	388	150.5	119.25	118.25

(b) **Absorption rates**

Department	North	East	West
Fixed overhead	£150,500	£119,250	£118,250
Labour hours	35,000	45,000	55,000
Absorption rate (per hour)	£4.30	£2.65	£2.15

(c) **Standard cost card**

Weber PM2

	£	£
Materials		28.50
Labour: North (2 hours at £2.80)	5.60	
East (4 hours at £2.60)	10.40	
West (3 hours at £2.50)	7.50	
		23.50
Variable overheads		19.85
		71.85
Fixed overheads: North (2 × £4.30)	8.60	
East (4 × £2.65)	10.60	
West (3 × £2.15)	6.45	
		25.65
		97.50
Profit (35/65)		52.50
Selling price		150.00

Comments

In part (b), the basis of absorption is labour hours, and so the hourly absorption rate is the total cost divided by the number of labour hours, for each department.

In part (c), some students may wish to delay their attempt until some standard costing has been studied. However, the production of the standard cost card in this question simply puts together all the details about the different costs per unit, and the good student should earn extra marks here.

4

(a) **Current overhead absorption rate**

Budgeted production overhead	£225,000	
Budgeted direct wages cost	£150,000	
Current overhead absorption rate	£225,000	i.e., 150% of direct wages cost
	£150,000	

(b) **Production overhead charged to job No. 657**

150% of direct wages cost i.e. 150% × £170 = £255

Production cost of job No. 657:	£
Direct material	190
Direct wages	170
Production overhead	255
	615

Expected gross profit: $^1/_3$ of production cost £205

(c) (i) The calculation of overhead absorption rates for each department would lead to more accurate job costs where the spread of production overheads between each department is not even. In this factory, department A's heavy use of machine time results in high production overheads, whereas department B's overheads are low. Where jobs are done in different departments, the cost will be more fairly established by attaching departmental rates.

(ii)

Department	Basis of Absorption	Absorption rate	Reason
A	Machine hours	£120,000 / 40,000 = £3 per hour	The department is heavily dependent on machine time. The production overhead will include machine costs, such as depreciation and maintenance.
B	Direct labour hours	£30,000 / 50,000 = £0.6 per hour	Production is labour-dominated. A rate per hour is preferred to a percentage of cost to avoid the problems of differing rates of pay.
C	Direct labour hours	£75,000 / 25,000 = £3 per hour	As for department B.

(d) **Job No. 657: overhead**

		£
Department A	40 hours × £3.00	120
Department B	40 hours × £0.60	24
Department C	10 hours × £3.00	30
		174

(e) (i) **Current rate**

	Department A £	Department B £	Department C £	Total £
Actual overhead	130,000	28,000	80,000	238,000
Overhead absorbed (Based on wages)	45,000	120,000	45,000	210,000
Over/(Under) absorption	(85,000)	92,000	(35,000)	(28,000)

(ii) **Suggested rates**

	Department A £	Department B £	Department C £	Total £
Actual overhead	130,000	28,000	80,000	238,000
Overhead absorbed	135,000	27,000	90,000	252,000
Over/(Under) absorption	5,000	(1,000)	10,000	14,000

Comments

This is a good example of an examination question, in that it seeks to test understanding in more than one area — in this case, overheads and job costing. Some students may wish to spend time studying job costing before attempting this question, although the marks are to be earned for an appreciation of overheads.

An alternative answer to part (e) could use budgeted instead of actual overhead, as follows:

(e) (i) **Current rate**

	Department A £	Department B £	Department C £	Total £
Budgeted overhead	120,000	30,000	75,000	225,000
Overhead absorbed	45,000	120,000	45,000	210,000
Over/(Under) absorption	(75,000)	90,000	(30,000)	(15,000)

(ii) **Suggested rates**

	Department A £	Department B £	Department C £	Total £
Budgeted overhead	120,000	30,000	75,000	225,000
Overhead absorbed	135,000	27,000	90,000	252,000
Over/(Under) absorption	15,000	(3,000)	15,000	27,000

5

Report to the board: overhead absorption

As requested, the report sets out five methods of overhead absorption, and their merits in relationship to the company.

(a) **Rate per unit of output**

This is perhaps the simplest rate to use, calculated by dividing budgeted production overhead by the number of units of output budgeted. It is also easy to apply, attaching overheads to units produced.

However, it is only suitable where one product is made, since a differing range of products require differing times and skills. For this reason, this method should not be adopted by a multi-product company such as ours.

(b) **Percentage of materials cost**

The calculation of this second method is achieved by dividing the budgeted production overhead by the budgeted materials cost. This percentage can then be applied to every pound actually spent on materials to determine the overhead absorbed.

This method should be adopted only when the value of the materials is considered for all products to have some relationship to the overhead. It is best suited to organisations where material cost is a high percentage of total cost.

However, it has two weaknesses; firstly, most overheads are incurred through the passage of time, and thus have no connection with materials cost; and secondly, two similar materials of differing costs would absorb differing overhead charges.

(c) **Percentage of labour cost**

This is calculated by dividing budgeted overhead by the budgeted labour cost, and is straightforward to apply. This method is suitable where it is considered that relationship between overhead and wages is firm, and where wages cost is a high percentage of total cost.

However, the two weaknesses of method (b) apply here — a combination of time-based overhead and differing grades of labour render this method unsuitable.

Methods (d) and (e) recognise the idea that overheads are incurred through the lapse of time.

(d) **Rate per direct labour hour**

This is calculated by dividing budgeted overhead by budgeted labour hours. Every time an hour is worked, the overhead rate is applied.

Adoption of this method indicates that overheads are incurred because labour hours are being worked. This is, therefore, suitable for a stage of production that is predominantly manual. It will produce more accurate results than the labour cost percentage method, where different rates of pay are used.

(e) **Rate per machine hour**

This necessitates the recording of machine times, since it is calculated by dividing budgeted overhead by budgeted machine hours. However, this extra work is useful in that this method should be used only when machines play an important part in production.

For a capital-intensive operation, the overhead cost will consist, to a large extent, of machine-connected costs, such as depreciation, maintenance and power, and this method provides the most suitable basis of absorption.

Conclusion

An overhead absorption rate should be calculated for each department, using a rate per machine hour for capital-intensive departments, such as the machining department, and using a rate per direct labour hour for departments where

6

(a)   **Calculation of budgeted manufacturing costs**

(i)   **Product A**

		£	£
Direct material			7.00
Direct labour		£	
Cutting — skilled	3 × 4.00	12.00	
— unskilled	6 × 2.50	15.00	
Machining	½ × 3.00	1.50	
Pressing	2 × 3.00	6.00	
			34.50
Overheads			
Cutting	9 × 2.25	20.25	
Machining	2 × 3.50	7.00	
Pressing	2 × 2.00	4.00	
			31.25
			72.75

(ii)   **Product B**

		£	£
Direct material			4.00
Direct labour			
Cutting — skilled	5 × 4.00	20.00	
— unskilled	1 × 2.50	2.50	
Machining	¼ × 3.00	0.75	
			23.25
Overheads			
Cutting	6 × 2.25	13.50	
Machining	1½ × 3.50	5.25	
			18.75
			46.00

Workings

1 Apportionment of service department overheads

	Cutting £		Machining £		Pressing £		Engineering £		Personnel £
	154,482		64,316		58,452		56,000		34,000
(20%)	11,200	(45%)	25,200	(25%)	14,000		(56,000)	(10%)	5,600
	165,682		89,516		72,452		—		39,600
(55%)	21,780	(10%)	3,960	(20%)	7,920	(15%)	5,940		(39,600)
	187,462		93,476		80,372		5,940		—
(20%)	1,188	(45%)	2,673	(25%)	1,485		(5,940)	(10%)	594
	188,650		96,149		81,857		—		594
(55%)	327	(10%)	59	(20%)	119	(15%)	89		(594)
	188,977		96,208		81,976		89		—
(20%)	17	(45%)	41	(25%)	22		(89)	(10%)	9
	188,994		96,249		81,998		—		9
(55/85)	6	(10/85)	1	(25/85)	2		—		(9)
	189,000		96,250		82,000		—		—

Comment

Using this method of repeated reapportionment the service department costs are gradually reduced. The final distribution ignores the benefit received by engineering from personnel, since the effect is immaterial.

A neater apportionment may be achieved using algebra, as follows:

Let the total cost of the engineering department = E
and the total cost of the personnel department = P

Then
$$E = 56,000 + 0.15P$$
$$P = 34,000 + 0.1E$$

Solving simultaneously:

$$P = 34,000 + 0.1 (56,000 + 0.15P)$$
$$0.985\ P = 39,600$$
$$P = 40,203$$
$$E = 56,000 + (0.15 \times 40,203)$$
$$= 62,030$$

Now the reapportionment may be done in one step.

	Cutting £		Machining £		Pressing £		Engineering £		Personnel £
	154,482		64,316		58,452		56,000		34,000
E(20%)	12,406	(45%)	27,914	(25%)	15,507		(62,030)	(10%)	6,203
P(55%)	22,112	(10%)	4,020	(20%)	8,041	(15%)	6,030		(40,203)
	189,000		96,250		82,000		—		—

2 Calculation of overhead absorption rates

Although selection of bases for absorbing overheads is to a certain extent arbitrary, it would appear that the following are the most equitable:

Cutting   Direct labour hours
Machining   Machine hours
Pressing   Direct labour hours (although labout cost would give the same result)

(i) Cutting	A £	B £	C £	Total £
Labour hours — skilled	12,000	15,000	12,000	39,000.
— unskilled	24,000	3,000	18,000	45,000
				84,000

(ii) Machining Machine hours	8,000	4,500	15,000	27,500

(iii) Pressing Labour hours	8,000	9,000	24,000	41,000

Hence the overhead absorption rates are:

Cutting $\dfrac{189,000}{84,000} = £2.25$ per labour hour

Machining $\dfrac{96,250}{27,500} = £3.50$ per machine hour

Pressing $\dfrac{82,000}{41,000} = £2.00$ per labour hour

(b) A credit balance on a production overhead control account indicates that the amount of overhead actually absorbed exceeds the amount incurred.

The possible reasons for this are:

(i)   The actual activity level was greater than that budgeted.
(ii) The actual amount incurred was less than that budgeted.
(iii) Activity is seasonal and the first month is a month of higher than average activity.
(iv) Similarly, the first month's actual costs are less than average.

7

(a) The company costing system provides a whole range of information, and one particular piece of information provides the answer to the question: 'How much does it cost to make one unit of production?'

The cost of production may be split into two sorts of cost, direct and indirect. The direct costs — materials and labour — incurred in the manufacture of one unit are relatively easy to ascertain, since direct costs by their nature may be attached to individual products. Indirect costs, or overheads, such as factory rent, depreciation and power, do not relate to one unit of production, and so the overhead cost per unit is not readily available.

The overhead absorption rate is a means of attaching overhead cost to each unit of production. Our company uses direct wages cost as a basis for absorbing overheads. To calculate the overhead absorption rate, two estimates are made; firstly, an estimate of the overhead likely to be incurred during the coming year; and secondly, an estimate of the direct wages costs expected over the same year. For instance, in 1976 we estimated an overhead of £4 million and direct wages cost of £2 million, giving a rate of 200%.

In computing the cost of a unit produced, we now have a means of attaching overheads to the unit, since for every £1 incurred on direct wages we add £2 for production overhead; thus the overhead rate is used to help build up the cost of each unit.

(b) It is instructive to express the overhead rate as a fraction:

$$\frac{\text{budgeted overhead cost}}{\text{budgeted direct wages cost}}$$

The rate will increase in any of the following circumstances:

  (i)   Inflation, where overhead increases at a greater rate than direct wages.
  (ii) The method of production changes; more use is made of machines, and less of labour.
  (iii) There is a reduction in output; direct wages costs will fall proportionately, but overhead costs fall to a lesser extent, since the fixed part of the overhead cannot be altered in the short term.
  (iv) Expansion in service departments without a corresponding increase in direct wages.

(c) The control of overhead costs is an important part of costing, and a rise of 50% in the absorption rate seems excessive. However, part (b) of the report suggested four possible factors, which might explain the increase in this case.

  (i)   *Increased mechanisation.* Where this leads to a lower unit cost, the nature of the cost incurred is immaterial. Production cost will now be mainly overhead costs (maintenance, depreciation, etc.), and the present basis of absorption is not very useful — a rate per machine hour would be more appropriate.
  (ii) *Inflation.* Where a large increase in overheads is caused by external factors, such as rate increases, it is unavoidable, and cannot be regarded as unacceptable, although a very high inflation rate in one particular area of production (such as rates) may mean a shift in long-term planning.
  (iii) *Service department expansion.* Where this results in a better and more marketable product then the rate increase caused is acceptable.

(iv) *Reduction in output.* Contraction of the company's activities may be unavoidable. In the short term, overheads may remain high, but if the reduction is permanent, then steps must be taken to bring down the level of overheads.

8

(a) (i) **Cost per unit**

	W	X	Y	Z
	£	£	£	£
Prime cost	40	70	50	60
Fixed overhead A	30	35	15	20
B	56	84	28	28
	126	189	93	108

(ii) **Total budgeted profit**

	W	X	Y	Z	Total
	£	£	£	£	£
Selling price per unit	148	218	117	148	
Cost per unit	126	189	93	108	
Profit per unit	22	29	24	40	
Budgeted units	300	200	600	400	
Budgeted profit	6,600	5,800	14,400	16,000	42,800

Workings

Calculation of overhead cost per hour

	W	X	Y	Z	Total
Units	300	200	600	400	
Cost centre:					
A Hours/unit	12	14	6	8	
Total	3,600	2,800	3,600	3,200	13,200
B Hours/unit	16	24	8	8	
Total	4,800	4,800	4,800	3,200	17,600
					30,800

Overheads

	A	B	GS
	£	£	£
	26,400	52,800	15,400
	6,600	8,800	(15,400)
Total	33,000	61,600	
Labour hours	13,200	17,600	
Rate per hour	£2.50	£3.50	

Calculation of overhead cost per unit

	W	X	Y	Z
A: Hours	12	14	6	8
at £2.50	£30	£35	£15	£20
B: Hours	16	24	8	8
at £3.50	£56	£84	£28	£28

(b) Although the question does not make this explicit, it is important to realise that the loss on second-quality products (to be charged to GS) is to be calculated *before* absorbing any overheads. In this way, only first-quality products recover fixed overheads.

Calculation of loss	W	X	Y	Z	Total
	£	£	£	£	£
Selling price	30	36	35	30	
Prime cost	40	70	50	60	
Loss per units	10	34	15	30	
Units sold (10%)	30	20	60	40	
Total loss	300	680	900	1,200	3,080

Cost centre overheads	A	B	GS
	£	£	£
	26,400	52,800	15,400
Add: Loss			3,080
			18,480
	7,920	10,560	(18,480)
Total	34,320	63,360	
Labour hours (90%)	11,880	15,840	
Rate per hour	£2.89	£4.00	

Calculation of overhead cost per unit

	W	X	Y	Z
A: Hours	12	14	6	8
at £2.89	£34.67	£40.44	£17.33	£23.11
B: Hours	16	24	8	8
at £4.00	£64	£96	£32	£32

(i) **Cost per unit**

	W	X	Y	Z
	£	£	£	£
Prime cost	40	70	50	60
Fixed overhead: A	34.67	40.44	17.33	23.11
B	64	96	32	32
	138.67	206.44	99.33	115.11

(ii) **Total budgeted profit**

	W £	X £	Y £	Z £	Total £
Selling price	148	218	117	148	
Cost	138.67	206.44	99.33	115.11	
Unit profit	9.33	11.56	17.67	32.89	
Budgeted units (90%)	270	180	540	360	
Budgeted profit	2,520	2,080	9,540	11,840	25,980

(c)

	W	X	Y	Z	Total £
Sales revenue:					
Firsts: units	270	180	540	360	
SP	£148	£218	£117	£148	
	39,960	39,240	63,180	53,280	195,660
Seconds: units	30	20	60	40	
SP	£30	£36	£35	£30	
	900	720	2,100	1,200	4,920
					200,580
Cost: all units (from a(i))					
units	300	200	600	400	
unit cost	126	189	93	108	
	37,800	37,800	55,800	43,200	174,600
Budgeted profit					25,980

(d) **Details of seconds**

	W	X	Y	Z
Sales	25	17	51	34
Closing stock	5	3	9	6
Production	30	20	60	40
	£	£	£	£
Selling price	30	36	35	30
Prime cost	40	70	50	60

Each second-quality product sustains a loss on manufacture. If only the cost of products sold in the year is charged against sales, then part of the loss is carried forward, which is not prudent accounting policy (and closing stock would be valued at a figure higher than net realisable value).

Thus, choice (i) is preferred.

6 Cost book-keeping

Like overhead allocation (chapter 5), this is an area of high-mark questions which can be dealt with by the logical application of double-entry procedures; but you must have a clear appreciation of the distinction between interlocking and integrated cost and financial accounts. The question will specify which system is required.

Where T accounts are called for, or can be helpful in arriving at your answer, set them out clearly and give yourself plenty of space so that your display is not cramped and you have room for arithmetical corrections should they be necessary.

STUDY REQUIREMENTS

(a) Cost book-keeping using double entry.
(b) Interlocking and integrated accounts.
(c) Notional overheads (such as interest or rental charges).

QUESTIONS

1 Belinda has been talking to a trainee accountant, Martin, who has been teaching her double-entry. He tried to show Belinda the difference between integrated accounts and interlocking accounts; however, Belinda is still puzzled, and asks you in your capacity as a cost accountant for a further demonstration.

(a) Describe briefly what you understand by the terms:

    (i) Integrated cost accounts.
    (ii) Interlocking cost accounts.   *(6 marks)*

(b) Tabulate the advantages and disadvantages of integrated cost accounts.
                           (9 marks)
                    (Total 15 marks)

2 Draw a flowchart or diagram to show the typical accounting entries for the cost ledger in an interlocking system, where separate cost and financial accounts are kept.

Treat all materials and wages as direct costs.   *(12 marks)*

3 'I've got a problem', Alastair tells you at the squash club. 'My financial accountant tells me we've made a profit of £12,000 this month, but my cost accountant insists that the figure should be £16,000. Which one is right?'

You ascertain that Alastair's company keeps its financial and cost accounts separate, and you note the following information:

(a) Stock valuations:

	Financial accounts £	Cost accounts £
Raw materials: opening	20,000	16,000
closing	24,000	22,000
Finished goods: opening	50,000	51,000
closing	60,000	61,500

(b) The following items do not appear in the cost accounts:

	£
Donations: Prestbury Bowls Club	700
OXFAM	300
Profit on sale of Fiat 500	2,000
Exchange rate losses	2,500
Bad debt written off	500
Discounts allowed	500
Discounts received	400
Rents receivable	600

You are required to prepare a statement reconciling the two profit figures.

                              (15 marks)

4 K Limited operates separate cost accounting and financial accounting systems. The following manufacturing and trading statement has been prepared from the financial accounts for the *quarter* ended 31 March:

	£	£
Raw materials:		
Opening stock	48,000	
Purchases	108,800	
	156,800	
Closing stock	52,000	
Raw materials consumed		104,800
Direct wages		40,200
Production overhead		60,900
Production cost incurred		205,900
Work-in-progress:		
Opening stock	64,000	
Closing stock	58,000	
		6,000
Cost of goods produced carried down		211,900
Sales		440,000
Finished goods:		
Opening stock	120,000	
Cost of goods produced brought down	211,900	
	331,900	
Closing stock	121,900	
Cost of goods sold		210,000
Gross profit		230,000

From the cost accounts, the following information has been extracted:

	£
Control account balances at 1 January:	
Raw material stores	49,500
Work-in-progress	60,100
Finished goods	115,400
Transactions for the quarter:	
Raw materials issued	104,800
Cost of goods produced	222,500
Cost of goods sold	212,100
Loss of materials damaged by flood (insurance claim pending)	2,400

A notional rent of £4,000 *per month* has been charged in the cost accounts. Production overhead was absorbed at the rate of 185% of direct wages.

You are required:

(a) to prepare the following control accounts in the cost ledger:

raw materials stores;
work-in-progress;
finished goods;
production overhead;   *(10 marks)*

(b) to prepare a statement reconciling the gross profit as per the cost accounts and the financial accounts;   *(11 marks)*

(c) to comment on the possible accounting treatment(s) of the under- or over-absorption of production overhead, assuming that the financial year of the company is 1 January to 31 December.   *(4 marks)*
                                                           (Total 25 marks)

5 Gooch uses an integrated system. You are required to write up the appropriate ledger accounts for the year (including profit and loss account) and prepare a balance sheet as at 31 December from the following information:

Balance sheet as at 1 January

	£	£	£
Fixed assets:	**Cost**	**Depreciation**	
Plant and machinery	50,000	10,000	40,000
Current assets:	£	£	
Stocks:			
Raw materials	6,000		
Work-in-progress	8,000		
Finished goods	9,000	23,000	
Balance at bank		4,000	
		27,000	
Current liabilities:			
Trade creditors	6,000		
Accrual for PAYE	1,000	7,000	
			20,000
			60,000
Financed by:			
Gooch: Capital account			60,000

Data for the year

	£
Materials purchased	48,000
Materials issued to production	44,000
Net wages and salaries paid	60,000
PAYE paid	8,000
Production wages (direct)	40,000
Indirect production wages and salaries	17,000
Non-production wages and salaries	12,000
Deductions for PAYE	9,000
Depreciation charge	5,000
Indirect production expenses	14,000
Non-production expenses	30,000
Payments for expenses	39,000
Production overhead recovered	40,000
Cost of completed production	85,000
Factory cost of sales	76,000
Cash sales	150,000
Trade creditors owing at 31 December	5,000

(25 marks)

6 B Limited operates an integrated accounting system and the following details given relate to one year.

You are required, from the details given:

    (a)   to enter in the appropriate ledger accounts the transactions for the year;

    (b)   to prepare a profit and loss account for the year; and

    (c)   to prepare a balance sheet as at the end of the year.

Trial balance at beginning of the year:

	£ thousands	£ thousands
Capital	—	1,000
Reserves	—	200
Creditors	—	150
Expense creditors	—	20
Freehold buildings, at cost	500	—
Plant and machinery, at cost	300	—
Provision for depreciation of plant and machinery	—	100
Stock of: raw materials	220	—
work-in-progress	40	—
finished goods	60	—
Debtors	200	—
Bank	150	—
	1,470	1,470

The following data for the year are given:

	£ thousands
Materials: purchased on credit	990
returned to suppliers	40
issued to production	850
Production: wages incurred	250
salaries	60
expenses incurred	320
Carriage inwards	45
Provision for depreciation of plant and machinery	50
Production: overhead absorbed	425
Production, at standard cost	1,600
Administration: salaries	100
expenses incurred	260
overhead absorbed in finished goods	380
Selling and distribution: salaries	80
expenses incurred	120
absorbed in cost of sales	210
Finished goods sold	2,000
Sales on credit	2,500
Sales returns	60
Variance: direct material: price (adverse)	35
usage (favourable)	20
direct wages rate (favourable)	15
direct labour efficiency (favourable)	30
production overhead: expenditure (adverse)	25
efficiency (favourable)	40
Abnormal loss of raw material stock, insurance claim agreed and cash received	60
New machinery purchased, paid by cheque	50
Paid: creditors	895
expense creditors	730
Cash discount received from trade creditors	25
Paid wages and salaries	425
Deduction from wages and salaries	50
Received cheques from debtors	2,350
Cash discount allowed	35
Bad debts written off	25

All 'price' variances (i.e., direct material price, direct wages rate, production overhead expenditure) are recorded in the relevant expenditure accounts; 'quantity' variances (i.e., direct material usage, direct labour efficiency, production overhead efficiency) are recorded in the work-in-progress account.

(35 marks)

ANSWERS

1

(a)   (i) **Integrated cost accounts**

This is a unified accounting system combining the cost accounts and the financial accounts. One set of books is kept, one profit figure is generated, and information from the accounting records is used for both financial and managerial purposes.

(ii) **Interlocking cost accounts**

Two separate accounting systems are kept, one for cost accounts and one for financial accounts. Interlocking is achieved by a control account in each system, which acts as a check between the two systems.

(b) **Integrated cost accounts**

Advantages	Disadvantages
1 Easier to maintain.	1 No independent check on the accounting records.
2 Quicker and therefore less costly to manage.	2 Two bases for stock valuation cannot be employed.
3 No 'division' of staff into costing and finance.	3 Insufficient details available for complex production processes.
4 No need for reconciliations.	4 Only one classification of costs available.
	5 No scope for notional charges.

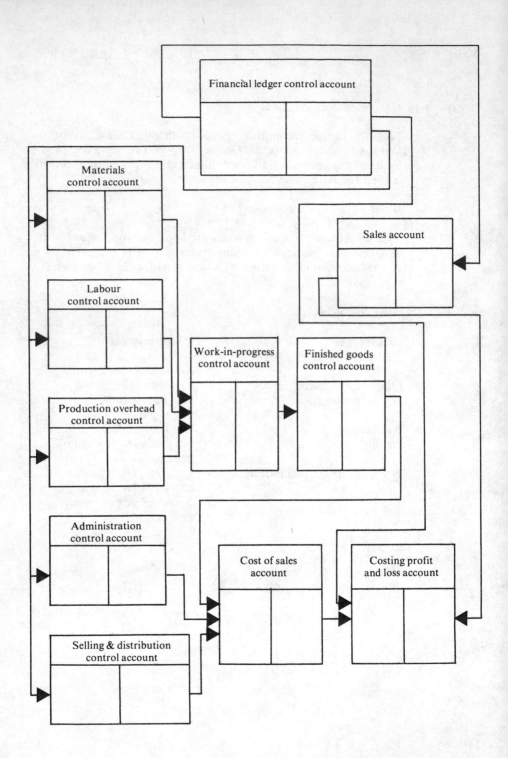

3 Reconciliation of financial profit and costing profit

	£ Add	£ Less	£
Profit per financial accounts			12,000
Differences in stock valuations:			
Raw materials: opening	4,000		
closing		2,000	
Finished goods: opening		1,000	
closing	1,500		
	5,500	3,000	2,500
			14,500
Items appearing on financial accounts only:			
Charges:			
Donations to charities	1,000		
Exchange rate losses	2,500		
Discounts allowed	500		
Bad debts	500		
Credits:			
Profit on sale of motor car		2,000	
Discounts received		400	
Rents receivable		600	
	4,500	3,000	1,500
Profit per cost accounts			16,000

4

(a) Cost ledger control accounts

Raw material stores

	£		£
Balance b/f	49,500	Issued to WIP	104,800
Purchases	108,800	Less: flood damage	2,400
		Balance c/d	51,100
	158,300		158,300

Work-in-progress

	£		£
Balance b/f	60,100	Finished goods	222,500
Raw materials	104,800	Balance c/d	56,970
Direct wages	40,200		
Production overhead	74,370		
	279,470		279,470

Finished goods

	£		£
Balance b/f	115,400	Cost of goods sold	212,100
WIP	222,500	Balance c/d	125,800
	337,900		337,900

Production overhead

	£		£
Cost ledger control	60,900	WIP (40,200 × 185%)	74,370
Notional rent	12,000		
Costing PL a/c (over-absorption)	1,470		
	74,370		74,370

(b) **Reconciliation of cost accounts and financial accounts**

Cost accounts	£	£
Sales		440,000
Less: cost of goods sold		212,100
Gross profit		227,900
Less: stock loss		2,400
		225,500
Add: production overhead over-absorbed	1,470	
Notional rent	12,000	
		13,470
		238,970

Differences in stock valuations	Less	Add	
Raw materials: opening stock	1,500		
closing stock	900		
WIP: opening stock		3,900	
closing stock	1,030		
Finished goods: opening stock		4,600	
closing stock		3,900	
	3,430	12,400	8,970
Financial accounts gross profit			230,000

(c) The over-absorbed production overhead may be treated in one of the following ways:

    (i)   Credited to cost accounting profit and loss account.

    (ii) Carried forward as a credit balance in the production overhead control account.

    (iii) Apportioned between cost of goods sold and closing stock of finished goods.

Method (i) is usually adopted as in part (b). Perhaps the only circumstances which would justify method (ii) would be seasonal fluctuations in overhead costs. Method (iii) implies doubt about the validity of the basis of absorption since under this method the cost accounts fall in line with the financial accounts.

5

PLANT AND MACHINERY

Balance b/f	50,000	Balance c/d	50,000

PROVISION FOR DEPRECIATION

		Balance b/f	10,000
Balance c/d	15,000	Production overhead	5,000
	15,000		15,000

RAW MATERIALS

Balance b/f	6,000	WIP	44,000
Creditors	48,000	Balance c/d	10,000
	54,000		54,000

WORK-IN-PROGRESS

Balance b/f	8,000		
Materials	44,000	Finished	
Wages	40,000	goods	85,000
Overhead	40,000	Balance c/d	47,000
	132,000		132,000

FINISHED GOODS

Balance b/f	9,000	Cost of sales	76,000
WIP	85,000	Balance c/d	18,000
	94,000		94,000

BANK

Balance b/f	4,000	Wages and salaries	60,000
Sales	150,000	PAYE	8,000
Balance c/d	2,000	Expenses	39,000
		Trade creditors	49,000
	156,000		156,000

TRADE CREDITORS

Bank	49,000	Balance b/f	6,000
Balance c/d	5,000	Materials	48,000
	54,000		54,000

PAYE AND NIC

Bank	8,000	Balance b/f	1,000
Balance c/d	2,000	Wages	9,000
	10,000		10,000

GOOCH: CAPITAL ACCOUNT

		Balance b/f	60,000
Balance c/d	96,000	P & L A/C	36,000
	96,000		96,000

WAGES AND SALARIES

Bank	60,000	WIP	40,000
PAYE	9,000	Production overhead	17,000
		Non-production overhead	12,000
	69,000		69,000

PRODUCTION OVERHEAD

Wages	17,000	WIP	40,000
Depreciation	5,000		
Expenses	14,000		
Over-recovery	4,000		
	40,000		40,000

NON-PRODUCTION EXPENSES

Wages	12,000	COS	42,000
Expenses	30,000		
	42,000		42,000

EXPENSES

Bank	39,000	Production	14,000
Balance c/d	5,000	Non production	30,000
	44,000		44,000

COST OF SALES

Finished goods	76,000		
Expenses	42,000	P & L A/C	118,000
	118,000		118,000

SALES

P & L A/C	150,000	Bank	150,000

PROFIT AND LOSS ACCOUNT

Cost of sales	118,000	Sales	150,000
Net profit:		Over-recovery of production overhead	4,000
Gooch	36,000		
	154,000		154,000

Balance sheet as at 31 December

Fixed assets:	Cost £	Depreciation £	£
Plant and machinery	50,000	15,000	35,000
Current assets:	£	£	
Stocks:			
Materials	10,000		
Work-in-progress	47,000		
Finished goods	18,000	75,000	
Current liabilities:			
Trade creditors	5,000		
Accrued expenses	5,000		
Accrued PAYE	2,000		
Bank	2,000	14,000	
			61,000
			96,000
Financed by:			
Gooch: Capital account			96,000

Comment

A good question to practice ledger entries.

6

(a) **Ledger accounts in £ thousands**

CAPITAL

Balance c/d	1,000	Balance b/d	1,000

RESERVES

Balance c/d	200	Balance b/d	200

CREDITORS

Returns	40	Balance b/d	150
Bank	895	Raw materials	990
Cash discount	25		
Balance c/d	180		
	1,140		1,140

EXPENSE CREDITORS

Bank	730	Balance b/d	20
Balance c/d	35	Production expenses	320
		Carriage inwards	45
		Administration expenses	260
		Selling and distribution expenses	120
	765		765

FREEHOLD BUILDINGS, AT COST

Balance b/d	500	Balance c/d	500

PLANT AND MACHINERY, AT COST

Balance b/d	300	Balance c/d	350
Bank	50		
	350		350

PROVISION FOR DEPRECIATION OF PLANT AND MACHINERY

		Balance b/d	100
Balance c/d	150	Production overhead	50
	150		150

RAW MATERIAL CONTROL

Balance b/d	220	Returns	40
Creditors	990	Work-in-progress	850
		Price variance	35
		Abnormal loss	60
		Balance c/d	225
	1,210		1,210

WORK-IN-PROGRESS CONTROL

Balance b/d	40	Finished goods	1,600
Raw material	850	Balance c/d	55
Salaries and wages control	250		
Production overhead	425		
Material usage variance	20		
Labour efficiency variance	30		
Production overhead efficiency variance	40		
	1,655		1,655

FINISHED GOODS CONTROL

Balance b/d	60	Cost of sales	2,000
Work-in-progress	1,600	Balance c/d	40
Administration overhead	380		
	2,040		2,040

DEBTORS

Balance b/d	200	Sales returns	60
Sales	2,500	Bank	2,350
		Cash discount	35
		Bad debts	25
		Balance c/d	230
	2,700		2,700

BANK

Balance b/d	150	Plant and machinery	50
Abnormal (Loss)	60	Creditors	895
Debtors	2,350	Expense creditors	730
		Salaries and wages control	425
		Balance c/d	460
	2,560		2,560

SALARIES AND WAGES CONTROL

Wages rate variance	15	Work-in-progress	250
Bank	425	Production overhead	60
Deductions	50	Administration control	100
		Selling and distribution control	80
	490		490

PRODUCTION OVERHEAD CONTROL

Salaries and wages control	60	Work-in-progress	425
Expense creditors	320	Expenditure variance	25
*Expense creditors (carriage)	45	Capacity variance	25
Provision for depreciation	50		
	475		475

*Carriage inwards may be charged to raw material control.

ADMINISTRATION OVERHEAD CONTROL

Salaries and wages control	100	Finished goods	380
Expense creditors	260		
Variance	20		
	380		380

SELLING AND DISTRIBUTION OVERHEAD CONTROL

Salaries and wages control	80	Cost of sales	210
Expense creditors	120		
Variance	10		
	210		210

COST OF SALES

Selling and distribution	210	Profit and loss	2,210
Finished goods	2,000		
	2,210		2,210

SALES

Returns	60	Debtors	2,500
Profit and loss	2,440		
	2,500		2,500

ABNORMAL LOSS

Raw material	60	Bank	60

CASH DISCOUNT RECEIVED

Profit and loss	25	Creditors	25

DEDUCTIONS FROM SALARIES AND WAGES

Balance c/d	50	Salaries and wages control	50

CASH DISCOUNT ALLOWED

Debtors	35	Profit and loss	35

BAD DEBTS

Debtors	25	Profit and loss	25

Comments

(a) 'Production: wages incurred' is the charge to production (i.e., work-in-progress) for wages.

(b) The following expenses comprise production overhead:

   (i)   Production salaries.
   (ii) Production expenses.
   (iii) Depreciation charge.
   (iv) Carriage inwards.

   They are absorbed into work-in-progress.

(c) 'Production at standard cost' is the amount to transfer from work-in-progress to finished goods.

(d) Administration salaries and expenses are absorbed into finished goods. (which is unorthodox).

(e) All variances have been transferred directly to profit and loss account, where they have been shown in detail.

(f) Deductions from wages and salaries have been treated as unpaid at the year end, since no details of payment are given.

(g) When closing off the ledger accounts the following accounts will have a closing balance, which will appear on the balance sheet:

Capital	Raw material
Reserves	Work-in-progress
Creditors	Finished goods
Expense creditors	Debtors
Freehold	Bank
Plant and machinery	Deductions
Provision for depreciation	

There is a further variance (capacity) on the production overhead account, and a variance closes off both the administration and the selling and distribution accounts.

All remaining accounts are closed off to the profit and loss account.

(b) Profit and loss account for the year

	£ thousands	£ thousands	£ thousands
Sales			2,440
Cost of sales			2,210
			230

Variances	£ thousands Favourable	£ thousands Adverse	£thousands
Direct material: price		35	
usage	20		
Direct wages: rate	15		
Direct labour efficiency	30		
Production overhead:			
expenditure		25	
efficiency	40		
capacity		25	
Administration	20		
Selling and distribution	10		
	135	85	50
			280
Add: Discounts received			25
			305
Less: Discounts allowed		35	
Bad debts		25	60
Net profit			245

(c) **Balance sheet as at year end**

Employment of capital:

Fixed assets:

Freehold buildings, at cost		500
Plant and machinery, at cost	350	
Less: Depreciation	150	200
		700

Current assets:

Stocks: Raw materials	225	
Work-in-progress	55	
Finished goods	40	
	320	
Debtors	230	
Bank	460	1,010

Current liabilities:

Creditors	180	
Expense creditors	35	
Deductions from salaries and wages	50	265
Net current assets		745
		1,445

Financed by:

Capital		1,000
Profit	245	
Reserves	200	445
		1,445

7 Process costing

This chapter is concerned with basic process costing. Questions on process losses are in Chapter 8; and those on joint products and by-products are in Chapter 18.

You are concerned in this chapter with the cost of units transferred from one process to another or emerging from the final process; and the valuation of uncompleted work-in-process. You must be completely familiar with the method of identifying 'equivalent units' and their cost.

At various stages of calculation you will need column headings for input units and unit cost; material cost; labour cost (and possibly overheads); total cost; output units, including equivalent units; and output unit cost. Use double-width analysis paper if it is available. Some questions will also call for T accounts.

STUDY REQUIREMENTS

    (a)   Continuous output costing.
    (b)   Equivalent (or 'effective') units.
    (c)   Process costing.

QUESTIONS

1 The Allbutt Brewery processes a range of beers including its prize-winning 'Dunn's Pedigree', which passes through the malting, hopping and skimming departments before completion.

Details for the hopping department for May 19X0 are as follows:

Quantity transferred from malting department 1,000 litres, cost £1,250
Quantity transferred to skimming department 600 litres
Costs added:

Materials	£2,000
Labour	£1,260
Overhead	£570

Closing work-in-progress: Degree of completion

Materials	50%
Labour	60%
Overhead	40%

There was no opening work-in-progress, and no losses occurred during the month.

You are required to calculate:

    (a)   The cost of the quantity transferred to skimming department; and
    (b)   The value of closing work-in-progress.

Assume no increase or decrease in volume due to addition of materials.

(10 marks)

2 Bewley Ltd has developed a process for the manufacture of after-shave. Materials are added at the beginning of the process and conversion costs are incurred uniformly. Details for the month ended 30 June 19X5 are as follows:

Work-in-progress at 1 June 19X5: 4,000 litres, 75% complete
Work-in-progress at 30 June 19X5: 15,000 litres, 60% complete
Materials added in June: 30,000 litres

	Materials	Conversion costs
Value of opening work-in-progress	£10,800	£8,500
Costs added in June	£30,000	£47,500

You are required to prepare a cost of production report for the process for June, showing:

    (a)   a quantity schedule;
    (b)   costs charged to the process;
    (c)   cost of finished goods;
    (d)   value of closing work-in-process; and

any additional computations necessary.

N.B. Assume a weighted average basis is to be used.   *(18 marks)*

3 Using the details in question 2, prepare a similar cost of production report, but this time assuming a FIFO basis is used.

(18 marks)

4 Product B is made by means of three processes. Material is put into process at the start of process 1 and the output transferred to process 2. The output of process 2 is transferred to process 3 and the completed product of process 3 is transferred to finished goods stock.

Data for the week ended 31 October 19X0 relating to product B are given below:

Process		Units	Stage of completion	Cost £
1	Work in process, at start	20	50%	270
	Input: Material	270		3,240
	Labour and overhead			840
	Output: Transferred to process 2	290		
2	Input: Material added			530
	Labour and overhead			1,540
	Output: Transferred to process 3	240		
	Work in process, at end:			
	Material added	50	{50%	
	Labour and overhead		{80%	
3	Work in process, at start:	90		
	Transferred cost			2,025
	Labour and overhead		33¹/₃%	105
	Input: Labour and overhead			1,015
	Output: Transferred to finished goods stock	300		
	Work in process, at end	30	66²/₃%	
	Finished goods:			
	Stock at start	100		2,700
	Sold	324		

No units were lost in production and the weighted average basis of pricing is to be used.

You are required to prepare for the week ended 31 October 19X0:

(a)   the three manufacturing process accounts, showing in each:

    (i)   the unit cost;
    (ii)   the value of work in process; and
    (iii) the cost of production transferred; and

(b)   the finished goods stock account.

(30 marks)

5 The Godwin company makes plastic ducks. Details for the month ending 31 December 19X1 are as follows:

Work-in-progress at 1 December 19X1:

200 units, cost	£1,250	
Degree of completion:	Materials	75%
	Labour	50%
	Overhead	30%

Costs added during December:

	£
Materials	10,250
Labour	8,000
Overhead	5,895

Work-in-progress at 31 December 19X1:

500 units		
Degree of completion:	Materials	60%
	Labour	40%
	Overhead	25%

The company completed 1,900 units during December.

You are required to calculate the cost of units completed.

(12 marks)

6 The following figures relate to process X for the week ending 26 February 19X2:

Opening work-in-process:	
3,000 units	£
Costs: From process W	39,000
Materials	7,000
Labour and overhead	3,600
	49,600

Units transferred from process W = 39,000, cost £507,000

Costs added: Materials	£242,600
Labour and overhead	£445,200

Closing WIP: 2,000 units

Degree of completion: Materials	80%
Labour and overhead	40%

Unfortunately, Alastair, the cost accountant, has thrown away details of the degree of completion of opening WIP.

You are required to prepare, for the week ending 26 February 19X2, the process X account, assuming no production losses.

(15 marks)

ANSWERS

1

Flow of product

Opening WIP + transfers from malting = transfer to skimming + closing WIP
NIL + 1,000 = 600 + 400

Equivalent units	litres	Materials		Labour		Overhead	
Transferred out	600	100%:	600		600		600
Closing WIP	400	50%:	200	60%:	240	40%:	160
			800		840		760

Cost per equivalent unit

		Materials	Labour	Overhead
Total cost		£2,000	£1,260	£570
Unit cost		£2.50	£1.50	£0.75

Cost of product transferred to skimming department

	£	
Transferred-in cost	1.25	
Materials	2.50	
Labour	1.50	
Overhead	0.75	
	6.00 × 600 litres =	£3,600

Value of closing WIP

	Equivalent units	Unit costs £		
Transferred-in	400	1.25	500	
Materials	200	2.50	500	
Labour	240	1.50	360	
Overhead	160	0.75	120	£1,480

2 Cost of production report for the process for June 19X5

(a) **Quantity schedule**	litres	litres
Quantity in process at 1 June 19X5	4,000	
Quantity added in process during June	30,000	34,000
Quantity completed and transferred to finished goods	19,000	
Quantity in process at 30 June 19X5	15,000	34,000

87

(b) Costs charged to the process	Total cost £	Unit cost £
Work-in-progress at 1 June 19X5:		
Materials	10,800	
Conversion costs	8,500	
Costs added during June:		
Materials	30,000	1.20
Conversion costs	47,500	2.00
	96,800	3.20

(c) Costs accounted for as follows:	£
Transferred to finished goods	60,800
Work-in-progress at 30 June 19X5	36,000
	96,800

Workings

Flow of product

Opening WIP + started = completed + closing WIP
4,000 + 30,000 = 19,000 + 15,000

Calculation of equivalent units

	litres	Materials	Conversion costs
Completed	19,000	100%: 19,000	100%: 19,000
Closing WIP	15,000	100%: 15,000	60%: 9,000
		34,000	28,000

Total costs	£	£
b/f	10,800	8,500
Added	30,000	47,500
	40,800	56,000

Unit costs	£1.20	£2.00

Cost of finished goods
19,000 × £3.20 = £60,800

(d) Value of closing WIP	Equivalent units	Unit cost	£
Materials	15,000	£1.20	18,000
Conversion costs	9,000	£2.00	18,000
			36,000

3   Cost of production report for the process for June 19X5

(a) **Quantity schedule**

	litres	litres
Quantity in process at 1 June 19X5	4,000	
Quantity added in process during June	30,000	34,000
Quantity completed and transferred to finished goods	19,000	
Quantity in process at 30 June 19X5	15,000	34,000

(b) **Costs charged to the process**

	Total cost	Unit cost
	£	£
Work-in-progress at 1 June 19X5:		
Materials	10,800	
Conversion costs	8,500	
Costs added during June:		
Materials	30,000	1.20
Conversion costs	47,500	2.00
	96,800	3.20

(c) **Costs accounted for as follows:**

	£
Transferred to finished goods	64,700
Work-in-progress at 30 June 19X5	32,100
	96,800

Workings

Calculation of equivalent units

	litres	Materials		Conversion costs	
Opening WIP to completion	4,000	NIL	—	25%:	1,000
Started and completed	15,000	100%:	15,000	100%:	15,000
Closing WIP	15,000	100%:	15,000	60%:	9,000
Equivalent units for June			30,000		25,000
Current costs added in June			£30,000		£47,500

4

(a) **Process 1**

	Units	£		Units	£
WIP b/f	20	270	Transfer: Process 2	290	4,350
Material	270	3,240	(at £15 per unit)		
Labour and overhead	—	840			
	290	4,350		290	4,350

Process 2

	Units	£		Units	£
Transfer: Process 1	290	4,350	Transfer: Process 3	240	5,400
Material	—	530	(at £22.50 per unit)		
Labour and overhead	—	1,540	WIP c/d	50	1,020
	290	6,420		290	6,420

Process 3

	Units	£		Units	£
WIP b/f	90	2,130	Transfer: Finished		
Transfer: Process 2	240	5,400	goods	300	7,800
Labour and overhead	—	1,015	(at £26 per unit)		
			WIP c/d	30	745
	330	8,545		330	8,545

(b) Finished goods

	Units	£		Units	£
Opening stock	100	2,700	Transfer: cost of sales	324	8,505
Transfer: Process 3	300	7,800	(at £26.25 per unit)		
			Closing stock	76	1,995
			(at £26.25)		
	400	10,500		400	10,500

Workings

Process 2: Calculation of unit cost

	Units	Materials		Labour and overhead	
Completed	240	100%:	240	100%:	240
Closing WIP	50	50%:	25	80%:	40
Equivalent units			265		280
Costs added			£530		£1,540
Cost per unit			£2		£5.50

Process 2: Application of costs

	Equivalent units	Unit cost	Value £
Closing WIP:			
Transferred-in cost	50	£15.00	750
Materials	25	£2.00	50
Labour and overhead	40	£5.50	220
			1,020

Transferred to process 3:	£	
Transferred-in cost	15.00	
Materials	2.00	
Labour and overhead	5.50	
	22.50 × 240 units	£5,400

Process 3: Calculation of unit cost

	Units	Labour and overhead	
Completed	300	100%:	300
Closing WIP	30	66²/₃%:	20
Equivalent units			320
			£
Costs: b/f			105
Added			1,015
			1,120
Cost per unit			£3.50

Process 3: Application of costs

	Equivalent units	Unit cost	Value £
Closing WIP:			
Transferred-in cost	30	£22.50	675
Labour and overhead	20	£3.50	70
			745

Transferred to finished goods:	£	
Transferred-in cost	22.50	
Labour and overhead	3.50	
	26.00 × 300 units	£7,800

Finished goods: Calculation of unit cost

			£
Opening stock	100	at £27	2,700
Added	300	at £26	2,800
	400	at £26.25	10,500

Comment

Process 1 has no closing WIP, so the unit cost is simply:

$$\frac{\text{total cost}}{\text{number of units of output}}$$

Process 2 has no opening WIP, so there is only one basis for calculating unit costs.

Process 3 has both opening and closing WIP. The weighted average basis is to be used. This method calculates unit cost as follows:

$$\frac{\text{total costs}}{\text{number of equivalent units}} = \frac{\text{opening costs} + \text{costs added}}{\text{opening EUs} + \text{EUs added}}$$

5

Equivalent units	**Units**	**Materials**		**Labour**		**Overhead**	
Opening WIP							
To complete	200	25%:	50	50%:	100	70%:	140
Started and completed	1,700		1,700		1,700		1,700
Closing WIP	500	60%:	300	40%:	200	25%:	125
			2,050		2,000		1,965
Current costs			£10,250		£8,000		£5,895
	Total						
Unit costs	£12		£5		£4		£3

Calculation of cost of units transferred to refining department

		£	£
Opening WIP			
Costs, b/f			1,250
Costs to complete:			
Material	50 × £5	250	
Labour	100 × £4	400	
Overhead	140 × £3	420	1,070
			2,320
Started and completed			
1,700 × £12			20,400
			22,720

Comment

The FIFO basis must be adopted to answer this question, since no details of the cost of opening WIP are given.

6   PROCESS X ACCOUNT
                 For week ending 26 February 19X2

	Units	£		Units	£
WIP b/f	3,000	49,600	Completed and		
From process W	39,000	507,000	transferred	40,000	1,200,000
Materials	—	242,600	WIP c/d	2,000	44,400
Labour and					
overhead	—	445,200			
	42,000	1,244,400		42,000	1,244,400

Comment

The FIFO basis cannot be used, since there are no details of work already performed or opening WIP before this week. The question must be answered using the weighted average basis.

Flow of units

opening WIP + added = completed + closing WIP
3,000 + 39,000 = 40,000 + 2,000

Equivalent units		Materials			Labour and overhead	
Completed	40,000	100%:	40,000	100%:	40,000
Closing WIP	2,000	80%:	1,600	40%:	800
			41,600		40,800

Total costs

	£	£
Brought forward	7,000	3,600
Added	242,600	445,200
	249,600	448,800

Unit costs

	£6.00	£11.00

Application of costs

Completed units:	£
From process W	13
Materials	6
Labour and overhead	11
	30 × 40,000

£1,200,000

Closing WIP:

	Equivalent units	Unit costs £	Value £
From process W	2,000	13	26,000
Materials	1,600	6	9,600
Labour and overhead	800	11	8,800
			44,400

8 Process costing losses

Spoilage and waste are likely to occur in all manufacturing operations, and can give rise to saleable scrap material. However, the most common type of examination question on the subject is concerned with abnormal losses (or gains) in process operations; and will usually call for T accounts. Careful reading of the question will enable the candidate to identify what are normal losses, if these are not specifically stated, after that no conceptuali difficulties should arise.

STUDY REQUIREMENTS

Accounting for material losses.

QUESTIONS

1 You have recently been appointed chief cost accountant of Squelch Chemicals plc, a company which converts a raw material known as Aad into a finished product, the Zyb. For every ten litres of Aad put in, one litre is expected to be spoiled. Spoiled Aad can be sold for £1 per litre.

During December 19X2, 5,000 litres of Aad were used at a cost of £1.80 each. Labour costs amounted to £7,500, overheads incurred totalled £3,600, and incidental costs of processing came to £2,900. The actual output of Zyb was 4,100 litres.

    (a) State the features which distinguish process costing from job costing.
    (b) Write up the process account, the normal spoilage account, and the abnormal spoilage account.

(15 marks)

2

    (a) MA Chemicals Limited process a range of products including a detergent 'Washo', which passes through three processes before completion and transfer to the finished goods warehouse. During April, data relating to this product were as shown:

	Process 1	Process 2	Process 3	Total
	£	£	£	£
Basic raw material (10,000 units)	6,000	—	—	6,000
Direct materials added in process	8,500	9,500	5,500	23,500
Direct wages	4,000	6,000	12,000	22,000
Direct expenses	1,200	930	1,340	3,470
Production overhead				16,500
(Production overhead is absorbed as a percentage of direct wages)				
	units	units	units	
Output	9,200	8,700	7,900	
	%	%	%	
Normal loss in process, of input	10	5	10	
	£	£	£	
All loss has a scrap value, per unit, of	0.20	0.50	1.00	

There was no stock at start or at end in any process.

You are required to prepare the following accounts:

    (i)   process 1;
    (ii) process 2;
   (iii) process 3;
    (iv) abnormal loss;
    (v) abnormal gain.

(b) Define briefly the following:

  (i) normal loss;
  (ii) abnormal loss;
  (iii) abnormal gain;
  (iv) scrap;
  (v) waste.

(30 marks)

3 Incisor plc produces bulk quantities of toothpaste from two raw materials, S and R. Material S is introduced into process 1 from which the output goes to process 2 when material R is introduced. During November 19X0 the company purchased 40,000 kg of material S which was introduced into process 1. The process 1 production details are as follows:

40,000 kg of raw material S purchased at	60p per kg
Processing cost (excluding labour)	30 hours at £42 per hour
Labour cost	£400
General overheads recovered at	125% of labour cost
Standard yield	90% of input
Waste from this process sold at	15p per kg

The actual output from this process was 35,000 kg which was transferred to process 2.

The company used the 35,000 kg from process 1 together with 15,000 kg of purchased material R. The process 2 production details and costs are as follows:

15,000 kg of material R purchased at	20p per kg
Processing cost (excluding labour)	20 hours at £30 per hour
Labour cost	£200
General overheads recovered at	50% of labour cost
Standard yield	95% of input
Waste from this process sold at	10p per kg

The actual output of process 2 was 48,000 kg which was transferred to finished store.

There was an enquiry for a quantity of 850 kg of specially prepared waste material from process 1. This material would have to be specially processed and packed incurring the following cost:

Processing	9p per kg
Packing	4p per kg

This specially prepared waste incurs no processing waste and could be sold for 32p per kg.

(a) Record the information in the process cost accounts, *before the enquiry was received,* and show the overall profit or loss transferred to the profit

and loss account from the abnormal gains or losses in processing.
(15 marks)

(b)   Advise management on whether or not they should produce the 850 kg of specially prepared waste material from process 1 and the effect on the overall results of the company. *(5 marks)*

(Total 20 marks)

4   Trepan Treatment Co. plc processes used tin cans. From every 50 tonnes of used cans 40 tonnes of metal is recovered and 10 tonnes of ash is produced which can be sold for £10 per tonne.

During the month of October 19X1 the following processing occurred:

	£
Materials (60 batches of 2,500 kg) delivery costs	750
Labour costs	2,500
Processing costs	1,600
Overheads	2,650

You are required to calculate the cost per tonne of metal produced and write up the process account and an ash account if:

(a)   110 tonnes of metal and 40 tonnes of ash were produced.
(b)   140 tonnes of metal and 10 tonnes of ash were produced.

You may assume that the ash was sold at the expected price of £10 per tonne.
(15 marks)

5   As cost accountant at Adina Ltd, a drug manufacturer, you are provided with the following information relating to production of the drug 'Poptup' during the month of July 1983:

(a)   The drug passes through three separate processes, in each of which there is a degree of wastage. This is estimated as follows:

Process:	1	2	3
Percentage of waste	4%	6%	10%

The waste percentage is calculated on the number of units entering production. The waste in process 1 is valueless; that from processes 2 and 3 is sold at £1 and £1.50 per litre respectively.

(b)   4,200 litres of raw material at a cost of £2.50 per litre were introduced to process 1 on 1 July. During the month, as the process continued, other materials with a cost of £2,400 were introduced to process 2, and further materials with a cost of £2,720 were introduced to process 3.

(c)   Direct labour and other direct expenses were incurred as follows:

Process:	1	2	3
Labour (£):	4,250	1,750	1,925
Other expenses (£):	1,755	425	400

(d)　The output, excluding waste, from each process during the month was as follows:

Process:	1	2	3
Output (litres):	4,000	3,960	3,450

(e)　Stock was as follows:

Process:	1	2	3
1 July (litres):	1,200	1,000	1,500
31 July (litres):	1,000	900	1,750

(f)　The values of stock as per the standard cost prices were as follows:

Process:	1	2	3
Value of stock:			
(£ per litre)	4.20	5.20	7.50

(g)　During July 3,200 litres were transferred from process 3 to finished stock.

You are required to prepare the process and stock accounts for the month of July 1983.　　　　　　　　　　　　　　　　　　　　　　*(18 marks)*

6　Sharpless plc manufactures a range of sugar confectionery. The main elements of cost, which accrue evenly, are incurred in the first process, the conversion of raw materials into bulk finished goods. The goods are then transferred for finishing, inspection and final packing to a central warehouse.

As the accountant at the manufacturing unit you are required to report weekly to the head office accountant. Your staff provide you with the following information in respect of a week's production:

	£
Direct wages	18,570
Direct materials	28,125
Production overheads	9,485

Opening stock: 800 dozen cartons: 75 per cent complete as regards labour and material and 50 per cent complete as regards overheads.
Closing stock: 900 dozen cartons: 50 per cent complete as regards materials and 40 per cent complete as regards labour and overheads.

During the week production commenced on 10,000 dozen cartons, 8,400 dozen cartons were passed to finishing. Production losses in the first process are usually negligible. However, because of incorrect mixing an abnormal loss took place during the week and goods were rejected when 75 per cent complete.

You are required to prepare a financial report on the week's production for the head office accountant.

　　　　　　　　　　　　　　　　　　　　　　(15 marks)

7   A manufacturing company makes a product by two processes and the data below relate to the second process for the month of April.

A work-in-progress balance of 1,200 units brought forward from March was valued, at cost, as follows:

	£
Direct materials, complete	10,800
Direct wages, 60% complete	6,840
Production overhead, 60% complete	7,200

During April 4,000 units were transferred from the first process to the second process at a cost of £7.50 each, this input being treated as direct material within the second process.

Other costs incurred by the second process were:

	£
Additional direct materials	4,830
Direct wages	32,965
Production overhead	35,538

3,200 completed units were transferred to finished goods store. A loss of 520 units, being normal, occurred during the process. The average method of pricing is used.

Work-in-progress at the end of April consisted of 500 completed units awaiting transfer to the finished goods store and a balance of unfinished units which were complete as regards direct material and 50% complete as regards direct wages and production overhead.

You are required:

(a)   to prepare for the month of April the account for the second process;
(14 marks)

(b)   to present a statement for management setting out the:

(i)   cost per unit of the finished product, by element of cost and total;
(ii)   cost of production transferred to finished goods;
(iii) cost of production of completed units awaiting transfer to finished goods;
(iii) cost of uncompleted units in closing work-in-progress, by element of cost and in total. *(6 marks)*
(Total 20 marks)

ANSWERS

1

(a) The features which distinguish process costing from job costing are:

   (i) The continuous nature of the process as opposed to the discrete nature of the job.

  (ii) Smaller volume of paperwork brought about by the less frequent issues of material, charging of the process labour as an entity.

 (iii) Individual units of output of a process cannot be identified with specific items of cost: units of output are costed by dividing total cost of process by total output.

 (iv) Evaluation of work-in-process requires estimates to be made of stage of completion in relation to the various cost elements.

  (v) The output of one process often forms the raw material of a subsequent process; in some cases it can be sold without further processing.

 (vi) Waste or by-products may emerge at each stage of processing.

(vii) Joint products may be produced which, in view of the continuous nature of the process, cannot be costed separately although there are various methods of apportioning costs.

(b)

PROCESS ACCOUNT

	litres	£		litres	£
Raw material: Aad	5,000	9,000	Normal spoilage	500	500
Labour		7,500	Finished goods	4,100	20,500
Overheads		3,600	Abnormal spoilage	400	2,000
Processing costs		2,900			
	5,000	23,000		5,000	23,000

NORMAL SPOILAGE ACCOUNT

	litres	£		litres	£
Process account	500	500	Cash	900	900
Abnormal spoilage	400	400			
	900	900		900	900

ABNORMAL SPOILAGE ACCOUNT

	litres	£		litres	£
Process account	400	2,000	Normal spoilage	400	400
			Profit and loss account		1,600
	400	2,000		400	2,000

Workings

	litres	£
Cost of normal output		
Input: Aad	5,000	9,000
Labour		7,500
Overheads		3,600
Processing costs		2,900
	5,000	23,000
Normal spoilage	(500)	(500)
	4,500	22,500

i.e., £5 per litre

2

(a)

PROCESS 1 ACCOUNT

	Units	£		Units	£
Basic raw material	10,000	6,000	Output: process 2	9,200	23,000
Direct materials	—	8,500	Normal loss	1,000	200
Direct wages	—	4,000			
Direct expenses	—	1,200			
Production overhead	—	3,000			
Abnormal gain	200	500			
	10,200	23,200		10,200	23,200

PROCESS 2 ACCOUNT

	Units	£		Units	£
Input: process 1	9,200	23,000	Output: process 3	8,700	43,500
Direct materials	—	9,500	Normal loss	460	230
Direct wages	—	6,000	Abnormal loss	40	200
Direct expenses	—	930			
Production overhead	—	4,500			
	9,200	43,930		9,200	43,930

PROCESS 3 ACCOUNT

	Units	£		Units	£
Input: process 2	8,700	43,500	Finished goods	7,900	71,100
Direct materials	—	5,500	Normal loss	870	870
Direct wages	—	12,000			
Direct expenses	—	1,340			
Production overhead	—	9,000			
Abnormal gain	70	630			
	8,770	71,970		8,770	71,970

ABNORMAL LOSS ACCOUNT

	Units	£			Units	£
Process 2	40	200		Scrap	40	20
				Profit and loss	—	180
	40	200			40	200

ABNORMAL GAIN ACCOUNT

	Units	£			Units	£
Scrap	200	40		Process 1	200	500
Scrap	70	70		Process 3	70	630
Profit and loss	—	1,020				
	270	1,130			270	1,130

(b)   (i)   **Normal loss**

Normal loss is the loss expected under efficient operating conditions. It is an inherent part of the production process and the cost is typically viewed as part of the cost of good production.

   (ii)   **Abnormal loss**

This is any actual loss not expected under efficient operating conditions, i.e. any loss over and above the normal loss. It is not an inherent part of the process and the cost is typically treated as a charge to profit and loss account.

   (iii)   **Abnormal gain**

This is an unexpected gain in output, i.e. where the actual loss is less than the normal loss. The 'saving' is credited to profit and loss account.

   (iv)   **Scrap**

The residue from a manufacturing operation is called scrap if it has a relatively small recovery value.

   (v)   **Waste**

Waste is material that evaporates, shrinks or is lost during a manufacturing process, or is residue with no recovery value.

Appendix

Calculation of cost of normal output

		Units	£	
(a)	Process 1			
	Raw material	10,000	6,000	
	Material added	—	8,500	
	Wages	—	4,000	
	Expenses	—	1,200	
	Overhead (75% of wages)	—	3,000	
		10,000	22,700	
	Normal loss, at scrap value	(1,000)	200	
		9,000	22,500	£2.50 per unit
(b)	Process 2	Units	£	
	From process 1	9,200	23,000	
	Materials	—	9,500	
	Wages	—	6,000	
	Expenses	—	930	
	Overhead	—	4,500	
		9,200	43,930	
	Normal loss, at scrap value	(460)	(230)	
		8,740	43,700	£5.00 per unit
(c)	Process 3	Units	£	
	From process 2	8,700	43,500	
	Materials	—	5,500	
	Wages	—	12,000	
	Expenses	—	1,340	
	Overhead	—	9,000	
		8,700	71,340	
	Normal loss, at scrap value	(870)	870	
		7,830	70,470	£9.00 per unit

3

(a) *Process accounts*

PROCESS 1 ACCOUNT

	kg	£		kg	£
Material S	40,000	24,000	Process 2	35,000	24,850
Processing	—	1,260	Normal waste	4,000	600
Labour	—	400	Abnormal waste	1,000	710
Overheads	—	500			
	40,000	26,160		40,000	26,160

$$\text{Cost per unit} = \frac{£26,160 - £600}{40,000 \times 0.90} = 71\text{p per kg}$$

PROCESS 2 ACCOUNT

	kg	£		kg	£
Process 1	35,000	24,850	Finished goods	48,000	28,800
Material R	15,000	3,000	Normal waste	2,500	250
Processing	—	600			
Labour	—	200			
Overheads	—	100			
	50,000	28,750			
Abnormal yield	500	300			
	50,500	29,050		50,500	29,050

$$\text{Cost per unit} = \frac{£28,750 - £250}{50,000 \times 0.95} = 60\text{p per kg}$$

Calculation of profit/loss from abnormal gains and losses

	£	£
Process 1:		
Cost of abnormal loss = 1,000 kg at 71p	(710)	
Less: Revenue from extra waste:		
1,000 kg at 15p	150	(560)
Process 2:		
Credit for abnormal gain = 500 kg at 60p	300	
Less: Revenue lost: 500 kg at 10p	(50)	250
Overall loss		(310)

(b) The specially prepared waste should be sold because the additional revenue exceeds the additional costs.

		Pence per kg
Revenue from sales		32
Less: Revenue lost from sale of waste		(15)
Additional revenue		17
Additional costs: Processing	9	
Packing	4	(13)
		4

Additional profit = 4p × 850 = £34

4 The unit cost of metal produced will not be affected by any abnormal losses or yields and is therefore the same for parts (a) and (b).

	£
Cost of process:	
Materials (150 tonnes)	750
Labour	2,500
Processing	1,600
Overheads	2,650
	7,500
Less: Proceeds of normal loss of ash (30 tonnes at £10)	(300)
	7,200

$$\text{Cost per tonne} = \frac{£7,200}{120} = £60$$

(a)

PROCESS ACCOUNT

	tonnes	£		tonnes	£
Materials	150	750	Metal stock	110	6,600
Labour	—	2,500	Normal ash	30	300
Processing	—	1,600	Abnormal ash	10	600
Overheads	—	2,650			
	150	7,500		150	7,500

ASH ACCOUNT

	tonnes	£		tonnes	£
Process account	30	300	Cash	40	400
Process account	10	600	Profit and loss account	—	500
	40	900		40	900

(b)

PROCESS ACCOUNT

	tonnes	£		tonnes	£
Materials	150	750	Metal stock	140	8,400
Labour	—	2,500	Normal ash	30	300
Processing	—	1,600			
Overheads	—	2,650			
	150	7,500			
Abnormal ash	20	1,200			
	170	8,700		170	8,700

ASH ACCOUNT

	tonnes	£		tonnes	£
Process account	30	300	Process account	20	1,200
Profit and loss account	—	1,000	Cash	10	100
	30	1,300		30	1,300

Comment

(a) Ash has been treated as scrap.

(b) Cost of abnormal scrap (per tonne):

	£
Cost of good production	60
Less: scrap value	(10)
	50

5

PROCESS 1 ACCOUNT

	litres	£		litres	£
Raw material	4,200	10,500	Output	4,000	16,800
Labour	—	4,250	Normal waste	168	—
Expenses	—	1,755	Abnormal waste	32	134
Variance	—	429			
	4,200	16,934		4,200	16,934

PROCESS 1 STOCK ACCOUNT

	litres	£		litres	£
Balance b/f	1,200	5,040	Process 2	4,200	17,640
Process 1	4,000	16,800	Balance c/d	1,000	4,200
	5,200	21,840		5,200	21,840

PROCESS 2 ACCOUNT

	litres	£		litres	£
Process 1 stock	4,200	17,640	Output	3,960	20,592
Materials	—	2,400	Normal waste	252	252
Labour	—	1,750	Variance	—	1,433
Expenses	—	425			
Abnormal gain	12	62			
	4,212	22,277		4,212	22,277

PROCESS 2 STOCK ACCOUNT

	litres	£		litres	£
Balance b/f	1,000	5,200	Process 3	4,060	21,112
Process 2	3,960	20,592	Balance c/d	900	4,680
	4,960	25,792		4,960	25,792

PROCESS 3 ACCOUNT

	litres	£		litres	£
Process 2 stock	4,060	21,112	Output	3,450	25,875
Materials	—	2,720	Normal waste	406	609
Labour	—	1,925	Abnormal waste	204	1,530
Expenses	—	400			
Variance	—	1,857			
	4,060	28,014		4,060	28,014

PROCESS 3 STOCK ACCOUNT

	litres	£		litres	£
Balance b/f	1,500	11,250	Finished goods	3,200	24,000
Process 3	3,450	25,875	Balance c/d	1,750	13,125
	4,950	37,125		4,950	37,125

Comment

This question combines process costing with standard costing, so a knowledge of both areas is necessary. The assumption that transfers are made at standard cost has been made although there are several acceptable approaches to this question.

6
Quantity schedule

	Dozen	Dozen
Opening stock of cartons	800	
Started during the week	10,000	10,800
Completed and passed to finishing	8,400	
Closing stock	900	
Rejected cartons	1,500	10,800

Costs added during the week

	Total £	Per unit £
Direct wages	18,570	2.00
Direct materials	28,125	3.00
Production overhead	9,485	1.00
	56,180	6.00

Costs accounted for as follows:

	£
Cost of cartons:	
Completed and passed to finishing	47,000
Value of closing stock	2,430
Cost of rejected cartons	6,750
	56,180

Additional computations

Equivalent units for the week

	Dozen cartons	Labour £		Materials £		Overhead £	
Opening stock, to complete	800	25%	200	25%	200	50%	400
Started and completed	7,600		7,600		7,600		7,600
Closing stock	900	40%	360	50%	450	40%	360
Rejected cartons	1,500 75%		1,125		1,125		1,125
			9,285		9,375		9,485
Costs added during week			18,570		28,125		9,485
Unit costs for week			2.00		3.00		1.00

Application of costs
Completed:

Opening stock	200 × £2	400	
To complete	200 × £3	600	
	400 × £1	400	1,400
Started and completed	7,600 × £6		45,600
			47,000
Closing stock	360 × £2	720	
	450 × £3	1,350	
	360 × £1	360	2,430
Rejected cartons	1,125 × £6		6,750

Comment

No information is given about the cost of opening stock; therefore the FIFO basis must be used.

The cost of cartons completed and passed to finishing excludes this (unknown) cost brought forward.

Care has to be taken with the 1,500 rejected units. They are to be treated as an abnormal loss and so the cost of this loss must be ascertained. Because they are rejected when 75% complete, the 1,500 units were worth 1,125 equivalent units (for all cost components). These equivalent units are included in the calculation of unit costs.

7

(a)

SECOND PROCESS ACCOUNT

	Units	£		Units	£
Balance b/f:			Normal loss	520	—
Materials	1,200	10,800			
Wages	—	6,840	Transfer to		
Overheads	—	7,200	finished goods	3,200	94,240
	1,200	24,840	Balance c/d		
From first process	4,000	30,000	Completed units	500	14,725
Cost incurred:			WIP		
Materials	—	4,830	Materials	980	9,555
Wages	—	32,965	Wages	—	4,655
Overheads	—	35,538	Overheads	—	4,998
	5,200	128,173		5,200	128,173

Workings

Calculation of equivalent units

	Units	Materials		Wages		Overheads
Completed	3,700	3,700		3,700		3,700
Closing WIP	980	980	50%:	490	50%:	490
	4,680	4,680		£4,190		£4,190

	£	£	£
Total costs			
b/f	10,800	6,840	7,200
added	34,830	32,965	35,538
	45,630	39,805	42,738
Costs per equivalent unit	£9.75	£9.50	£10.20
Total			£29.45

(b) (i) **Cost per unit of finished product**

	£
Direct materials	9.75
Direct wages	9.50
Production overhead	10.20
Total	29.45

(ii) **Cost of production transferred to finished goods**
3,200 × £29.45 — 94,240

(iii) **Cost of completed units awaiting transfer**
500 × £29.45 — 14,725

(iv) **Cost of uncompleted units in closing WIP**

Direct materials	980 × £9.75	9,555
Direct wages	490 × £9.50	4,655
Production overhead	490 × £10.20	4,998
		19,208

Comment

The normal loss is spread over good production and so does not have to be costed out.

9 Operation and service costing

Operation and service costing involves merely the application of 'job' or 'continuous output' costing methods to non-manufacturing activities. The main problem lies in identifying the cost units and cost centres with which costs are to be associated.

Few questions have been set on this subject, probably because any major question would require some experience of the particular service industry or activity concerned. Therefore, only three brief questions are given in this chapter.

STUDY REQUIREMENTS

Cost ascertainment for non-manufacturing activities.

QUESTIONS

1 Malcolm, a tax consultant, is staying in the St Alice's Hotel while visiting a client. During the course of the evening he engages in conversation with Mr Nance, the hotel accountant. Among other things, it transpires that the hotel's costing system is quite different from that used by Malcolm. 'I'm surprised,' says Malcolm. 'We both offer a service, so our accounting should be the same.'

(a) Suggest the two different costing methods in use.
(b) Explain why the two different operations use different costing methods.

(10 marks)

2 List six types of service industries that are likely to use a service costing method, and for each suggest the cost unit that would be adopted.

(12 marks)

3 The Greenstreet Company operates several production and several service departments. The canteen department is a separate cost centre, providing free lunches to all employees of the company.

(a) Draw up a pro-forma cost sheet for the canteen, listing typical expenses.
(b) Suggest a basis for charging canteen costs to user departments.

(15 marks)

ANSWERS

1

   (a) St Alice's Hotel would use service costing. The tax consultancy would use job costing.

   (b) An hotel offers a standardised service (the provision of accommodation on a daily basis). Each guest is treated in the same way, and the service provided results from a sequence of continuous and repetitive activities (booking, breakfast, room cleaning, heat, light, telephone, television). Calculation of the cost of a room per day is an averaging process, and no attempt is made to relate individual costs to individual room-days.

By contrast, tax consultancy work responds to the individual request of the client, and Malcolm can directly attribute some of his costs to each job (hours put in, any incidental expenses, and travelling).

2

Service	Cost unit
Hotel accommodation	Occupied room-day
Hospital	Patient-day
Freight	Tonne-mile
Carriage of passengers	Passenger mile
Restaurant	Meal
Holiday camp	Camper-day
College	Full-time student
Gas	Therm
Electricity	Kilowatt-hour

3

(a)

Account code No.	Expense item	Total costs This year Last year £ £	Costs per meal This year Last year £ £	Increase or decrease

	Food: Meats
	      Fruit and veg.
	      Bread, flour, etc.
	      Sundries
	Drink: Milk
	       Tea and coffee
	Cleaning materials
	Cutlery and crockery
	Laundry
	Assistants' wages
	Supervisor's salary
	Maintenance: Equipment
	Depreciation
	Rent and rates
	Insurance
	Heat and light			

	TOTAL			
MEALS SERVED		TOTAL CONSUMPTION		

(b) The best cost unit is the meal, so the best basis is on consumption of meals in each user department. Otherwise, canteen costs could be apportioned on the basis of the number of employees in each department.

10 Job costing

Questions on job costing as an historical cost-finding technique are seldom set in examinations, since they would involve merely the re-presentation and summarisation of data provided in the question.

One essay-type and three numerical examples are given in this chapter.

The related technique of batch costing, however, is sometimes illustrated in questions on standard costing or budgetary control.

STUDY REQUIREMENTS

(a)   Product costing in jobbing industries.
(b)   Batch costing.

QUESTIONS

1

(a) (i)   Set out the features of job costing. *(3 marks)*
   (ii) List the features needed within the job costing system to ensure that it operates efficiently. *(5 marks)*
   (iii) Suggest two types of business where job costing would be appropriate. *(2 marks)*

(b) (i)   Compare and contrast batch costing and job costing. *(3 marks)*
   (ii) Suggest two types of business where batch costing would be appropriate. *(2 marks)*

(Total 15 marks)

2 Hancock receives an order to supply his local farmer with a delivery of cattle feed.

The job passes through three departments, collecting costs as follows:

Mixing department	100 kg of Owen at £2 per kg 50kg of Howe at £1 per kg 20 kg of Benn at 50p per kg 10 hours of labour at £4 per hour
Boiling department	20 hours of labour at £3 per hour 60 hours of the boiling machine
Cooling and skimming department	50 hours of labour at £2 per hour Hire of giant thermometer and scoop £200

The job does not disrupt normal activity levels, which are as follows:

Department	Labour hours	Machine hours	Budgeted overheads £
Mixing	200	—	1,600
Boiling	250	700	9,100
Cooling	550	—	4,950

Basis of absorption: Mixing: labour hours
                     Boiling: machine hours
                     Cooling: labour hours

Selling and administrative expenses are 30% of factory cost.

You are required to prepare a statement showing the profit or loss on the job, if the price agreed is £2,500.

(20 marks)

3   Draw up a job cost sheet to record the following information on job No. 789:

Customer	Quinn & Company
Description of product	Typewriter
Date started	27 February 19X2
Completion date	5 March 19X2
Job price	£400

Already charged to job at 1 March 19X2:	£
Direct materials	40
Direct labour	20
Overhead	10

Costs added during week ending 5 March 19X2:

Date		
2.3	Material requisition XC 2	5 units at £7
3.3	Material requisition GB 17	7 items at £6
	Labour work ticket M 25	
5.3	10 hours at £4	40
	Labour work ticket M 29	
5.3	8 hours at £3	24
	Overhead	
5.3	10 hours at £2	20
5.3	8 hours at £1.50	12

(15 marks)

4   You are required to prepare, using the information set out below:

(a) The cost account for job No. 544.
(b) The factory overhead control account.
(c) The work-in-progress control account.

The Start Company has a 30 June year-end. By 29 June all work had been completed except job No. 544.

At 29 June:

	£
Total factory overhead incurred to date	45,000
Direct labour applied to work-in-progress	36,000
Direct material applied to work-in-progress	54,000

For 30 June:

Factory overhead incurred	250
Direct labour for job No. 544	400
Direct materials for job No. 544	100

At 29 June: Job cost sheet details for job No. 544:
        Direct materials   2,000
        Direct labour   1,500

Factory overhead is applied to jobs at 120% of direct labour.

(15 marks)

ANSWERS

1

(a) (i) Features of job costing:
   (1) Each job is of a comparatively short duration.
   (2) Work is undertaken to customers' specific requirements.
   (3) Each job moves through stages as a continuously identifiable unit.

   (ii) Necessary features for efficient operation:
   (1) A suitable system for booking time to jobs.
   (2) Comprehensive documentation for materials.
   (3) Clearly defined cost centres.
   (4) Adequate labour analysis.
   (5) Suitable bases for the absorption of overheads.

   (iii) Examples include special machinery, house extensions, accountancy firms, plumbers.

(b) (i) Batch costing can be regarded as a form of job costing. Instead of one unit being made in response to a customer's request, a batch of identical units is made. The procedures are the same as for job costing, with the batch constituting the unit.

   (ii) Examples include: footwear, clothing, printing, engineering components.

2

		£	£
Mixing department			
Materials: Owen	100 kg at £2	200	
Howe	50 kg at £1	50	
Benn	20 kg at 50p	10	260
Labour:	10 hours at £4		40
Overhead:	10 hours at £8		80
			380
Boiling department			
Labour:	20 hours at £3	60	
Overhead:	60 hours at £13	780	840
Cooling and skimming department			
Labour:	50 hours at £2	100	
Overhead:	50 hours at £9	450	
Direct expense:		200	750
Factory cost			1,970
Add: Selling and administration 30% × £1,970			591
			2,561
Price agreed			2,500
Loss			(61)

Appendix: overhead absorption rates

Mixing £1,600 ÷ 200 = £ 8 per labour hour
Boiling £9,100 ÷ 700 = £13 per machine hour
Cooling £4,950 ÷ 550 = £ 9 per labour hour

3

JOB COST SHEET

CUSTOMER:	Quinn and Company	JOB NO.: 789
DESCRIPTION:	Typewriter	
DATE STARTED:	27.2.X2	
DATE COMPLETED:	5.3.X2	JOB PRICE: £400

MATERIAL					LABOUR					OVERHEAD		
Date	Req. No.	Qty	Price £	Cost £	Date	Work ticket No.	Hrs.	Rate £	Cost £	Lab. Hrs.	OAR £	Cost £
1.3	b/f			40	1.3	b/f			20	b/f		10
2.3	XC2	5	7	35	5.3	M25	10	4	40	10	2	20
3.3	GB17	7	6	42	5.3	M29	8	3	24	8	1.5	12
				117					84			42

SUMMARY		COMMENTS
	£	
Material	117	
Labour	84	
Overhead	42	
	243	
Job price	400	
Job profit	157	

Comment

A job cost sheet can be designed in a number of ways. Marks will be awarded in an examination provided all the details are there.

4

COST ACCOUNT: JOB NO. 544

		£			£
29.6	Balances b/f:				
	Materials	2,000			
	Labour	1,500			
	Overhead	1,800			
		5,300			
30.6	Materials	100			
	Labour	400	30.6	Balance c/d	6,280
	Overhead	480			
		6,280			6,280

FACTORY OVERHEAD CONTROL ACCOUNT

		£			£
29.6	Balance b/f	45,000	29.6	Applied to WIP	43,200
				(£36,000 × 120%)	
30.6	Charges	250	30.6	Applied to WIP	480
			30.6	Underapplied	1,570
		45,250			45,250

WORK-IN-PROGRESS CONTROL ACCOUNT

		£			£
29.6	Balances b/f	5,300	30.6	Balance c/d	6,280
30.6	Added	980			
		6,280			6,280

Comment

This question tests three things: a knowledge of job order costing, bookkeeping skills and the ability to deal with overheads.

Notice that the balance in the work-in-progress control account consists of the only unfinished job.

11 Contract costing

A contract, for this purpose is a large job; often extending over more than one financial year. Because of the significant amounts of money involved, detailed cost estimates will be prepared, and the contract may be broken down into stages or phases. This facilitates control though there may be problems in measuring site activities and progress achieved. You might get a narrative question on control techniques but the most common type of question on contract costing relates to the amount of profit to be taken year by year during the progress of the contract. The general principle of profit-taking is laid down in a statement of Standard Accounting Practice (SSAP 9, 'Stocks and Work in Progress'). The application of this principle will depend on the facts of the case, which will be given in the question.

STUDY REQUIREMENTS

(a) Contract costing and control.
(b) Profit taking on contracts.
(c) SSAP 9, 'Stocks and Work in Progress'.

QUESTIONS

1

    (a) Set out the main distinguishing features of contract costing.

(10 marks)

    (b) Give five examples of jobs where contract costing would be appropriate.

(5 marks)

(Total 15 marks)

2 Outline the major problems in controlling the costs of a contract.

(12 marks)

3 A construction company is currently undertaking three separate contracts and information relating to these contracts for the previous year, together with other relevant data, is shown below.

	Contract MNO £ thousands	Contract PQR £ thousands	Contract STU £ thousands	Construction services dept overhead £ thousands
Contract price	800	675	1,100	
Balances b/f at beginning of year:				
Cost of work completed	—	190	370	—
Material on site	—	—	25	—
Written down value of plant and machinery	—	35	170	12
Wages accrued	—	2	—	—
Profit previously transferred to profit and loss a/c	—	—	15	—
Transactions during year:				
Material delivered to sites	40	99	180	—
Wages paid	20	47	110	8
Payments to subcontractors	—	—	35	—
Salaries and other costs	6	20	25	21
Written down value of plant:				
issued to sites	90	15	—	—
transferred from sites	—	8	—	—
Balances c/f at the end of year:				
Material on site	8	—	—	—
Written down value of plant and machinery	70	—	110	5
Wages accrued	—	5	—	—
Prepayments to subcontractors	—	—	15	—
Value of work certified at end of year	90	390	950	—
Cost of work not certified at end of year	—	—	26	—

The cost of operating the construction services department, which provides technical advice to each of the contracts, is apportioned over the contracts in proportion to wages incurred.

Contract STU is scheduled for handing over to the contractee in the near future and the site engineer estimates that the extra costs required to complete the contract in addition to those tabulated above, will total £138,000. This amount includes an allowance for plant depreciation, construction services and for contingencies.

You are required:

(a) to construct a cost account for each of the three contracts for the previous year and show the cost of the work completed at the year end.
(9 marks)

(b) to recommend how much profit or loss should be taken, for each contract, for the previous year, and explain the reasons for each of your recommendations.
(13 marks)
(Total 22 marks)

4 Contractors plc undertook short-term 'A' contracts, all of which were subcontracted, and long-term 'B' contracts.

Only one long-term contract, B1 commenced on 1 October, was undertaken in 19X0.

Each subcontractor rendered an invoice for every section of work on each A contract on the date when the section was finished. Subsequently a corresponding part of the contract price was invoiced to the customer.

The following figures as on 31 December 19X0, were taken from the company's ledger:

	£
Total of subcontractors' invoices	15,750
Total of sales invoices dated in 19X0: A contracts	19,800
Debtors	4,160
Expenditure on contract B1:	
Materials	8,760
Wages	10,220
Direct expenses	640
Plant purchased 1 October	6,000
Cash received in respect of contract B1 representing the contract price of work certified in 19X0 less 10 per cent retention money	18,000

The contract price of B1 was £80,000 and on 31 December 19X0, it was estimated that the contract would be finished on 30 June 19X1 and that further expenditure would total £35,000. It was decided that depreciation of the plant purchased for contract B1 should be charged by the straight-line method, calculated by reference to an estimated residual value of £1,800 on 30 June 19X1.

The following are particulars of all A contracts which, on 31 December 19X0, had not been fully charged to customers:

127

Contract No.	Subcontractor's invoice Date	£	Related sales invoice Date	£	Date paid by customer
A21	20 November 19X0	466	2 December 19X0	574	15 December 19X0
	15 December 19X0	248	2 January 19X1	304	8 January 19X1
	24 January 19X1	156	3 February 19X1	224	10 February 19X1
A22	8 December 19X0	185	1 January 19X1	237	4 January 19X1
A23	4 December 19X0	329	21 December 19X0	441	8 January 19X1
	18 January 19X1	97	27 January 19X1	135	5 February 19X1

Contract 'A22' was completed on 8 December 19X0.

The annual accounts for the year 19X0 were to be prepared on the basis of taking credit for:

(a) the proportion of the estimated profit on contract B1 which the contract price of the work certified in 19X0 bore to the total contract price, and

(b) the profit on completed A contracts and, as regards uncompleted A contracts the apparent profit on work invoiced by the subcontractor up to 31 December 19X0 less a provision of 25 per cent against contingencies.

You are required:

(a) To prepare an account for contract B1 for the year 19X0. *(8 marks)*

(b) To prepare the trading account for A contracts for the year 19X0.
(8 marks)

(c) To show the debtors and work-in-progress (in respect of uncompleted contracts) as they should appear in the balance sheet as on 31 December 19X0. *(4 marks)*
(Total 20 marks)

ANSWERS

1

(a) The main distinguishing features of contract costing are:

    (i) The work will be of a relatively long duration.

    (ii) The work is undertaken to customer's specific requirements.

    (iii) The price is usually fixed in advance.

    (iv) The completion date is usually fixed in advance, and penalties follow delays.

    (v) The work is usually site-based.

    (vi) The end product is usually guaranteed, and final payment is only received after testing.

    (vii) Payments on account are often made against work certified.

    (viii) Most costs can be classified as direct, since they can be identified with the contract.

    (ix) A certain amount of profit is taken at the year-end on uncompleted contracts.

    (x) Special plant is often purchased for the contract.

(b) Shipbuilding; motorway construction; factory construction; building of an oil rig; renovating old buildings.

2 Some of the problems which could be mentioned in an answer to this question include:

(a) *Materials*

Usage	Actual usage may exceed estimates.
Price	As the contract progresses, purchase prices may rise above those budgeted.
Losses	Through deterioration, mishandling or pilferage.
Location of stores	If materials are kept on site, special facilities may be required.

(b) *Labour*

Time	Estimated hours may be exceeded by actual time taken.
Rate	High wage rises may invalidate budgeted rates.
Utility	Productive time may be wasted by delays, setting-up time, stoppages, travelling time.

(c) *Plant and tools*

Damage	Accidental or vandalism.
Pilferage	On unattended sites.
Breakdowns	Causing delays and penalties.

(d) *Unexpected costs*

Rectification work.
Penalties for late completion.
Changes in Government legislation.

(e) *General problems*

Inability to predict costs far into the future.
Diseconomies of scale affecting large contracts.
Bad weather.
Strikes.

3

(a) **Cost accounts**

Contract MNO

	£ thousands		£ thousands
Material	40		
Wages	20		
Salaries	6	Materials c/f	8
Plant	90	Plant c/f	70
Construction services	4	Cost of work completed c/f	82
	160		160

Contract PQR

	£ thousands		£ thousands
Cost of work completed b/f	190	Wages b/f	2
Plant b/f	35	Plant returned	8
Materials	99	Cost of work completed c/f	411
Wages	47		
Salaries	20		
Plant	15		
Construction services	10		
Wages c/f	5		
	421		421

Contract STU

	£ thousands		£ thousands
Cost of work completed b/f	370	Plant c/f	110
Material b/f	25	Prepayment c/f	15
Plant b/f	170	Cost of work completed c/f	812
Materials	180		
Wages	110		
Subcontractors	35		
Salaries	25		
Construction services	22		
	937		937

Working

Apportionment of construction services department overhead

	£ thousands
Plant b/f	12
Wages	8
Salaries	21
	41
Plant c/f	(5)
	36

	£ thousands
To **MNO**: $36 \times \dfrac{20}{177}$	4
To **PQR**: $36 \times \dfrac{47}{177}$	10
To **STU**: $36 \times \dfrac{110}{177}$	22
	36

(a) **Profit to be taken**

(i) **Contract MNO**
The value of work certified to date is £90,000, and the final contract price is £800,000. This contract, therefore, is in its infancy so it is too early to take any profit

Recommended profit   **NONE**

(ii) **Contract PQR**

	£
Contract price	675,000
Costs to date	411,000
Value of work certified	390,000

So far the contract had incurred a loss of £21,000. Prudence dictates that the whole of this loss should be written off immediately.

Recommended loss   £21,000

Comment

Further information should be requested. An estimate of future costs should be made to arrive at the total loss over the entire contract. It would then be prudent to make a provision against the entire loss at this intermediate stage.

(iii) **Contract STU**

	£
Contract price	1,100,000
Cost to date	812,000
Value of work certified	950,000
Add: Costs not yet certified	26,000
	976,000

Contract STU is nearing completion and it appears that the outcome can be predicted with reasonable certainty. In such circumstances, it is permissible under SSAP 9 to spread the profit over the life of the contract, rather than wait until completion when the profit is actually realised.

The profit earned to date is £164,000. Profit over the entire contract may be calculated as follows:

	£	£
Contract price		1,100,000
Costs: to date	812,000	
estimated to complete	138,000	
		950,000
Contract profit		150,000
Recommended profit		
£150,000 × ⅔		100,000
Less: already taken		(15,000)
		85,000

Comment

There are a variety of answers which would be satisfactory here. For instance the profit of £150,000 could be scaled down by the fraction

$$\frac{£950,000}{£1,100,000}$$

representing the ratio of work certified to final contract price. The fraction ⅔ is arbitrary, although frequently used.

4

(a)   CONTRACT ACCOUNT: CONTRACT B1

	£		£
Materials	8,760	Work-in-progress,	
Wages	10,220	carried down	26,315
Direct expenses	640		
Depreciation	1,400		
	21,020		
Profit and loss account,			
estimated profit	5,295		
	26,315		26,315

Workings

	£
Depreciation	
Cost of plant, 31 December 19X0	6,000
Residual value, 30 June 19X1	1,800
Depreciation for 9 months	4,200
Depreciation 1 October 19X0 to 31 December 19X0: one-third	1,400
Value of work certified	
Cash received	18,000
Add: 10% retention £18,000 × 10/90	2,000
	20,000

	£	£
Estimated profit		
Contract price		80,000
Total expenditure incurred so far	21,020	
Further depreciation	2,800	
Further expenditure	35,000	
		(58,820)
Total estimated profit		21,180
Earned so far: $\frac{20,000}{80,000} \times £21,180$		5,295

(b)   TRADING ACCOUNT FOR A CONTRACTS
year ended 31 December 19X0

	£	£
Sales (completed contracts)		19,022
Less: Subcontractors' cost	15,750	
Work in progress, at cost	1,043	
		(14,707)
Gross profit on completed contracts		4,315
Gross profit on incomplete contracts		207
Total gross profit		4,522

Workings

| | Complete | | Incomplete | |
	Cost	Sales invoices	Cost	Sales invoices
	£	£	£	£
Per question	15,750	19,800		
Transfer to incomplete:				
A21	(466)	(574)	466	574
	(248)		248	304
A23	(329)	(441)	329	441
	(1,043)	(1,015)		
	14,707	18,785	1,043	1,319
A22		237		(1,043)
		19,022	Gross profit	276
			Less: 25% for contingencies	(69)
				207

(c) Extract from balance sheet at 31 December, 19X0

Work-in-progress, at cost, plus interim profit	27,565
Less: Cash on account	18,574
	8,991
Debtors	3,956
	12,947

Workings

Work-in-progress:	
Cost plus interim profit: B1	26,315
A's (£1,043 + £207)	1,250
	27,565
Cash on account: B1	18,000
A's (the only invoice paid before the year-end)	574
	18,574
Debtors: per question	4,160
Add: Invoice re A22	237
	4,397
Less: Unpaid invoice re A23	(441)
	3,956

There can be taken out of debtors *only* those invoices dated 19X0 relating to incomplete contracts which were *unpaid* at 31 December 19X0. The A21 invoice for £574 will not be in the debtors figure because it has already been paid.

12 Introduction to budgetary control

This chapter contains specimen essay-type questions on the basic principles and practice of budgetary control.

Arithmetical questions on budget preparation are in Chapter 13, and questions on variance analysis are in Chapters 14 and 19.

STUDY REQUIREMENTS

(a) Principles of budgetary control.
(b) Administration of budgetary control.
(c) Identification of principal budget factor.

QUESTIONS

1 Discuss briefly:

    (a) How budgetary control assists management.
    (b) The requirements of an effective system of budgetary control.

(20 marks)

2 With reference to the administration of budgetary control:

    (a) List the general duties of a budget officer.
    (b) Set out the functions of the budget committee.
    (c) Set out the main headings which are likely to be contained within the budget manual.

(20 marks)

3 In general, budget preparation is started by the identification of a 'limiting factor' or the 'principal budget' factor.

    (a) List five possible limitations on activity that could be principal budget factors.
    (b) For each, suggest two means of overcoming the limitation.
    (c) State which limitation will be most frequently encountered, and hence choose the first of the individual budgets to be prepared.

(15 marks)

ANSWERS

1

(a) Budgetary control assists management in the following ways:

   (i)   It compels planning. Plans are defined and evaluated, resources are allocated, and any problems, such as limiting factors, are faced in advance.

   (ii) It promotes communication and co-ordination. The organisation will be split into various segments. The aims of the organisation are communicated downwards and the segment limitations are communicated upwards. Individual budgets have to be linked together to form the master budget, co-ordinating the efforts of the different segments.

   (iii) It provides definite expectations. Subsequent performance can be measured against planned targets. The budget defines areas of responsibility for achieving plans, and the comparison of actual results against budget serves as a control device over the various segments.

(b) The requirements of an effective system of budgetary control are:

   (i)   A clearly defined organisational structure, which emphasises areas of responsibility.

   (ii) Adequate accounting records and procedures, so that measurement of performance may be relied on.

   (iii) Participation by individuals within the budgeting process.

   (iv) An awareness by management of the uses of the budgetary system.

   (v) An awareness by top management of the problems of budgetary control, and especially of the reaction of individuals to budgets.

   (vi) Flexibility, so that plans and objectives may be revised.

2

(a) General duties of a budget officer:

   (i)   Co-ordination of individuals involved in preparing budgets.

   (ii) Preparation of budget reports.

   (iii) Recommendation of courses of action on the strength of the budgets.

   (iv) Analysis of the budget system, and revision of it where appropriate.

(b) Functions of the budget committee:

   (i)   Establishment of budget procedures and timetables.

   (ii) Review, revision and acceptance of individual budgets.

   (iii) Co-ordinating decisions.

   (iv) Review of performance reports.

   (v) Recommendation of action, where appropriate.

(c)   Main headings within the budget manual:

   (i)   The objectives of the business.
   (ii)   Its organisation structure.
   (iii) The role of the budget officer and budget committee.
   (iv)   Time periods for budgets.
   (v)   Procedures for budget preparation.
   (vi)   Bases to be adopted, methods of calculation, accounting policies, etc.
   (vii) Copies of forms to be used.

Comment

The budget officer has the primary responsibility for administration. A budget committee will be assembled in large companies, where co-ordination and review are important. It is essentially an advisory committee, and the budget officer will usually be its secretary.

The budget manual has two functions:

   (a) Gives individuals an appreciation of the budget system.
   (b) Provides detailed instructions, so that all budgets are prepared on a consistent basis.

3

(a) **Limitation**	(b) **Means of overcoming limitation**
1 Market demand for products or services.	Extra advertising, new products, or new markets.
2 Availability of material supplies.	Alternative supplies, or different raw materials.
3 Availability of skilled labour.	Higher rates of pay or increased mechanisation.
4 Availability of machines.	Capital expenditure, subcontracting.
5 Factory space.	Extension or different location.
6 Cash.	Issue of capital, shortening of debt-collecting period, or restructuring of debts.

   (c) Market demand. Sales budget.

13 Preparation of budgets

Past questions on budget preparation have been based on two main themes:

(a) Cash budgets, illustrated in Questions 1 to 6 in this chapter. Given data on sales, expenses, credit periods, inventory changes and possibly capital expenditure, candidates are required to prepare a cash-flow budget and also, in most cases, a budgeted profit and loss account and forecast year-end balance sheet. The procedure has similarities with the preparation of accounts from incomplete records in financial accounting papers. Two interesting variations on this theme are illustrated. Question 4 calls for a flexible profit and loss budget, at alternative levels of activity. Question 6 requires the preparation of a cash flow statement from a profit and loss account and opening and closing balance sheets.

(b) Product line budgets, illustrated in questions 7 to 10. Given data on quantities and prices, and changes in stock holdings, candidates are required to prepare production, material usage and purchases budgets; plus in some cases sales budgets or labour utilisation budgets. There may also be a requirement to summarise this information into a trading or profit and loss account.

You should study the model answers carefully as a basis for your own approach to such questions and, as always with numerical questions, give yourself plenty of space for a clear presentation.

STUDY REQUIREMENTS

(a) Budgeting for sales, material, labour and expenses.
(b) Cash forecasts and budgets.
(c) Fixed and flexible budgets.

QUESTIONS

1 On 31 March 19X5 the balance sheet of Schubert Ltd, retailers of musical instruments, was as follows:

	£		£	£
Ordinary shares of £1		Equipment at cost	2,000	
each fully paid	2,000	Less: Depreciation	(500)	
Unappropriated profit	1,000			1,500
Trade creditors	4,000	Stock		2,000
Proposed ordinary		Trade debtors		1,500
dividend	1,500	Balance at bank		3,500
	8,500			8,500

The company is developing a system of forward planning and on 1 April 19X5 supplies the following information:

Month	Credit sales £	Cash sales £	Credit purchases £
March, 19X5 (actual)	1,500	1,400	4,000
April, 19X5 (budgeted)	1,800	500	2,300
May, 19X5 (budgeted)	2,000	600	2,700
June, 19X5 (budgeted)	2,500	800	2,600

All trade debtors are allowed one month's credit and are expected to settle promptly; the trade creditors are paid in the month following delivery.

On 1 April 19X5, all the equipment was replaced at a cost of £3,000. £1,400 was allowed on the old equipment and a net payment made of £1,600. Depreciation is to be provided at the rate of 10% per annum.

The proposed dividend will be paid in June 19X5.

The following expenses will be paid:
Wages: £300 per month
Administration: £150 per month
Rent: £360 for year to 31 March 19X6 (to be paid in April 19X5).

The gross profit percentage on sales is estimated at 25%.

You are required:

(a) To prepare a cash budget for each of the months April, May and June, 19X5.
(b) To prepare a budgeted trading and profit and loss account for the three months ended 30 June 19X5.

(c)   To explain the reasons for the difference between budgeted profitability and budgeted liquidity for the period.

(18 marks)

2

(a)   The following information relates to XY Limited:

Month	Wages incurred £ thousands	Material purchases £ thousands	Overheads £ thousands	Sales £ thousands
February	6	20	10	30
March	8	30	12	40
April	10	25	16	60
May	9	35	14	50
June	12	30	18	70
July	10	25	16	60
August	9	25	14	50
September	9	30	14	50

(i)   It is expected that the cash balance on 31 May will be £22,000.
(ii)   The wages may be assumed to be paid within the month they are incurred.
(iii) It is company policy to pay creditors for materials three months after receipt.
(iv)   Debtors are expected to pay two months after delivery.
(v)   Included in the overhead figures is £2,000 per month which represents depreciation on two cars and one delivery van.
(vi)   There is a one-month delay in paying the overhead expenses.
(vii) 10% of the monthly sales are for cash and 90% are sold on credit.
(viii) A commission of 5% is paid to agents on all the sales on credit but this is not paid until the month following the sales to which it relates; this expense is **not** included in the overhead figures shown.
(ix)   It is intended to repay a loan of £25,000 on 30 June.
(x)   Delivery is expected in July of a new machine costing £45,000 of which £15,000 will be paid on delivery and £15,000 in each of the following months.
(xi)   Assume that overdraft facilities are available if required.

You are required to prepare a cash budget for each of the three months of June, July and August.   *(14 marks)*

(b)   'Experts stress that one of the most vital uses of management accounts is regularly to monitor cash flow — moneys coming into the company each month minus moneys going out.' *(Financial Times, 8 March 1983)*

You are required to comment on the above statement and include in your answer the chief benefits obtained from the preparation of cash budgets.   *(6 marks)*
(Total 20 marks)

141

3   On 1 January 19X1 Faust acquired the goodwill of a wholesale fancy goods business for the sum of £10,000 and paid £3,500 premium for a lease of warehouse premises at a rent of £1,000 per annum. The lease is to expire on 31 December 19X5. The finance for the goodwill, the premium on the lease and the first year's rent payment was transferred from Faust's building society account into the business bank account. He asked you to assist him in projections of the trading position over the first six months of the business.

Faust provides you with the following additional information:

(1)   A gross profit of 20% on gross sales before discount can be achieved and maintained.
(2)   Sales before discount, and purchases are budgeted as follows:

	Gross sales before discounts £	Goods purchased £
January	12,000	36,800
February	16,000	16,000
March	18,000	19,200
April	20,000	24,000
May	24,000	25,600
June	30,000	16,000

(3)   60% of sales will be on credit terms. The remainder will be for cash. Credit terms are settlement at the end of the month after sale. A 5% settlement discount is available for debts settled on those terms.

Faust anticipates that 20% of his credit customers will not take advantage of these terms and will settle one month later.
(4)   Purchases will be made from two suppliers in equal proportions. One supplier requires payment in the month of delivery; the second requires payment in the month following delivery.
(5)   Rates totalling £960 will be payable on 30 June 19X1 for the year ended 31 March 19X2. Rates of £240 for the three months to 31 March 19X1 were paid privately by Faust.
(6)   Wages will be £300 per month.
(7)   An electricity bill will be paid in April estimated at £250 to cover the first three months' supplies.
(8)   Postages will be £50 per month.
(9)   A van will be purchased for £2,400 on 1 April 19X1 which is to be written off over four years. Three months' depreciation is to be provided.

You are required to prepare:

(a)   A forecast of monthly cash flow for the six months ending on 30 June 19X1.
(b)   A forecast trading and profit and loss account for the six months ending on 30 June 19X1.
(c)   A budgeted balance sheet as at 30 June 19X1.

(23 marks)

4 The balance sheet of Lady Jane Fashions at 31 December 19X1 is summarised below:

	£ thousands	£ thousands
Fixed assets		700
Current assets:		
Stock of finished goods	44.8	
Debtors	200.0	
Cash	157.6	
	402.4	
Current liabilities	2.4	
Net current assets		400
Capital employed		1,100

Following an advertising campaign around Christmas time the firm expects sales to rise in 19X2 but it is not known precisely to what level. It is anticipated that 12,000 items will be sold in the year at an average price of £100, though, with the uncertainty that exists over this figure, you have been asked to produce a flexible budget showing the profit if sales are 80%, 90%, 100%, 110% and 120% of 12,000. You have also been asked to produce a cash budget showing the balance at the end of each quarter of 19X2 and a budgeted balance sheet at 31 December 19X2 on the assumption that the 12,000 sales figure is achieved.

You are told that:

(1) The level of demand is expected to be constant during 19X2 though the actual level achieved will not be confirmed until the end of the first quarter. Production will be 1,000 garments per month during the first quarter; production in the second quarter will be sufficient to bring the end of June stock levels to two months; and in the remaining two quarters production will match demand.

(2) Although it is intended to maintain the average sales price of £100 per item, if sales are to reach the 120% level, it is felt that a quantity discount of 10% will need to be given on 20% of sales made.

(3) All sales are on credit, 50% of debtors pay two months after sale and 50% pay three months after sale. Sales in 19X1 had been constant throughout the year.

(4) Materials cost is £20 per item. In order to achieve this purchase price stocks have to be bought in bulk on the first day of each quarter and payment made within thirty days. For orders in excess of £50,000 this cost will fall by 5%.

(5) Labour costs are based on piece-work scales of £3 per item, though the management of Lady Jane Fashions have recently been reminded of a productivity bonus of 60p per item if monthly production from the work-force of 10 reaches 1,000 items. Labour costs are paid one month after they are incurred.

(6) Overhead costs are partly fixed and partly variable. The variable element amounts to £5 per item payable in the month incurred. The fixed element is expected to be £500,000 of which £100,000 is

depreciation of existing fixed assets. Half of the balance is payable monthly, a quarter at the end of June and a quarter at the end of December. If sales reach 120% it will be necessary to purchase additional machinery costing £240,000 on 1 April 19X2 and this will be depreciated at 10% p.a.

(7) Opening stock represents 1,600 items at unit variable cost. Creditors are for wages.

(8) Tax and interest charges can be ignored.

(25 marks)

5 Othello Industries Ltd intends to diversify its product range and, on 1 January 19X9 it sets aside £75,000 for working capital to manufacture a new product.

The standard marginal cost per unit of the new product is as follows:

	£
Direct material	3
Direct wages	2
Variable overhead	1
	6

Fixed overheads are budgeted at £92,000 for the year commencing 1 January 19X9. These will be incurred in equal amounts during each month from 1 February 19X9. The fixed overheads for the month of January are budgeted at 50% of a normal month.

Production is to commence in January and sales from 1 February 19X9.

The sales budget for the period to 31 May 19X9 is as follows:

	Units	Sales value
		£
February	2,000	20,000
March	4,000	40,000
April	6,000	60,000
May	10,000	110,000

The following data are available:

(1) Direct wages are paid in the month in which they are incurred.
(2) Direct materials: 80% of direct materials required for each month's production are purchased in the previous month and 20% in the current month. These are paid for in the month following purchase.
(3) Variable overhead: 25% is paid in the month of usage and the balance in the following month.
(4) Fixed overhead: 50% is paid in the month in which it is incurred and 20% in the following month; the balance is depreciation of fixed assets.

(5) Sales: 25% of each month's invoiced sales units are produced in the month of sale and 75% in the previous month. There is to be a 10% price increase on all sales from 1 May 19X9.

(6) Debtors:
10% received in the month of sale
60% received in the following month
20% in the third month
5% in the fourth month
3% in the fifth month
2% is not received.

You are required to prepare a monthly cash budget for the period to 30 April 19X9.

(20 marks)

6 The budgeted profit and loss account for the year ending 31 October 19X1 together with the actual and budgeted balance sheets as at 31 October 19X0 and 19X1 respectively for BC Limited are given below.

You are required, using the data given, to prepare a budgeted cash-flow statement for the year ending 31 October 19X1.

(20 marks)

Budgeted profit and loss account for the year ending 31 October 19X1

	£ thousands	£ thousands
1 November 19X0		
Balance brought down		120
31 October 19X1		
Net profit		200
		320
Less:		
Reserves	30	
Dividends	100	
Corporation Tax	80	(210)
Balance		110

145

Balance sheets as at 31 October

Assets:	Actual 19X0 £ thousands	Actual 19X0 £ thousands	Budgeted 19X1 £ thousands	Budgeted 19X1 £ thousands
Freehold buildings	600		600	
Less: Depreciation	50	550	50	550
Plant and machinery	500		700	
Less: Depreciation	150	350	200	500
Motor vehicles	200		180	
Less: Depreciation	80	120	120	60
		1,020		1,110
Investments		150		180
Stock: Raw materials	180		140	
Work-in-progress	60		65	
Finished goods	120	360	135	340
Debtors		30		40
Bank		40		20
		1,600		1,690
Capital and liabilities:				
Issued share capital		800		1,000
Reserves		80		110
Profit and loss, balance		120		110
Debentures		300		200
Corporation tax		100		60
Creditors		70		90
Dividends		120		—
Accruals		10		20
Bank loan		—		100
Total		1,600		1,690

7 Fasolt Limited manufactures children's toys and its range consists of four different models: a school, a house, a boat and a caravan. Over 90% of the sales are made in two months of the year and for this reason the establishment of accurate budgets is essential.

You are provided with the following information relating to projections for October and November 19X2:

(1) Sales	School	House	Boat	Caravan
Quantity	12,000	15,500	9,000	8,500
Price	£10	£14	£20	£12

(2) Material usage

	School £	House £	Boat £	Caravan £
Moulded plastic	4	6	8	5
Accessories (bought in)	2	2	1	1
Packing (per toy)	2	2	1	1

(3) Wages costs will be £1 per unit for each of the models.

(4) Stocks of raw materials and work-in-progress are to be zero at the beginning and end of the period. Finished stocks will be built up during the earlier part of the year and it is anticipated that some stocks will be on hand at 30 November.

	Estimated stocks (units)	
Finished goods	1 October 19X2	30 November 19X
Schools	6,000	1,500
Houses	8,000	2,000
Boats	6,000	1,000
Caravans	4,500	500

You are required to prepare:

(a) Budgets for sales, production, materials usage and purchases for the two months ended 30 November 19X2. *(11 marks)*
(b) A budgeted trading account for the two months ended 30 November 19X2. *(4 marks)*
(Total 15 marks)

8 Kes Manufacturing Ltd makes a range of falconry equipment mainly for export. When producing the budget for 19X2 the company realises that its principal budget factor is sales, and forecasts the following sales:

Product name	Kent	Essex	Sussex
Sales	1,000	2,000	500
Selling price	£50	£75	£100

The unit direct costs of manufacturing each type of equipment are:

	Kent	Essex	Sussex
Materials			
Leather (at 10p/m)	5 m	6 m	7 m
Wire (at £2/kg)	1.2 kg	1.3 kg	1.4 kg
Labour			
Stitchers (at £2/hour)	$1/2$ hour	$3/4$ hour	1 hour
Assemblers (at £3/hour)	$1/2$ hour	$1/2$ hour	1 hour

The company has stock of finished goods of 200 Kents, 200 Essexes and 100 Sussexes and raw materials stocks of 1,000 m of leather and 500 kg of wire. It feels that 19X2's sales figures could well be repeated in 19X3 and wishes to have sufficient stock of finished goods to cope with 10% of this demand and raw materials to cope with 20% of this demand.

You are required to produce:

(a) Sales budget.
(b) Production budget (in numbers of Kent, Essex and Sussex).
(c) Materials usage budgets (for leather and wire).
(d) Materials purchases budgets.
(e) Labour utilisation budget.

(15 marks)

9 XYZ Ltd manufactures three products: P1, P2 and P3. These are made in three production departments from four materials M1, M2, M3 and M4. The following information is supplied:

Material	Used in department	Cost per unit £	P1	P2	P3
			Units per article		
M1	D1	0.5	—	1	2
M2	D2	0.2	1	—	2
M3	D2	0.4	2	1	—
M4	D3	0.3	2	2	1

	P1	P2	P3
Rejection on final inspection at end of process considered normal	5%	10%	10%
Budget details			
Sales for the year in thousands	£260	£580	£450
Sales price each	£5	£10	£6
Stocks of finished goods			
1 January	5,000	10,000	15,000
31 December	10,000	15,000	30,000

Stocks of raw materials (units)	M1	M2	M3	M4
1 January	30,000	40,000	10,000	60,000
31 December	40,000	30,000	20,000	50,000

You are required to prepare:

(a) The production budget.
(b) Production cost budgets for direct materials for departments D1, D2 and D3.
(c) The purchasing budget.

(25 marks)

10 Rigoletto Ltd manufactures three products from three basic raw materials in three departments. The company operates a budgetary control system and values its stock of finished goods on a total cost basis. From the data given below, you are required to produce for the month of October 19X9 the following budgets:

(a) Production.
(b) Material usage.
(c) Purchases.
(d) Profit and loss account for each product and in total.

Budgeted data, for October 19X9:

	Product		
	A	**B**	**C**
Sales	£1,500,000	£1,080,000	£1,680,000
Stock of finished products at 1 October 19X9 in units	3,000	2,000	2,500

	Department		
	I	**II**	**III**
Fixed production overhead	£239,000	£201,300	£391,200
Direct labour hours	47,800	67,100	65,200

	Direct material		
	M1	**M2**	**M3**
Stock at 1 October 19X9 in units	24,500	20,500	17,500

The company is introducing a new system of inventory control which should reduce stocks. The forecast is that stocks at 31 October 19X9 will be reduced as follows: raw materials by 10% and finished products by 20%.

Fixed production overhead is absorbed on a direct labour hour basis. It is expected that there will be no work-in-progress at the beginning or end of the month.

Administration cost is absorbed by products at a rate of 20% of production cost and selling and distribution cost is absorbed by products at a rate of 40% of production cost.

Profit is budgeted as a percentage of total cost as follows: product A 25%; product B 12$\frac{1}{2}$% and product C 16$\frac{2}{3}$%.

Standard cost data, per unit of product:

	Price per unit £	Product A units	Product B units	Product C units
Direct material				
M1	2.00	5	—	12
M2	4.00	—	10	9
M3	1.00	5	5	—

	Rate per hour £	hours	hours	hours
Direct wages				
Department I	2.50	4	2	2
Department II	2.00	6	2	3
Department III	1.50	2	4	6
		£	£	£
Other variable costs		10	20	15

(25 marks)

ANSWERS

1

(a) **Cash budget for April, May and June, 19X5**

	April £	May £	June £
Receipts			
Sales: Credit	1,500	1,800	2,000
Cash	500	600	800
	2,000	2,400	2,800
Payments	£	£	£
Purchases: Credit	4,000	2,300	2,700
Equipment	1,600	—	—
Dividend	—	—	1,500
Wages	300	300	300
Administration	150	150	150
Rent	360	—	—
	6,410	2,750	4,650
Cash flow	(4,410)	(350)	(1,850)
Opening balance	3,500	(910)	(1,260)
Closing balance	(910)	(1,260)	(3,110)

(b) **Budgeted trading and profit and loss account for the three months ended 30 June 19X5**

	£	£
Sales		8,200
Less: Cost of sales: Opening stock	2,000	
Purchases	7,600	
	9,600	
Less: Closing stock	(3,450)	(6,150)
Gross profit		2,050
Less: Wages	900	
Administration	450	
Rent	90	
Depreciation on equipment	75	
Loss on sale of old equipment	100	(1,615)
Net profit		£435

(c) **Reasons for difference between budgeted profitability and budgeted liquidity for the period**

			£	£
(i)	Changes in working capital:			
	Stock has increased by		1,450	
	Debtors have increased by		1,000	
	Repayments have increased by		270	
	Creditors have decreased by		1,400	4,120
(ii)	Payments of a non-revenue nature:			
	Dividends		1,500	
	Equipment		1,600	3,100
(iii)	Charges of a non-cash nature:			
	Depreciation		75	
	Loss on sale of equipment		100	(175)
				7,045

		£	£
Cash outflow:			
Opening balance in hand		3,500	
Closing balance overdrawn		3,110	
			6,610
Net profit			435
			7,045

2

(a) Cash budgets for June, July and August

	June £ thousands	July £ thousands	August £ thousands
Opening balance	22	1.75	(16.40)
Receipts:			
Cash sales	7	6	5
Debtors	54	45	63
	83	52.75	51.60
Payments:			
Wages	12	10	9
Creditors	30	25	35
Overhead	12	16	14
Commission	2.25	3.15	2.70
Loan	25	—	—
Machine	—	15	15
	81.25	69.15	75.70
Closing balance	1.75	(16.40)	(24.10)
	83.00	52.75	51.60

(b) While statements of profitability are central to any form of accounting, it is recognised that other financial information provides an important supplement. Cash flow statements therefore augment profit statements.

Indeed, for some companies cash flow may be more important than profit, at least in the short term. Many companies have run into liquidity problems while still profitable, for instance through over-trading or by being too reliant on fixed interest borrowings. The monitoring of cash flow helps to avoid such problems.

The chief benefits obtained from the preparation of cash budgets are as follows:

  (i)   Future cash shortages are identified in plenty of time to raise finance;
  (ii) cash as a resource is utilised efficiently;
  (iii) future cash surpluses may be predicted so that investment plans may be made.

3 (a) Forecast of monthly cash flow for the six months ended 30 June 19X1

	January £	February £	March £	April £	May £	June £	Total £
Receipts							
Building society	14,500	—	—	—	—	—	14,500
Sales:							
Cash	4,800	6,400	7,200	8,000	9,600	12,000	48,000
One month's credit	—	5,472	7,296	8,208	9,120	10,944	41,040
Two months' credit	—	—	1,440	1,920	2,160	2,400	7,920
	19,300	11,872	15,936	18,128	20,880	25,344	111,460
Payments							
Initial payments	14,500	—	—	—	—	—	14,500
Purchases:							
Same month	18,400	8,000	9,600	12,000	12,800	8,000	68,800
Following month	—	18,400	8,000	9,600	12,000	12,800	60,800
Rates	—	—	—	—	—	960	960
Wages	300	300	300	300	300	300	1,800
Electricity	—	—	—	250	—	—	250
Postage	50	50	50	50	50	50	300
Van	—	—	—	2,400	—	—	2,400
	33,250	26,750	17,950	24,600	25,150	22,110	149,810
Net cash flow	(13,950)	(14,878)	(2,014)	(6,472)	(4,270)	3,234	(38,350)
Opening balance	—	(13,950)	(28,828)	(30,842)	(37,314)	(41,584)	—
Closing balance	(13,950)	(28,828)	(30,842)	(37,314)	(41,584)	(38,350)	(38,350)

(b) **Forecast trading and profit and loss account for six months ended 30 June 19X1**

	£	£
Sales		120,000
Purchases	137,600	
Closing stock	(41,600)	
Cost of sales		(96,000)
Gross profit		24,000
Expenses:		
Discount allowed	2,880	
Wages	1,800	
Rates (£240 + $\frac{1}{4} \times$ £960)	480	
Electricity (£250 + £250)	500	
Postage	300	
	5,960	
Depreciation: Van (£2,400 ÷ 16)	150	
Lease (£3,500 ÷ 10)	350	
Rental	500	
		(6,960)
		17,040

(c) **Budgeted balance sheet as at 30 June 19X1**

Assets employed

	Cost	Depreciation	
Fixed assets	£	£	£
Lease premium	3,500	350	3,150
Motor van	2,400	150	2,250
	5,900	500	5,400
			10,000
Goodwill			
Current assets			
Stock		41,600	
Debtors (£18,000 × 0.8 × 0.95			
+ £18,000 × 0.2 + £14,400 × 0.2)		20,160	
Prepayments ($\frac{3}{4}$ × £960 + £500)		1,220	
		62,980	
Current liabilities			
Creditors	8,000		
Accruals	250		
Bank overdraft	38,350		
		(46,600)	
Net current assets			16,380
			31,780

Financed by:
Proprietor's interest
Capital introduced (£14,500 + £240)   14,740
Profit for the period   17,040

Balance at 30 June 19X1   31,780

Debtors have been valued net of discount expected to be allowed, discount allowed has been based on all six months' sales.

Comments

Cash-flow forecast

Firstly, sales have to be converted into receipts, for example:

January sales £		£	January receipts £	February receipts £	March receipts £
12,000	40% cash		4,800		
	60% credit:				
	60% × 80% next month	5,760			
	Less: 5% discount	(288)		5,472	
	60% × 20% month later				1,440

Secondly, purchases have to be converted into payments, for example:

January purchases £		January payments £	February payments £
36,800	½ paid in month of delivery	18,400	
	½ paid in month following delivery		18,400

The remaining figures are easy to slot in, but remember, there are several marks to be gained here.

Forecast trading account

Closing stock is by deduction: the percentage gross profit is known.

Three items are easily forgotten: discount, depreciation and rent.

4

(a) Flexible budget for 19X2

Activity level	80% £ thousands	90% £ thousands	100% £ thousands	110% £ thousands	120% £ thousands
Gross sales	960	1,080	1,200	1,320	1,440.0
Discount	—	—	—	—	28.8
	960	1,080	1,200	1,320	1,411.2
Variable production costs:					
Materials	189.00	209.00	235.60	262.20	288.80
Labour	30.60	34.80	44.64	49.68	54.72
Overheads	48.00	55.00	62.00	69.00	76.00
	267.60	298.80	342.24	380.88	419.52
Opening stock	44.80	44.80	44.80	44.80	44.80
	312.40	343.60	387.04	425.68	464.32
Closing stock	(44.80)	(48.60)	(55.20)	(60.72)	(66.24)
Cost of goods sold	267.60	295.00	331.84	364.96	398.08
Fixed costs	500.00	500.00	500.00	500.00	518.00
Total costs	767.60	795.00	831.84	864.96	916.08
Profit	192.4	285.0	368.16	455.04	495.12

(b) Cash budget for 19X2 (at 100% activity)

Quarter	1 £ thousands	2 £ thousands	3 £ thousands	4 £ thousands
Sales	300	300	300	300
Opening debtors	200	250	250	250
	500	550	550	550
Closing debtors	(250)	(250)	(250)	(250)
Receipts	250	300	300	300
Payments:				
Materials	57.00	64.60	57.00	57.00
Labour	9.60	11.76	11.28	10.80
Variable overhead	15.00	17.00	15.00	15.00
Fixed overhead	50.00	150.00	50.00	150.00
	131.60	243.36	133.28	232.80
Net cash flow	118.40	56.64	166.72	67.20
Balance brought forward	157.60	276.00	332.64	499.36
Balance carried forward	276.00	332.64	499.36	566.56

(c) **Budgeted balance sheet at 31 December 19X2**

	£ thousands	£ thousands
Fixed assets		600.00
Current assets		
Stock of finished goods	55.20	
Debtors	250.00	
Cash	566.56	
	871.76	
Current liabilities	(3.60)	
Net current assets		868.16
Net assets		1,468.16
Capital employed		
Balance at 1 January 19X2		1,100.00
Profit for the year		368.16
Balance at 31 December 19X2		1,468.16

Workings

Production (units)

	80%	90%	100%	110%	120%
Activity level					
Quarter 1					
Production	3,000	3,000	3,000	3,000	3,000
Opening stock	1,600	1,600	1,600	1,600	1,600
	4,600	4,600	4,600	4,600	4,600
Sales	(2,400)	(2,700)	(3,000)	(3,300)	(3,600)
Closing stock	2,200	1,900	1,600	1,300	1,000
Quarter 2					
Sales	2,400	2,700	3,000	3,300	3,600
Closing stock	1,600	1,800	2,000	2,200	2,400
	4,000	4,500	5,000	5,500	6,000
Opening stock	(2,200)	(1,900)	(1,600)	(1,300)	(1,000)
Production	1,800	2,600	3,400	4,200	5,000
Quarters 3 and 4					
Production	2,400	2,700	3,000	3,300	3,600
Total production for year	9,600	11,000	12,400	13,800	15,200

Materials cost (£ thousands)

Quarter 1	57	57	57	57	57
2	36	49.4	64.6	79.8	95
3	48	51.3	57	62.7	68.4
4	48	51.3	57	62.7	68.4
Total	189	209.0	235.6	262.2	288.8

Labour cost (£ thousands)

Quarter 1	10.8	10.8	10.8	10.80	10.80
2	5.4	7.8	12.24	15.12	18.00
3	7.2	8.1	10.80	11.88	12.96
4	7.2	8.1	10.80	11.88	12.96
Total	30.6	34.8	44.64	49.68	54.72

Closing stock

Units	1,600	1,800	2,000	2,200	2,400
Cost	£ thousands	£ thousands	£ thousands	£ thousands	£ thousands
Materials	32	34.2	38	41.8	45.6
Labour	4.8	5.4	7.2	7.92	8.64
Overhead	8	9	10	11	12
	44.8	48.6	55.2	60.72	66.24

Debtors represent $2\frac{1}{2}$ months' sales.
Labour payments are $\frac{2}{3}$ of each quarter's cost plus $\frac{1}{3}$ of previous quarter.

5 Cash budget 1 January 19X9 to 30 April 19X9

	January	February	March	April
Sales (units)	—	2,000	4,000	6,000
	£	£	£	£
Sales revenue	—	20,000	40,000	60,000
Receipts: February sales	—	2,000	12,000	4,000
March sales	—	—	4,000	24,000
April sales	—	—	—	6,000
	—	2,000	16,000	34,000
Production (units):				
Current month	—	500	1,000	1,500
Previous month	1,500	3,000	4,500	7,500
	1,500	3,500	5,500	9,000
	£	£	£	£
Materials used	4,500	10,500	16,500	27,000
Materials purchased	900	2,100	3,300	5,400
(£3,600 assumed pre January)	8,400	13,200	21,600	x
	9,300	15,300	24,900	5,400 + x
Payments for materials	3,600	9,300	15,300	24,900
Wages	3,000	7,000	11,000	18,000
Variable overhead: Current	375	875	1,375	2,250
Next	—	1,125	2,625	4,125
Fixed overhead: Current	2,000	4,000	4,000	4,000
Next	—	800	1,600	1,600
Total payments	8,975	23,100	35,900	54,875
Net cash flow	(8,975)	(21,100)	(19,900)	(20,875)
Balance brought forward	75,000	66,025	44,925	25,025
Balance carried forward	66,025	44,925	25,025	4,150

Workings

Fixed overheads $\dfrac{£92,000}{11.5} = £8,000$ per month

(January fixed overheads = £4,000)

6   Budgeted cash-flow statement for the year ending 31 October 19X1

	£ thousands	£ thousands	£ thousands
Net receipts from trading operations:			
Net profit for the year			200
Add: Decrease in stocks	20		
Less: Increase in debtors		10	
Add: Increase in creditors	20		
Add: Increase in accruals	10		
	50	10	40
			240
Add: Non-cash expenses			
Depreciation: Plant and machinery	50		
Motor vehicles	60		110
			350
Receipts from other sources:			
Issue of share capital	200		
Bank loan	100		300
			650
Payments (apart from trading):			
Purchase of plant and machinery		200	
Purchase of investments		30	
Redemption of debentures		100	
Payment of Corporation Tax		120	
Payment of dividends		220	
			670
Opening cash balance			40
Less: Net payments			(20)
Closing cash balance			20

Workings

Payments	Corporation Tax	Dividends
Liability brought forward	100	120
Add: Appropriation for the year	80	100
Less: Liability carried forward	(60)	—
Paid in the year	120	220

Comments

The cash-flow statement required is rather unusual for a cost-accounting question in that no details of sales, purchases, wages, etc. are known.

Movements in the two balance sheets may be taken as receipts or payments, and it is possible to calculate the cash generated from trading operations.

Motor vehicles costing £20,000 have been disposed of during the year. There are no details given of sale proceeds or accumulated depreciation. It has been assumed that the vehicles were disposed of for nil consideration, and were fully depreciated.

	19X0 Before disposal	19X0 After disposal	19X1	
	£ thousands	£ thousands	£ thousands	
Cost	200	180	180	
Depreciation	(80)	(60)	(120)	Increase in
	120	120	60	depreciation £60,000

7

(a)

Sales budget	School	House	Boat	Caravan	Total
Quantity	12,000	15,500	9,000	8,500	
Price	£10	£14	£20	£12	
	£120,000	£217,000	£180,000	£102,000	£619,000

Production budget					
Sales quantity	12,000	15,500	9,000	8,500	
Opening stocks	(6,000)	(8,000)	(6,000)	(4,500)	
Closing stocks	1,500	2,000	1,000	500	
Production Quantity	7,500	9,500	4,000	4,500	25,500

Materials usage and purchases budget					
Production quantity	7,500	9,500	4,000	4,500	
	£	£	£	£	£
Moulded plastic	30,000	57,000	32,000	22,500	141,500
Accessories	15,000	19,000	4,000	4,500	42,500
Packing	15,000	19,000	4,000	4,500	42,500
	60,000	95,000	40,000	31,500	226,500

(b) **Budgeted trading account for the two months ended 30 November 19X2**

	School	House	Boat	Caravan	Total
	£	£	£	£	£
Sales	120,000	217,000	180,000	102,000	619,000
Cost of sales	108,000	170,500	99,000	68,000	445,500
Gross profit	12,000	46,500	81,000	34,000	173,500

8

(a) **Sales budget**

	Kent	Essex	Sussex	Total
Quantities	1,000	2,000	500	3,500
Unit selling price	£50	£75	£100	
Revenue	£50,000	£150,000	£50,000	£250,000

(b) **Production budget**

	Kent	Essex	Sussex	Total
Sales	1,000	2,000	500	3,500
Closing stock	100	200	50	350
	1,100	2,200	550	3,850
Opening stock	(200)	(200)	(100)	(500)
Production	900	2,000	450	3,350

(c) **Materials usage**

	Kent	Essex	Sussex	Total
Leather (m)	4,500	12,000	3,150	19,650
Wire (kg)	1,080	2,600	630	4,310

(d) **Materials purchases**

	Leather		Wire		Total
	m	£	kg	£	£
Usage	19,650	1,965	4,310	8,620	10,585
Closing stock	4,100	410	900	1,800	2,210
	23,750	2,375	5,210	10,420	12,795
Opening stock	(1,000)	(100)	(500)	(1,000)	(1,100)
Purchases	22,750	2,275	4,710	9,420	11,695

(e) **Labour utilisation budget**

	Stitchers (hours)	Assemblers (hours)	Total (hours)
Kent (900 units)	450	450	900
Essex (2,000 units)	1,500	1,000	2,500
Sussex (450 units)	450	450	900
	2,400	1,900	4,300
Hourly rate	£2	£3	
Total cost	£4,800	£5,700	£10,500

(a) Production budget (in units)

	P1	P2	P3	Total
Sales	52,000	58,000	75,000	185,000
Opening stocks	(5,000)	(10,000)	(15,000)	(30,000)
Closing stocks	10,000	15,000	30,000	55,000
Production after rejects	57,000	63,000	90,000	210,000
Add: Rejects	3,000	7,000	10,000	20,000
Production before rejects	60,000	70,000	100,000	230,000

(b) Production cost budgets for direct materials

Department	D1		D2		D3		D4		
Material	M1		M2		M3		M4		Total cost
	Units	Cost £	Units	Cost £	Units	Cost £	Units	Cost £	£
P1 60,000	—	—	60,000	12,000	120,000	48,000	120,000	36,000	96,000
P2 70,000	70,000	35,000	—	—	70,000	28,000	140,000	42,000	105,000
P3 100,000	200,000	100,000	200,000	40,000	—	—	100,000	30,000	170,000
	270,000	135,000	260,000	52,000	190,000	76,000	360,000	108,000	371,000

(c) Purchasing budget

	M1	M2	M3	M4	Total
Used in production (units)	270,000	260,000	190,000	360,000	1,080,000
Opening stocks (units)	(30,000)	(40,000)	(10,000)	(60,000)	
Closing stocks (units)	40,000	30,000	20,000	50,000	
	280,000	250,000	200,000	350,000	
Cost	£140,000	£50,000	£80,000	£105,000	£375,000

Comment

The marks are earned in this question by the correct handling of rejected units. It is reasonable to assume that stocks of finished goods have been inspected and contain no future rejects. All rejects therefore come out of production. To calculate rejected units from the number of good units, the fractions $5/95$, $10/90$ and $10/90$ have been used for P1, P2 and P3, respectively.

10 Before any of the required budgets can be produced, budgeted sales must be found (in units). This may be done by finding the standard selling price, i.e. by producing standard cost cards.

	A £	A £	B £	B £	C £	C £
Materials: M1		10				24
M2				40		36
M3		5		5		
		15		45		60
Labour: Department I	10		5		5	
II	12		4		6	
III	3	25	6	15	9	20
		40		60		80
Other variable costs	10		20		15	
		50		80		95
Fixed costs:						
Department I (£5/hour)	20		10		10	
II (£3/hour)	18		6		9	
III (£6/hour)	12	50	24	40	36	55
Production cost		100		120		150
Administration	20		24		30	
Selling and distribution	40	60	48	72	60	90
		160		192		240
Profit		40		24		40
Selling price		200		216		280
Sales revenue		£1,500,000		£1,080,000		£1,680,000
Sales (in units)		7,500		5,000		6,000

(a) **Production budget**

	A (units)	B (units)	C (units)
Sales	7,500	5,000	6,000
Opening stock	(3,000)	(2,000)	(2,500)
	4,500	3,000	3,500
Closing stock	2,400	1,600	2,000
Production	6,900	4,600	5,500

(b) Materials usage budget

	M1 Quantity per unit of product	Total	M2 Quantity per unit of product	Total	M3 Quantity per unit of product	Total
Production of A	5	34,500	—	—	5	34,500
B	—	—	10	46,000	5	23,000
C	12	66,000	9	49,500	—	—
Total usage (units)		100,500		95,500		57,500

(c) Materials purchases budget

	M1 Units	£	M2 Units	£	M3 Units	£
Usage	100,500	201,000	95,500	382,000	57,500	57,500
Opening stock	24,500	49,000	20,500	82,000	17,500	17,500
	76,000	152,000	75,000	300,000	40,000	40,000
Closing stock	22,050	44,100	18,450	73,800	15,750	15,750
Purchases	98,050	196,100	93,450	373,800	55,750	55,750

(d) Budgeted profit and loss account

	A £ thousands	B £ thousands	C £ thousands	Total £ thousands
Sales	1,500	1,080	1,680	4,260
Cost of sales	(1,200)	(960)	(1,440)	(3,600)
Profit	300	120	240	660

Comment

This is a good example of a question where the starting point is hard to locate.

In this problem, in order to produce the production budget we use the equation:

opening stock in units + production in units =
sales in units + closing stock in units

To compute sales in units, budgeted sales revenue has to be divided by budgeted selling price per unit, and the only way this can be established is by constructing the standard cost card and then adding on the profit percentage.

14 Standard costing and basic variance analysis

These two subjects are linked because formal variance analysis applied to costs is only possible when standards are available.

Question 1 is a rare example of a narrative question on standard setting. The remaining questions in this chapter all require arithmetical calculations of the common material, labour and overhead variances; linked in some cases with a reconciliation between the budgeted and actual profit for a period. Provided you have learned the basic formulae for variance calculations, this type of question should not offer great difficulty. Note the use of T accounts in the workings to several of the model answers. Question 7 actually calls for a work-in-progress control account.

Question 5 calls for a commentary on reasons for variances occurring. Study this, bearing in mind that variance analysis is a practical management tool not merely a numerical exercise. With regard to overhead variances, question 7 requires the calculation of fixed overhead 'productivity' and 'capacity' variances. These sometimes cause difficulty. Make sure you understand them.

This chapter does not cover mix variances, which will be found in Chapter 19.

STUDY REQUIREMENTS

(a) Principles of standard costing.
(b) Concepts of capacity usage, activity and efficiency.
(c) Variance analysis and variance accounting.

QUESTIONS

1

(a) Explain briefly:

    (i)   how standards are compiled for material and labour costs for a product;

    (ii) the nature and purpose of material and labour variances.

(b) Calculate the material and labour variances from the data set out below and present your answers in the form of a statement for presentation to management.

	Standard
Weight to produce one unit	12 kg
Price, per kilogram	£9
Time to produce one unit	10 hours
Wages rate, per hour	£2

Actual production and costs for week ended 12 November 19X7:

Units produced	240
Material used	2,640 kg
Material cost	£26,400
Time worked	2,520 hours
Wages paid	£5,544

(25 marks)

2 Fischer Ltd manufactures a range of chess sets and operates a standard costing system. Information relating to the 'Spassky' design for the month of March 1985 is as follows:

1   Standard costs per 100 sets

	£
Raw materials:	
Plaster of paris: 20 kg at £8 per kg	160
Paint: ½ litre at £30 per litre	15
Direct wages: 2½ hours at £10 per hour	25
Fixed production overheads: 400% of direct wages	100
	———
	300
	———

2   Standard selling price per set   £3.80

3   Raw materials, work in progress and finished goods stock records are maintained at standard cost.

4   Stock levels at the beginning and end of March 1985 were as follows:

	1 March 1985	31 March 1985
Plaster of paris	2,800 kg	2,780 kg
Paint	140 litres	170 litres
Finished sets	900 sets	1,100 sets

There was no work in progress at either date.

168

5   Budgeted production and sales during the month were 30,000 sets. Actual sales, all made at standard selling price, and actual production were 28,400 and 28,600 sets respectively.

6   Raw materials purchased during the month were 5,400 kg of plaster of paris at a cost of £43,200 and 173 litres of paint at a cost of £5,800.

7   Direct wages were 730 hours at an average rate of £11 per hour.

8   Fixed production overheads amounted to £34,120.

You are required to prepare for the month of March 1985:

(a)   the cost ledger accounts for raw materials, work in progress and finished goods; and   *(10 marks)*

(b)   (i)   a budget trading statement;

           (ii) a standard cost trading statement;

           (iii) a financial trading statement; and

           (iv) a reconciliation between these statements identifying all relevant variances.   *(14 marks)*

(Total 24 marks)

3 K Ltd uses standard costs and flexible budgets for control purposes.

The standard material allowed per unit is 4 kg at a standard price of £0.75 per kg.

Budgeted direct labour hours for a four-week period were 80,000 hours at a budgeted cost of £152,000.

Budgeted variable production overhead for 80,000 hours was £96,000.

Details for the four-week period ended 29 April 19X8 were:

	£
Incurred	
Direct wages	163,800
Variances	
Direct wages rate	0.20 per hour adverse
Direct materials price (calculated on purchases at time of receipt at £0.05 per kg)	9,000 favourable
Direct materials usage	1,500 adverse
Variable production overhead	2,200 favourable
Variable production overhead efficiency	2,400 adverse

Production: 38,000 units

There were no stocks at the beginning of the period, but there were 26,000 kg of direct materials in stock at 29 April 19X8.

You are required to state for the period:

(a)   The number of kilograms of direct material purchased.

(b)   The number of kilograms of direct material used above the standard allowed.

(c)   The variable production overhead expenditure variance.

(d) The actual hours worked.

(e) The number of standard hours allowed for the production achieved.

(20 marks)

4 Bronte Ltd manufactures a single product, a laminated kitchen unit which has a standard cost of £80 made up as follows:

		£
Direct materials	15 square metres at £3 per square metre	45
Direct labour	5 hours at £4 per hour	20
Variable overheads	5 hours at £2 per hour	10
Fixed overheads	5 hours at £1 per hour	5
		80

The standard selling price of the kitchen unit is £100.

The monthly budget projects production and sales of 1,000 units.

Actual figures for the month of April are as follows:

Sales 1,200 units at £102
Production 1,400 units
Direct materials 22,000 square metres at £4 per square metre
Direct wages 6,800 hours at £5
Variable overheads £11,000
Fixed overheads £6,000

You are required to prepare a trading account reconciling actual and budgeted profit and showing all appropriate variances.

(13 marks)

5 The following are standard cost data for a company manufacturing a single product:

	Quantity	Price	£
Direct materials	50 kg	£4.20 per kg	210
Direct labour	20 hours	£3.50 per hour	70
Variable production overhead	20 hours	£1.20 per hour	24
Fixed production overhead	20 hours	£4.50 per hour	90
			394
Standard selling price			£600

Budgeted production for the month of April was 260 units and this figure was used in calculating the fixed overhead absorption rate. Overhead is absorbed into production on the basis of units produced but the variable overhead is deemed to vary with hours worked.

170

An abridged trading and profit statement prepared in the conventional way shows the following:

	£	£
Sales		165,000
Materials used	50,200	
Direct wages	22,400	
Production overhead, variable	6,600	
Production overhead, fixed	23,500	
		102,700
Gross profit		62,300
Selling and administration		29,300
Net profit		£33,000

Additional information appropriate to April:

Sales and production   250 units.
There was no work-in-progress.
Actual hours worked by direct labour   5,600.
Materials used cost £4.00 per kilogram.

You are required:

(a) to calculate the following variances:

      (i)   due to selling prices;
     (ii)   direct materials price;
   (iii)   direct materials usage;
   (iv)   direct wages rate;
    (v)   direct labour efficiency;
   (vi)   variable production overhead expenditure;
  (vii)   variable production overhead efficiency;
 (viii)   fixed production overhead expenditure;
   (ix)   fixed production overhead volume;

(b) to present a profit statement utilising standard costs and showing the variances;

(c)   (i)   to comment on two possible reasons for each of the variances you show for (a)(ii) and (a)(v) and to state who (job title) is responsible for the variance;
     (ii)   to state what ought to be done by the appropriate executive responsible for the direct labour efficiency variance.

(35 marks)

6   A company manufactures one product which passes through two processes before transfer to finished goods stock. Standard cost data for each process are as follows:

		Process A	Process B
		£	£	£
Direct materials	20 units at 0.30	6.00	
	14 units at 0.50		7.00
Direct wages	2 hours at 1.50	3.00	
	3 hours at 2.00		6.00
Production overheads	2 hours at 3.00	6.00	
	3 hours at 4.00		12.00
		15.00	25.00

Budgeted output for October was 5,000 units.

Actual costs incurred in October were:	£	£
Direct materials	30,720	31,740
Direct wages	15,840	25,650
Production overhead	31,680	58,425

An analysis of the production variances which had been calculated for October was as follows:

		£	£
Direct materials:	price	1,920(A)	2,760(F)
	usage	300(F)	550(A)
Direct wages:	rate	990(A)	2,850(F)
	efficiency	300(A)	600(F)
Production overhead:	expenditure	1,680(A)	1,575(F)
	capacity	300(A)	3,000(A)
	productivity	600(A)	1,200(F)

Adverse variances are indicated by (A), and favourable variances by (F).

From each of the questions 1 to 8 below, you are required to select the appropriate answer. You must support each answer with a reasoned explanation or calculation.

1 What was the actual output for the month?

   (a) 5,000
   (b) 5,120
   (c) 4,800
   (d) 5,440
   (e) None of the above. It is not possible to obtain an answer from data provided.
   (f) None of the above. In my opinion the output was .... units.

2 What was the actual price per unit of direct material used in process A?

   (a) £0.28
   (b) £0.30
   (c) £0.32
   (d) £0.34

(e) None of the above. It is not possible to obtain an answer from data provided.

(f) None of the above. In my opinion the price per unit was £..........

3 What was the total standard cost of direct materials in process B?

(a) £34,500
(b) £33,950
(c) £28,980
(d) £29,530
(e) None of the above. It is not possible to obtain an answer from data provided.
(f) None of the above. In my opinion the standard cost was £..........

4 What was the actual cost per labour hour in process B?

(a) £2.00
(b) £1.90
(c) £1.80
(d) £2.25
(e) None of the above. It is not possible to obtain an answer from data provided.
(f) None of the above. In my opinion the actual cost was £..........

5 What was the total standard cost of direct wages in process A?

(a) £14,550
(b) £14,850
(c) £15,830
(d) £16,130
(e) None of the above. It is not possible to obtain an answer from data provided.
(f) None of the above. In my opinion the standard cost was £..........

6 What was the cause of the overhead productivity variance in process B?

(a) The actual overhead incurred being less than the amount budgeted.
(b) The actual hours worked differing from those budgeted.
(c) The actual hours worked being greater than the standard hours.
(d) The actual capacity utilised being greater than budgeted.
(e) None of the above. It is not possible to obtain an answer from data provided.
(f) None of the above. In my opinion the variance was caused by........

7 What was the amount of the production overhead absorbed in both processes during the month?

    (a) £87,300
    (b) £90,000
    (c) £90,105
    (d) £89,895
    (e) None of the above. It is not possible to obtain an answer from data provided.
    (f) None of the above. In my opinion the amount absorbed was £..........

8 What was the actual profit realised in process B?

    (a) £50,000
    (b) £60,000
    (c) £121,250
    (d) £58,200
    (e) None of the above. It is not possible to obtain an answer from data provided.
    (f) None of the above. In my opinion the profit was £..........

(35 marks)

7 The cost accounting profit and loss statement for SC Limited for the four working weeks ended 28 October 19X9 is given below together with other relevant data.

Using the information given and showing clearly your workings, you are required:

    (a) To calculate the following:

        (i)   actual output in units;
        (ii) quantity of material E used in production;
        (iii) price per tonne of material E;
        (iv) man hours worked;
        (v) fixed overhead incurred.

    (b) To calculate the fixed overhead:

        (i) productivity variance;
        (ii) capacity variance.

    (c) To show the work-in-progress control account as it would appear in the cost ledger at 28 October 19X9. Direct materials price and direct wages rate variances are extracted before the prime cost items are charged to work-in-progress.

PROFIT AND LOSS STATEMENT
for four weeks ended 28 October 19X9

	£	£	£
Sales			177,500
Standard cost of sales:			
Direct materials		63,900	
Direct wages		28,400	
Fixed overhead		49,700	(142,000)
Standard profit on actual sales			35,500
Variances:			
Direct materials: price	1,440 (F)		
usage	900 (A)		
cost		540 (F)	
Direct wages: rate	1,375 (A)		
efficiency	900 (F)		
cost		475 (A)	
Fixed overhead: expenditure	150 (F)		
volume	700 (A)		
cost		550 (A)	(485) (A)
Net profit			35,015

Favourable variances indicated by (F) and adverse variances indicated by (A).

Other relevant data given are as follows:

(a) From the standard cost of the only product manufactured by SC Limited, direct material E at £360 per tonne is used to produce 400 units of the product; the basic wage rate of each employee is £2 per hour and the standard time allowed to produce one unit of product is 12 minutes.

(b) From the budget for the year:
Production, in units   900,000 per annum
Fixed overhead   £630,000 per annum
There are 50 working weeks in the year and in the production process it is planned that the 90 employees will work 40 hours each week.

(30 marks)

ANSWERS

1

(a) (i) **Compilation of standards for material costs**

The first stage is to define what quantity of material is required and should be used to produce one unit of output. This is a technical estimate and will take account of, among other things, expected losses during production. Once a standard for material usage has been set a standard price is determined, most commonly by forecasting the average price of the material over the period for which the standard is to be used. The standard cost per unit of output is then a multiple of the two standards set.

Compilation of standards for labour costs

Work study methods can establish the amount of productive time it should take to produce one unit of output after allowing for such factors as fatigue, spoilage and start-up time. This establishes the standard time allowed. To compile the standard labour cost for one unit, the standard time is then multiplied by the standard rate of pay per hour, again usually a forecast of the average rate over the life of the standard.

(ii) **Nature and purpose of material and labour variances**

Because two standards are established for materials, two variances from standard are possible. The usage variance shows the cost of any excess usage (or the benefit from any surplus) while the price variance shows the effect of buying material at a price higher or lower than the standard set.

Similarly, there are two labour variances, rate and efficiency. The first shows the effect of the difference between standard and actual rates of pay and the second measures whether or not the work has been performed at the expected speed.

The setting of standards establishes plans and expectations, and control over these plans may be exercised by comparing actual results with expected results. Variances are deviations from plans and any expectations highlighted in this way may be investigated and acted upon. Thus the major purpose of these variances is to assist management control.

(b) **Statement of material and labour variances for week ended 12 November 19X7**

Standard costs based on production of 240 units	£
Materials 240 × 12 kg × £9	25,920
Labour 240 × 10 hours × £2	4,800
	30,720

Variances	Favourable £	Unfavourable £	
Materials Price		2,640	
Usage	2,160		
Labour Rate		504	
Efficiency		240	
	2,160	3,384	1,224
			31,944
Actual costs			
Materials			26,400
Labour			5,544
			31,944

Ledger accounting

Materials	kg	£		kg	£
CLC	2,640	26,400	TFR : WIP	2,880	25,920
Usage variance	240	2,160	Price variance	—	2,640
	2,880	28,560		2,880	28,560
Labour	hours	£		hours	£
CLC	2,520	5,544	TFR : WIP	2,400	4,800
			Efficiency variance	120	240
			Rate variance	—	504
	2,520	5,544		2,520	5,544

Calculation of variances

Materials

Price	Actual cost – (Actual purchases × standard price)	
	£26,400 – (2,640 × £9)	£2,640 A
Usage	(Actual usage – expected usage) × standard price	
	(2,640 – 2,880) × £9	£2,160 F

Labour

Rate	Actual cost – (Actual hours paid × standard rate)	
	£5,544 – (2,520 × £2)	£504 A
Efficiency	(Actual hours worked – standard hours allowed) × standard rate	
	(2,520 – 2,400) × £2	£240 A

177

2

(a) Cost ledger accounts

RAW MATERIALS: PLASTER OF PARIS

	kg	£		kg	£
Balance b/f	2,800	22,400	WIP (28,600 sets)	5,720	45,760
Purchases	5,400	43,200	Balance c/d	2,780	22,240
Usage variance	300	2,400			
	8,500	68,000		8,500	68,000

RAW MATERIALS: PAINT

	litres	£		litres	£
Balance b/f	140	4,200	WIP	143	4,290
Purchases	173	5,800	Price variance	—	610
			Balance c/d	170	5,100
	313	10,000		313	10,000

WORK IN PROGRESS

	£		£
Materials:		Finished goods	
Plaster of paris	45,760	(28,600 sets)	85,800
Paint	4,290		
Wages	7,150		
Overheads	28,600		
	85,800		85,800

FINISHED GOODS

	sets	£		sets	£
Balance b/f	900	2,700	Cost of sales	28,400	85,200
WIP	28,600	85,800	Balance c/d	1,100	3,300
	29,500	88,500		29,500	88,500

(b) (i) Budget trading statement

	£
Sales: 300,000 sets at £3.80	114,000
Less: Standard cost, £3 per set	90,000
Budgeted profit	24,000

(ii) Standard cost trading statement

		£
Actual sales: 28,400 sets at £3.80		107,920

	sets	
Less: Standard cost of sales		
Opening stock	900	
Production	28,600	
	29,500	
Closing stock	(1,100)	
	28,400 at £3	85,200

		£
Standard profit for actual sales		22,720

(iii) Financial trading statement

	£	£	£
Sales			107,920
Less: Cost of sales			
Raw materials:			
Opening stock	26,600		
Purchases	49,000		
	75,600		
Closing stock	(27,340)		
		48,260	
Direct wages		8,030	
Production overheads		34,120	
Cost of production		90,410	
Add: Opening stock, finished goods		2,700	
		93,110	
Less: Closing stock, finished goods		3,300	
			89,810
Gross profit			18,110

(iv) **Reconciliation statement**

	£
Budgeted profit	24,000
Sales volume variance:	
1,600 sets at £0.80	1,280(A)

Cost variances	F £	A £
Raw materials		
Price		610
Usage	2,400	
Direct wages		
Rate		150
Efficiency		730
Fixed production overhead		
Expenditure		4,120
Volume		1,400
	2,400	7,010
		4,610
Actual profit		18,110

Comment

All variances have been identified through the appropriate ledger accounts; transfers to WIP are therefore taken at expected costs.

The materials usage, labour efficiency and overhead volume variances could have been isolated in the WIP ledger account as an alternative.

Workings

Cost ledger accounts

DIRECT WAGES

	hours	£		hours	£
Payroll	730	8,030	WIP	715	7,150
			Efficiency	15	150
			Rate	—	730
	730	8,030		730	8,030

FIXED PRODUCTION OVERHEADS

	Labour cost	£		Labour cost	£
Creditors	7,500	34,120	WIP		
			(400% × 7,150)	7,150	28,600
			Expenditure	—	4,120
			Volume	350	1,400
	7,500	34,120		7,500	34,120

3

(a) The materials price variance measures the difference between actual and standard price per kilogram multiplied by the number of kilograms purchased. So:

$9,000 = 0.05 \times$ number of kilograms purchased

$$\text{number of kilograms purchased} = \frac{90,000}{0.05} = 180,000$$

(b) The materials usage variance measures the difference between actual and standard usage multiplied by the standard price per kilogram. So:

$1,500 =$ excess kilograms used $\times 0.75$

$$\text{number of kilograms used above the standard allowed} = \frac{1,500}{0.75} = 2,000$$

(c) For variable production overhead:
total variance = expenditure variance + efficiency variance
£2,200 = expenditure variance – £2,400
variable production overhead expenditure variance = £4,600 F

(d) $$\text{actual hours worked} = \frac{\text{actual wages cost}}{\text{actual rate of pay}} \quad \text{(no idle time variances)}$$

actual rate of pay = standard rate of pay ± rate variance

$$= \frac{£152,000}{80,000 \text{ hours}} + £0.20 \text{ per hour} = £2.10 \text{ per hour}$$

$$\text{actual hours worked} = \frac{163,800}{2.10} = 78,000$$

(e) $$\text{excess time} = \frac{\text{overhead efficiency variance}}{\text{standard rate per hour}}$$

$$= \frac{£2,400}{£96,000 \div 80,000 \text{ hours}}$$

$= 2,000$ hours

standard hours allowed = actual hours worked – excess hours
$$= 78,000 - 2,000$$
$$= 76,000$$

4 Operating statement for April

	F £	A £	£
Budgeted profit			20,000
Sales margin variances			
Price	2,400		
Volume	4,000		6,400
			26,400
Cost variances			
Materials: price		22,000	
usage		3,000	
Labour: rate		6,800	
efficiency	800		
Variable overheads: expenditure	2,600		
efficiency	400		
Fixed overheads: expenditure		1,000	
volume	2,000		
	5,800	32,800	(27,000)
Actual loss			(600)

Workings

Calculation of actual loss		£	£
Sales	1,200 × £102		122,400
Cost of sales			
Materials	22,000 × £4	88,000	
Labour	6,800 × £5	34,000	
Variable overheads		11,000	
Fixed overheads		6,000	
		139,000	
Less: Closing stock at standard cost			
200 ×£80		(16,000)	(123,000)
			(600)

Ledger accounts

SALES ACCOUNT

	Units	£		Units	£
Profit and loss account	1,000	100,000	CLC	1,200	122,400
Price variance	—	2,400			
Volume variance	200	20,000			
	1,200	122,400		1,200	122,400

The sales *margin* volume variance is 200 × standard profit of £20 = £4,000

MATERIALS ACCOUNT

	square metres	£		square metres	£
CLC	22,000	88,000	TFR : WIP	21,000	63,000
			Price variance	—	22,000
			Usage variance	1,000	3,000
	22,000	88,000		22,000	88,000

LABOUR ACCOUNT

	hours	£		hours	£
CLC	6,800	34,000	TFR : WIP	7,000	28,000
Efficiency	200	800	Rate	—	6,800
	7,000	34,800		7,000	34,800

VARIABLE OVERHEADS ACCOUNT

	hours	£		hours	£
CLC	6,800	11,000	TFR : WIP	7,000	14,000
Expenditure	—	2,600			
Efficiency	200	400			
	7,000	14,000		7,000	14,000

FIXED OVERHEADS ACCOUNT

	hours	£		hours	£
CLC	5,000	6,000	TFR : WIP	7,000	7,000
Volume	2,000	2,000	Expenditure	—	1,000
	7,000	8,000		7,000	8,000

Calculation of variances

Sales

(a) Price — (actual price – standard price) × actual sales
($102 – $100) × 1,200 — £2,400 F

(b) Volume — (actual volume – budgeted volume) × standard profit
(1,200 – 1,000) × £20 — £4,000 F

Materials

(a) Price — (actual price – standard price) × actual purchases
(£4 – £3) × 22,000 — £22,000 A

(b) Usage — (actual usage – expected usage) × standard price
(22,000 – 15 × 1,400) × £3 — £3,000 A

Labour

(a) Rate   (actual rate – standard rate) × actual hours paid
              (£5 – £4) × 6,800   £6,800 A

(a) Rate   (actual rate – standard rate) × actual hours paid
              (£5 – £4) × 6,800   £6,800 A

(b) Efficiency   (actual hours worked – standard hours allowed) ×
                                                   standard rate
              (6,800 – 5 × 1,400) × £4   £800 F

Variable overheads

(a) Expenditure   actual expenditure – (actual hours worked × standard rate)
                     £11,000 – (6,800 × £2)   £2,600 F

(b) Efficiency   (actual hours worked – standard hours allowed) ×
                                                 standard rate
             (6,800 – 7,000) × £2   £400 F

Fixed overheads

(a) Expenditure   total actual cost – total budgeted cost
                     £6,000 – £5 × 1,000   £1,000 A

(b) Volume   (actual hours absorbed – budgeted hours) × standard rate
                     (5 × 1,400 – 5 × 1,000) × £1   £2,000 F

Note

The fixed overhead volume variance may be further analysed into an efficiency variance and a capacity variance, as follows:

Efficiency   (actual hours worked – standard hours allowed) ×
                                                      standard rate
            (6,800 – 7,000) × £1   £200 F

Capacity   (budgeted hours – actual hours worked) × standard rate
            (5,000 – 6,800) × £1   £1,800 F

5

(a) Calculation of variances

                                                                     £

(i) Selling price   (actual price – standard price) × actual sales
                             (£660 – £600) × 250   15,000 F

(ii) Direct materials price   (actual price – standard price) × actual purchases
                             (£4.00 – £4.20) × 12,550   2,510 F

(iii) Direct materials usage   (actual usage – expected usage) × standard price
                             (12,550 – 250 × 50) × £4.20   210 A

(iv) Direct wages rate   (actual rate – standard rate) × actual hours paid
                             (£4.00 – £3.50) × 5,600   2,800 A

(v) Direct labour efficiency   (actual hours worked – standard hours
                             allowed) × standard rate
                             (5,600 – 20 × 250) × £3.50   2,100 A

(vi) Variable production   actual expenditure – (actual hours worked ×
     overhead expenditure   standard rate)
                             £6,600 – (5,600 × £1.20)   120 F

(vii)	Variable production overhead efficiency	(actual hours worked − standard hours allowed) × standard rate $(5,600 - 5,000) \times £1.20$				720 A
(viii)	Fixed production overhead expenditure	total actual cost − total budgeted cost $£23,500 - (£90 \times 260)$				100 A
(ix)	Fixed production overhead volume	(actual production − budgeted production) × standard rate $(250 - 260) \times £90$				900 A

Comment

The cost variances could be calculated using ledger accounts:

MATERIALS ACCOUNT

	kg	£		kg	£
CLC	12,550	50,200	WIP	12,500	52,500
Price	—	2,510	Usage	50	210
	12,550	52,710		12,550	52,710

WAGES ACCOUNT

	hours	£		hours	£
CLC	5,600	22,400	WIP	5,000	17,500
			Rate	—	2,800
			Efficiency	600	2,100
	5,600	22,400		5,600	22,400

VARIABLE PRODUCTION OVERHEAD ACCOUNT

	hours	£		hours	£
CLC	5,600	6,600	WIP	5,000	6,000
Expenditure	—	120	Efficiency	600	720
	5,600	6,720		5,600	6,720

FIXED PRODUCTION OVERHEAD ACCOUNT

	units	£		units	£
CLC	260	23,500	WIP	250	22,500
			Expenditure	—	100
			Efficiency	10	900
	260	23,500		260	23,500

(b) **Profit statement for April**

	£
Sales at standard prices: 250 units at £600	150,000
Less: Standard costs: 250 units at £394	(98,500)
Standard profit for 250 units	51,500
Add: Selling prices variance	15,000F
	66,500

Cost variances	F £	A £
Direct materials: Price	2,510	
Usage		210
Direct wages: Rate		2,800
Efficiency		2,100
Variable production overheads: Expenditure	120	
Efficiency		720
Fixed production overheads: Expenditure		100
Volume		900
	2,630	6,830

	£
	4,200
Actual gross profit	62,300
Selling and administration	29,300
Actual net profit	33,000

Comment

A sales margin variance was not asked for in part (a), so the profit statement has been drafted using the actual sales volume of 250 units.

(c) (i) **Favourable materials price variance:**
Possible reasons: bulk buying
                lower than anticipated inflation
Responsibility: purchasing officer
Unfavourable labour efficiency variance:
Possible reasons: inefficient operatives
                inefficient machines
Responsibility: production manager

(ii) The direct labour efficiency variance is large and unfavourable. The variance should therefore be investigated so that the cause of the variance can be established; corrective action may then be taken.

For instance, if the variance is caused by an inefficient workforce, further investigation may reveal any of the following reasons: lack of experience, lack of supervision, lack of training, poor motivation, bad working conditions. Each cause would have its own remedy.

1 The number of units produced may be calculated from the direct wages element of the cost.

	Process A £	Process B £
Actual cost, which is:		
Actual hours at actual rate	15,840	25,650
Rate variance	(990) (A)	2,850 (F)
Actual hours at standard rate	14,850	28,500
Efficiency variance	(300) (A)	600 (F)
Standard hours at standard rate = standard cost	14,550	29,100
Standard wages cost per unit	£6	£12

$$\text{Hence actual output} = \frac{£14,550}{£6} + \frac{£29,100}{£12} = 4,850 \text{ (Answer: f)}$$

Comment

A similar calculation could have been performed using materials rather than wages. Perhaps the neatest approach though is to use production overheads.

	Process A £	Process B £
Capacity variance	300 (A)	3,000 (A)
Productivity variance	600 (A)	1,200 (F)
Volume variance	900 (A)	1,800 (A)
Standard absorption rate per unit	£6	£12
Hence units of output under-absorbed	150	
Budgeted units of output	5,000	
Actual units of output	4,850	

2 **Price of direct material in process A**

	units	£
Standard units of material at standard price = 4,850 × 20 × £0.30	97,000	29,100
Usage variance	(1,000)	(300) (F)
Actual units of material at standard price	96,000	28,800
Price variance	—	1,920 (A)
Actual units of material at actual price	96,000	30,720

$$\text{Hence actual price per unit} = \frac{£30,720}{96,000} = £0.32 \text{ (Answer: c)}$$

3 **Total standard cost of direct materials in process B**
actual output × standard cost per unit of output
= 4,850 units × £7 per unit = £33,950 (Answer: b)

4 **Cost per labour hour in process B**

	hours	£	
Standard hours at standard rate = 4,850 × 3 hours × £2 per hour	14,550	29,100	
Efficiency variance	(300)	(600)	(F)
Actual hours at standard rate	14,250	28,500	
Rate variance	—	2,850	(F)
Actual hours at actual rate	14,250	25,650	

Hence actual rate per hour $= \dfrac{£25,650}{14,250} = £1.80$ (Answer: c)

5 **Total standard cost of direct wages in process A**
actual output × standard cost per unit of output
= 4,850 units × £3 per unit = £14,550   (Answer: a)

6 An overhead productivity variance is an efficiency variance in respect of fixed production overhead. Therefore, because it was favourable, it was caused by the actual hours worked being less than the standard hours. (Answer: f)

7 **Amount of production overhead absorbed in both processes**
actual output × combined standard absorption rate
= 4,850 units × £18 per unit = £87,300   (Answer: a)

8 The actual profit realised in process B is impossible to obtain from the data, because no revenue figures are provided. (Answer: e)

Comment

An alternative method of finding the answers is to construct the ledger accounts for materials, wages and overhead for both processes.

PROCESS A MATERIALS

	units	£		units	£
CLC	96,000	30,720	Price	—	1,920
Usage	1,000	300	WIP	97,000	29,100
	97,000	31,020		97,000	31,020

PROCESS B MATERIALS

	units	£		units	£
CLC	69,000	31,740	Usage	1,100	550
Price	—	2,760	WIP	67,900	33,950
	69,000	34,500		69,000	34,500

Order of construction: (1) Actual cost: £ column. (2) Price variance: £ column and units column. (3) Usage variance: £ column and units column. (4) WIP: £ column and units. (5) Actual units: units column. (2), (3) and (4) at standard price.

PROCESS A WAGES

	hours	£		hours	£
CLC	9,900	15,840	Rate	—	990
			Efficiency	200	300
			WIP	9,700	14,550
	9,900	15,840		9,900	15,840

PROCESS B WAGES

	hours	£		hours	£
CLC	14,250	25,650	WIP	14,550	29,100
Rate	—	2,850			
Efficiency	300	600			
	14,550	29,100		14,550	29,100

PROCESS A OVERHEAD

	hours	£		hours	£
CLC	10,000	31,680	Expenditure	—	1,680
			Capacity	100	300
			Productivity	200	600
			WIP	9,700	29,100
	10,000	31,680		10,000	31,680

PROCESS B OVERHEAD

	hours	£		hours	£
CLC	15,000	58,425	Capacity	750	3,000
Expenditure	—	1,575	WIP	14,550	58,200
Productivity	300	1,200			
	15,300	61,200		15,300	61,200

All the answers can be quickly ascertained from these ledger accounts.

7

(a) (i) **Actual output in units**

Budgeted production
= 900,000 units p.a.
= 18,000 units per week
= 72,000 per 4 weeks

(assuming even production over the year)

189

Budgeted fixed overhead $= £630,000$ p.a.

$$= \frac{£630,000}{900,000} = 70\text{p/unit}$$

Fixed overhead volume variance $= £700$ (A)

$= 1,000$ units (A)

Actual production $= 72,000 - 1,000 = 71,000$ units

(**Note:** Actual sales are also 71,000 units since standard fixed overhead cost sales $= 71,000 \times 70$p and therefore actual production could have been found from the three components of standard cost of actual sales. This only applies here because production is at the same level as sales.)

(ii) **Quantity of material used**

	£		tonnes
Standard material cost of sales	63,900		177.5
Usage variance	900	(A)	2.5
Standard cost of actual usage	64,800		180
Price variance	1,440	(F)	
Actual cost of actual usage	63,360		

Actual quantity used $= 180$ tonnes

(iii) **Price per tonne**

From above:

$$\text{Price per tonne} = \frac{£63,360}{180} = £352/\text{tonne}$$

(iv) **Man hours worked**

	£		hours
Standard labour cost of sales	28,400		14,200
Efficiency variance	900	(F)	450
Standard cost of hours worked	27,500		13,750

Number of man hours worked $= 13,750$

(v) **Fixed overheads incurred**

	£	
Budgeted annual fixed overhead	630,000	
Budgeted four-weekly fixed overhead	50,400	
Expenditure variance	150	(F)
Actual fixed overhead $= £49,700 + £550 =$	50,250	

(b) (i) **Fixed overhead productivity variance**

This is probably the variance more commonly referred to as the fixed overhead efficiency variance.

Fixed overhead rate $\quad\quad\quad$ = 70p/unit
$\quad\quad\quad\quad\quad\quad\quad\quad\quad\quad$ = 70p $\times$ 12 = £3.50/hour
Labour efficiency variance $\quad$ = £900 (F)
$\quad\quad\quad\quad\quad\quad\quad\quad\quad\quad$ = £900 $\times$ $^1/_2$ = 450 hour
Fixed overhead efficiency variance = 450 $\times$ £3.50
$\quad\quad\quad\quad\quad\quad\quad\quad\quad\quad$ = £1,575 (F)

(ii) **Fixed overhead capacity variance**

Budgeted capacity = 40 hours $\times$ 90 $\times$ 4 = 14,400
Actual hours worked $\quad\quad\quad\quad\quad\quad$ = 13,750
Difference $\quad\quad\quad\quad\quad\quad\quad\quad\quad$ = $\quad$ 650 hours
Fixed overhead capacity variance = 650 $\times$ £3.5 = £2,275 (A)
(**Note:** also = £700 + £1,575)

(c) **Work-in-progress control account**

	£		£
Direct materials	64,800	Finished goods	142,000
Direct wages	27,500		
Fixed overhead	92,300		
Fixed overhead	50,250		
Wages efficiency	900	Materials usage	900
Fixed overhead		Fixed overhead	
$\quad$ expenditure	150	$\quad$ volume	700
	143,600		143,600

Note: Fixed overheads could be excluded from work-in-progress and transferred straight to (absorbed into) finished goods. The volume variance could be split into efficiency and capacity (£2,275 and £1,575).

15 Contribution analysis

All the questions in this chapter are based on the simple concept that costs can be analysed between those which will vary proportionately with sales volume and those which will remain fixed regardless of volume changes. From this analysis it is possible to identify the amount of 'contribution' per unit of sales and thus to calculate the effect on profit of changes in sales volume (or, in a multi-product business, of changes in sales mix).

Some of the questions also postulate that certain decisions on volume will be associated with changes in selling price or the level of costs.

STUDY REQUIREMENTS

(a) Cost behaviour patterns and the influence of volume or activity.
(b) The contribution concept.

QUESTIONS

1 A company manufactures three products X, Y and Z. The budgets are currently being prepared for 19X7 and estimates have been submitted for sales, costs and output.

From the data provided below you are required to prepare two statements to show:

(a) the expected profit if the original budget is pursued; and
(b) the expected profit at maximum sales demand.

The standard cost per unit is as follows:

	Product		
	X	Y	Z
	£	£	£
Direct materials: Aye	8	6	6
Bee	2	4	2
Cee	6	2	4
Direct wages	8	10	12
Variable overhead	6	8	8
Fixed overhead	12	15	18

Fixed overhead is absorbed as a percentage of direct wages and is based on the original budget.

	units	units	units
Budgeted output for 19X7	8,000	6,000	10,000
Maximum sales demand (estimated)	10,000	7,500	12,500
Sales price	£40	£50	£60

(15 marks)

2 A company located in London acts as a distributor for a range of specialist products which it sells to retailers throughout the United Kingdom.

The products vary considerably, and orders from retailers consist typically of a mixture of the products in the range. All dispatches are made to retailers by hired road transport.

Hitherto the company has sent goods to retailers without charging for delivery, but due to increases in carriage costs it now proposes to place a bottom limit on free delivery orders. The limit proposed is £20 per order.

Data on the company's products are as follows:

Product	Selling price per pack £	Direct cost per pack £	Weight per pack kg
A	1.50	0.75	1.0
B	7.50	5.50	6.0
C	6.50	4.20	13.5
D	15.00	8.50	12.0
E	16.00	11.60	16.0
F	4.50	3.50	4.0
G	3.50	3.00	5.0

Carriage costs per delivery, for an average distance of 150 miles are:

Weight (kg)	Cost £
10 or less	1.30
over 10 but not above 15	1.50
over 15 but not above 20	1.80
over 20 but not above 25	2.00
over 25 but not above 30	2.20
over 30 but not above 35	2.40
over 35 but not above 40	2.70
over 40 but not above 45	2.90

The company is considering making all sales to retailers in the North (200 or more miles from London) through a sub-distributor who has his own sales force. The company would make bulk deliveries fortnightly to the sub-distributor, but would continue to collect payment of accounts from retailers.

You are required:

(a) To show the percentage contribution to sales for each product and rank them in descending order.
(b) To calculate, to one decimal place, the profits that would result from each of seven free delivery orders (for an average distance of 150 miles), the first being for £20 worth of product A, the second for £20 worth of B, the third for £20 worth of C, and so on through to the seventh order for £20 worth of G. (Assume that packs can be split to make a £20 order.)
(c) To state for which products £20 would be a suitable limit for free delivery if the company's criterion is that carriage costs (for an average distance of 150 miles) should not exceed one-third of the contribution provided by that product.
(d) To list the costs that the company would need to consider if it wished to decide what commission it could afford to pay to the sub-distributor in the North.

(30 marks)

3

(a) XY Ltd is operating at a normal level of activity of 80% which represents an output of 5,600 units. The statement shown below gives basic details of cost and sales at three operating levels of activity. In view of the depressed market in which the company may have to operate in the near future, the production director believes that it may be necessary to operate at 60% level of activity.

As cost accountant of XY Ltd you are required to prepare a forecast statement to show the marginal costs and contribution at the proposed level of activity of 60%.

	Level of activity		
	70%	80%	90%
	£	£	£
Direct materials	73,500	84,000	94,500
Direct wages	44,100	50,400	56,700
Overhead	45,400	49,600	53,800
Sales	196,000	224,000	252,000

(b) Explain the meaning of contribution and discuss its relevance in a marginal costing system.

(20 marks)

4 The trading results for the year ending 30 June 19X8 of D Limited, a face cream manufacturer, are expected to be as follows:

	£ thousands	£ thousands
Sales (100,000 jars)		400
Costs:		
Material:	50	
Wages: direct	82	
indirect, fixed	19	
Production expenses: variable	25	
fixed	30	
Administration expenses: fixed	24	
Selling expenses: variable	20	
fixed	22	
Distribution expenses: variable	18	
fixed	10	(300)
Profit		100

Forecasts for the year ending 30 June 19X9 are given below:

(1) The sales price will be reduced to £3 per jar and this will increase sales volume by 50%.
(2) Material prices will remain unchanged except that, because of increased

quantities purchased, a 5% quantity discount will be obtained.
(3) Direct wage rates will increase by 10%.
(4) Variable selling costs will increase proportionately with sales value.
(5) Inflation will increase variable production and distribution expenses by 10%.
(6) All fixed costs will increase by 20%.
(7) There will be no stocks or work-in-progress at the beginning or end of the year.

You are required, using the information:

(a) To prepare a statement showing the profit forecast for the year ending 30 June 19X9 on a marginal costing basis.
(b) To comment on the result forecast in your answer to (a) above.
(c) To prepare an alternative profit statement for the year ending 30 June 19X9 based on a sales price increase of 10% on the 19X7/X8 price and a sales volume of 100,000 jars.
(d) To state the price increase per jar (as a percentage to three decimal places) needed, above the current sales price, for the year ending 30 June 19X9 to achieve a profit of £110,000.

(20 marks)

5   Freddie Kennedy, the owner of Port Street Holiday Camp, is presented with the latest financial figures by his accountant, Boardwell:

Year ended 30 September 19X1

	£ thousands	£ thousands
Fees: 500 bookings × 20 weeks × £100 per week		1,000
Costs:		
Food (variable)	300	
Cleaning (variable)	100	
Salaries (fixed)	400	
Mortgage interest (fixed)	50	
Administration (50% variable)	150	
Heat and light (50% variable)	50	
Advertising (fixed)	50	
Outside entertainers (fixed)	50	1,150
		(150)
Add:		
Bar receipts (average £10 per booked week)	100	
Less: Cost of sales (variable)	(50)	50
Loss		(100)

Freddie is concerned and says to Boardwell, 'This won't do. Let's raise fees by 25% next year — even though bookings will probably decrease by 20%.'

Boardwell says, 'Surely it would be better to generate more bookings, since we have the capacity to accommodate 1,000 bookings per week. We could average 90% capacity over our 20-week season if we reduced fees by 15%, and of course the bar income would increase.'

Freddie asks the rest of his staff for suggestions. The entertainments manager, Moffat, has this to say. 'The best way of filling the camp is to hire a famous act for the season. We could book that superb double act, Quas and Cohen, for £2,000 per week and I'm sure we would average 70% capacity. Of course, we would have to spend another £50,000 on advertising to publicise this, but we could still charge £100 per week.'

Little, the buildings and maintenance manager, gives this opinion. 'We're only receiving income for 20 weeks in the year. Why can't we open off-season, charging half the usual fee. We'd probably generate another 2,000 camper-weeks and fixed costs will only increase by about £10,000.'

The catering manager, Geisler, has something to say. 'Freddie, I'm concerned about food costs. If we used smaller plates, we could cut our food bills by 10% and I'm positive the campers wouldn't notice. Although it's not my responsibility, I've spoken to Edge, the cleaning manager, and he agrees that a similar cost-cutting exercise could be adopted there.'

You are required to produce:

(a) Five separate statements showing the revised profit or loss if the suggestions of Freddie, Boardwell, Moffatt, Little or Geisler were adopted.
(b) One statement combining the best of the suggestions.

(25 marks)

6 Andrew Scriver has been in business for two years making and selling machine tools and feels that he can improve his performance. He has shown you the summarised accounts for the first two years which his accountant has produced.

	Total £	Drill bits and reamers £	Saw blades £	Lathe bits £
19X0				
Sales	245,000	90,000	50,000	105,000
Cost of sales	(216,000)	(106,000)	(20,000)	(90,000)
Gross profit	29,000	(16,000)	30,000	15,000
Administration	(20,000)			
Profit	9,000			
19X1 (draft)				
Sales	505,000	270,000	60,000	175,000
Cost of sales	(456,000)	(294,000)	(22,000)	(140,000)
Gross profit	49,000	(24,000)	38,000	35,000
Administration	(22,000)			
Profit	27,000			

Each of the three product lines is sold in sets. The selling prices are £45 for a set of drill bits and reamers, £10 for a box of blades and £35 for a set of lathe bits. Andrew has not put up his prices over the two years as he feels that there has been a negligible rise in input costs, although administration expenses rose by 10% between 19X0 and 19X1 and will probably increase again by 10% in 19X2.

The cost of sales figure is made up of two elements: fixed costs and variable costs. The fixed costs total £37,000 and have been apportioned between the three product types by the accountant. The actual costs apportioned to each line have been exactly the same in 19X0 and 19X1.

Andrew has various ideas for developing the business in 19X2 based on these results including:

(a) Continuing as at present, in which case sales of each product line may well increase again though this time perhaps only by 1,000 units each.
(b) Discontinuing drill bits and reamers. Sales of the other two lines may still rise by 1,000 units each.
(c) Discontinuing drill bits and reamers with the result that Andrew will lose some of his market, in which case sales of the other two lines would stay at 19X1 levels.
(d) Switching production from drill bits and reamers to lathe bits. In this way sales of lathe bits could be doubled from their 19X1 levels. Sales of saw blades would stay at 19X1 levels.
(e) The switch proposed in (d) be carried out but this would only result in increased sales if the selling price was dropped from £35 to £29.

You are required to find the profit for 19X2 under each of these five schemes.
(3 marks each; total 15 marks)

7   Sachs Ltd manufactures high-class garden furniture, consisting of benches, tables and chairs. The production process involves three separate stages:

(1)   The raw materials, principally timber and metal fittings, are sorted into batches and the timber is treated with preservative.
(2)   The timber is machined, finished by hand and assembled. At this stage the metal fittings are fixed.
(3)   The products are painted and varnished prior to packaging in polythene and cardboard.

The principal features of the products are their high-quality finish and durability which are achieved by the skilled tradesmen employed in the machining and finishing department. Following an extensive advertising campaign, demand for the company's products is expected to increase. However, it has not proved possible to recruit any additional skilled tradesmen or to subcontract to increase capacity in the machining, finishing and assembling department (stage 2) and this seems likely to inhibit growth in the foreseeable future.

You are provided with the following additional information relating to production costs per unit:

	Benches	Tables	Chairs
	£	£	£
Raw materials: timber	10	12	2
metal fittings	3	4	7
fabric	—	—	6
Packing	2	2	1

Labour costs are based on the following estimated times (in minutes) required for each process:

	Stage 1	Stage 2	Stage 3
Benches	40	180	20
Tables	20	150	60
Chairs	20	60	40

The following rates of pay are anticipated:

	Stage 1	Stage 2	Stage 3
Per hour	£3	£4	£3

Variable overheads are anticipated at 100 per cent of direct labour.

You are provided with the following information relating to sales:

Estimated selling price:	Benches	£60
	Tables	£71
	Chairs	£45
Maximum predicted sales (units):	Benches	1,750
	Tables	1,500
	Chairs	2,750

Even working overtime for which no premium is paid, there are a maximum of 10,850 hours available in the year in the machining, finishing and assembling department (stage 2).

You are required to prepare a report for the managing director:

(a) Outlining the strategy which will maximise the company's profitability.
(8 marks)
(b) Enclosing a profit forecast based on the strategy you recommend.
7 marks)
(Total 15 marks)

8 The manager of a small business has received enquiries about printing three different types of advertising leaflet. Information concerning these three leaflets is shown below:

Leaflet type	A	B	C
	£	£	£
Selling price, per 1,000 leaflets	100	220	450
Estimated printing costs:			
Variable, per 1,000 leaflets	40	70	130
Specific fixed costs, per month	2,400	4,000	9,500

In addition to the specific fixed costs a further £4,000 per month would be incurred in renting special premises if any or all of the above three leaflets were printed.

The minimum printing order would be for 30,000 of each type of leaflet per month and the maximum possible order is estimated to be 60,000 of each leaflet per month.

Required:

(a) (i) Examine and comment upon the potential profitability of leaflet printing. Make whatever calculations you consider appropriate. *(8 marks)*

   (ii) Assuming that orders have been received to print each month 50,000 of both Leaflet A and Leaflet B calculate the quantity of Leaflet C which would need to be ordered to produce an overall profit, for all three leaflets, of £1,800 per month.
(4 marks)

(b) It is possible that a special type of paper used in printing the leaflets will be difficult to obtain during the first few months. The estimated consumption of this special paper for each type of leaflet is:

   Leaflet A   2 packs per 1,000 leaflets
   Leaflet B   6 packs per 1,000 leaflets
   Leaflet C   16 packs per 1,000 leaflets

Advise the manager on the quantity of each leaflet which should be printed in order to maximise profit in the first month, if 50,000 of each type of leaflet have been printed, there remains unfulfilled orders of 10,000 for each type of leaflet and there are 170 packs of special paper available for the rest of the month. *(5 marks)*

(c) 'If the manager of the above business wastes ten packs of special paper then the cost to the business of that waste is simply the original cost of that paper.'

Critically examine the validity of the above statement. *(5 marks)*

(Total 22 marks)

9

(a) Ben Halliday is an Exmoor farmer. He has set aside 100 acres of his land to grow four types of Christmas trees and has prepared the following budget:

	Porlock Pine	Oare Evergreen	Brendon Beauty	Countisbury Dwarf
Area to be occupied, in acres	25	25	25	25
Number of trees per acre	100	80	90	100
Selling price per tree	£4	£5	£6	£7
Variable costs per acre:	£	£	£	£
Seedlings	150	200	225	300
Direct wages	30	20	25	50
Fixed costs = £15,000				

You are required to prepare a statement showing the budgeted profit.

(b) Ben is thinking of varying his mix of trees. He has arranged to sell 600 Porlock Pines, 400 Oare Evergreens, 360 Brendon Beauties and 500 Countisbury Dwarfs to one customer, but apart from this he thinks demand for each type of tree will exceed 10,000.

You are required to prepare a statement showing the profit under the optimal mix of trees.

(c) Ben could cancel his sales arrangements by agreeing to let his customer take the 500 Countisbury Dwarfs half-price without the other trees, thus leaving the field open for any trees he wishes to grow.

Would this be worthwhile? *(17 marks)*

ANSWERS

1

	X £		Y £		Z £	
Sales per unit		40		50		60
Variable costs per unit						
Materials A	8		6		6	
B	2		4		2	
C	6		2		4	
Wages	8		10		12	
Overhead	6	30	8	30	8	32
Contribution per unit		10		20		28

Total fixed costs £12×8,000=96,000 £15×6,000=90,000 £18×10,000=180,000

(a) Profit statement based on original budget

	Total	X	Y	Z
Units	24,000	8,000	6,000	10,000
	£	£	£	£
Contribution	480,000	80,000	120,000	280,000
Fixed overhead	366,000	96,000	90,000	180,000
Profit	114,000	(16,000)	30,000	100,000

(b) Profit statement based on maximum sales demand

	Total	X	Y	Z
Units	30,000	10,000	7,500	12,500
	£	£	£	£
Contribution	600,000	100,000	150,000	350,000
Fixed overhead	366,000	96,000	90,000	180,000
Profit	234,000	4,000	60,000	170,000

2

(a)

	A	B	C	D	E	F	G
Selling price (£)	1.50	7.50	6.50	15.00	16.00	4.50	3.50
Variable cost (£)	0.75	5.50	4.20	8.50	11.60	3.50	3.00
Contribution (£)	0.75	2.00	2.30	6.50	4.40	1.00	0.50
Contribution to sales	50%	26.67%	35.38%	43.33%	27.50%	22.22%	14.29%
Ranking	1	5	3	2	4	6	7

(b)

	A	B	C	D	E	F	G
Sales value (£)	20.00	20.00	20.00	20.00	20.00	20.00	20.00
Contribution (£)	10.00	5.33	7.08	8.67	5.50	4.44	2.86
Weight of order (kg)	$\frac{20}{1.5}\times1$	$\frac{20}{7.5}\times6$	$\frac{20}{6.5}\times13.5$	$\frac{20}{15}\times12$	$\frac{20}{16}\times16$	$\frac{20}{4.5}\times4$	$\frac{20}{3.5}\times5$
=	13.33	16.00	41.54	16.00	20.00	17.78	28.57
Carriage costs (£)	1.50	1.80	2.90	1.80	1.80	1.80	2.20
Profit (£)	8.50	3.53	4.18	6.87	3.70	2.64	0.66

(c)

Ratio of carriage costs to contribution	A	B	C	D	E	F	G
	15%	34%	41%	21%	33%	41%	76%
Suitable products	A			D	E		

(d) Costs to be considered include:

    (i) Administration costs: Postages, telephone and the maintenance of accounting records.

    (ii) Distribution costs: Hire of transport.

    (iii) Selling costs: Cost of current sales force — salaries, commission and travel.

3

(a) Marginal cost and contribution statement at 60% activity:

	£	£
Sales		168,000
Variable costs:		
Direct materials	63,000	
Direct wages	37,800	
Overhead	25,200	126,000
Contribution		42,000

Comment

The question does not state the nature of the costs and so the first step is to decide whether the three costs are fixed, variable or partly variable.

Materials
The subtraction of 10% of activity reduces the cost by £10,500, as follows:

Activity	60%	50%	40%	30%	20%	10%	0%
Cost	£63,000	£52,500	£42,000	£31,500	£21,000	£10,500	NIL

Therefore this cost is entirely variable.

Wages
A similar exercise shows that wages cost is entirely variable.

Overhead
This cost contains a variable element and a fixed element, since reduction

204

of activity to nil does not result in nil cost. The neatest way to isolate the variable and fixed element is as follows:

Activity level	Units	Cost £
80%	5,600	49,600
70%	4,900	45,400
	700	4,200

Thus a decrease of 700 units results in a cost decrease of £4,200. The variable cost per unit is £6.

For 60% activity (4,200 units) the total variable cost is £25,200.

The fixed element may be calculated from the equation:

So at 80% activity: total costs – variable costs = fixed costs
£49,600 – £6 × 5,600 = £16,000

(b) By producing one extra unit, an organisation will increase some of its costs but not others since variable costs vary in total with output, whereas fixed costs remain fixed in total despite changes in output. The marginal cost of this unit is the amount by which total costs change, i.e. the extra variable cost of one unit.

Contribution is the difference between sales value and marginal cost. It may relate to one unit or to total sales.

A marginal costing system is one in which fixed and variable costs are segregated. Its features are:

(i) variable costs only are attached to products;
(ii) profit and loss accounts show contribution to profits;
(iii) stocks are valued at variable production cost; and
(iv) fixed costs are deducted in total from contribution for the period, i.e. they are charged as period costs.

This system is sometimes known as 'contribution analysis' since contribution is the central feature. Because fixed costs do not vary any increase in contribution will result in the same increase in profit and several techniques (e.g. profit-volume graphs; limiting factors) have been established to aid decision-making.

4

(a) **Profit forecast for the year ending 30 June 19X9**

	£	£
Sales (150,000 jars)		450,000
Variable costs:		
Material	71,250	
Direct wages	135,300	
Production expenses	41,250	
Selling expenses	22,500	
Distribution expenses	29,700	(300,000)
Contribution		150,000
Fixed costs		(126,000)
Profit		24,000

Notes

Variable costs per unit	1978		1979
	p		p
Material	50	× 95%	47.5
Direct wages	82	× 110%	90.2
Production expenses	25	× 110%	27.5
Selling expenses (5% of sales)	20	× 75%	15.0
Distribution expenses	18	× 110%	19.8
	195		200.0

Total fixed costs	£		£
Indirect wages	19,000		
Production expenses	30,000		
Administration expenses	24,000		
Selling expenses	22,000		
Distribution expenses	10,000		
	105,000	× 120%	126,000

(b) The profit forecast shows a fall in profit from £100,000 in 19X8 to £24,000 in 19X9. The change in selling price will cause the unit contribution to drop from £2.05 to £1 and although sales volume is increased by 50% the lower margin results in a drop in contribution from £205,000 in 19X8 to £150,000. Added to this is the 20% increase in fixed costs, a rise of £21,000.

The conclusion is that the price reduction is not worthwhile. To maintain profits of £100,000 under this scheme, the required contribution of £226,000 would need £678,000 worth of sales!

(c) **Alternative profit statement for the year ending 30 June 19X9**

	£	£
Sales (100,000 jars at £4.40)		440,000
Variable costs:		
Material (no quantity discount)	50,000	
Direct wages	90,200	
Production expenses	27,500	
Selling expenses (£440,000 × 5%)	22,000	
Distribution expenses	19,800	(209,500)
Contribution		230,500
Fixed costs		(126,000)
Profit		104,500

	£	
(d) Required profit	110,000	
Fixed costs	126,000	
Required contribution	236,000	
Variable costs for (100,000 jars at £4.40)	209,500	
Less: Selling expenses	22,000	
Variable costs excluding selling expenses	187,500	
Required sales value excluding selling expenses	236,000	
	187,500	
	423,500	95%
Add: Selling expenses (£423,500 × 5/95)	22,289	5%
Required sales value	445,789	100%
Current sales value	400,000	
Percentage increase required	11.447%	

Comment

Part (d) is difficult in that the variable costs include selling expenses and so the variable cost per unit depends on the selling price (which is not known). It is possible, though, to compute the required sales value after deduction of 5% selling expenses and then to calculate these expenses and add them on to net sales.

5

(a)   **Freddie's suggestion**

	£ thousands	£ thousands
Contribution £75 × 400 bookings × 20 weeks		600
Fixed costs		(650)
		(50)
Bar receipts (£10 × 400 × 20)	80	
Less: Costs	(40)	40
Loss		(10)

Boardwell's suggestion

Contribution £35 × 900 bookings × 20 weeks		630
Fixed costs		(650)
		(20)
Bar receipts (£10 × 900 × 20)	180	
Less: Costs	(90)	90
Profit		70

Moffat's suggestion

Contribution £50 × 700 bookings × 20 weeks		700
Fixed costs	650	
Booking fee	40	
Advertising	50	(740)
		(40)
Bar receipts (£10 × 700 × 20)	140	
Less: Costs	(70)	70
Profit		30

Little's suggestion

Loss for 20 weeks		(100)
Off-season income:		
Contribution (£nil × 2,000 camper-weeks)	nil	
Extra fixed costs	(10)	(10)
Bar receipts (£10 × 2,000)	20	
Less: Costs	(10)	10
Loss		(100)

Geisler's suggestion

Contribution £54 × 500 bookings × 20 weeks	540
Fixed costs	(650)
	(110)
Bar income	50
Loss	(60)

(b) The suggestions of Freddie, Boardwell and Moffat are alternatives and of these Boardwell's generates the highest income. It is possible, however, to combine this with both Little's and Geisler's suggestions as follows:

	In season £ thousands	Off-season £ thousands
Fees	85	50
Variable costs	(46)	(46)
Contribution	39	4

	£ thousands	£ thousands
Contribution £39 × 900 × 20		702
£4 × 2,000		8
		710
Fixed costs	650	
	10	(660)
		50
Bar income £5 × 900 × 20	90	
£5 × 2,000	10	100
Profit		150

Workings

(Per camper-week)		At present	Freddie's	Boardwell's	Moffat's suggestion	Little's	Geisler's
		£	£	£	£	£	£
Fees		100	125	85	100	50	100
Variable costs:							
Food	30					27	
Cleaning	10					9	
Administration	7.5					7.5	
Heat and light	2.5					2.5	
		(50)	(50)	(50)	(50)	(50)	(46)
Contribution		50	75	35	50	nil	54

Fixed costs (total)
Salaries	400
Interest	50
Administration	75
Heat and light	25
Advertising	50
Entertainers	50
	650

6

Comment

As with most questions in which various changes are suggested, the key is to identify the costs and revenues that will change. This usually means the calculation of any increase or decrease in contribution, although there may also be changes in fixed costs, as in this question.

A certain amount of careful thought is required in order to calculate the unit contribution for each product.

	Drill bits and reamers	Saw blades	Lathe bits
19X0			
Sales revenue	£90,000	£50,000	£105,000
Selling price	£45	£10	£35
Sales in units	2,000	5,000	3,000
19X1			
Sales revenue	£270,000	£60,000	£175,000
Selling price	£45	£10	£35
Sales in units	6,000	6,000	5,000
19X0–19X1			
Increase in unit sales	4,000	1,000	2,000
Increase in cost of sales	£188,000	£2,000	£50,000
(i.e. increase in variable cost of sales)			
Variable cost of sales per unit	£47	£2	£25
Contribution per unit	(£2)	£8	£10

			£	£
(a)	**Continuing as at present**			
	Change in contribution:	Drill bits 1,000 × (–£2)	(2,000)	
		Saw blades 1,000 × £8	8,000	
		Lathe bits 1,000 × £10	10,000	16,000
	Increase in administration expenses			2,200
	Increase in profit			13,800
	Profit for 19X1			27,000
	Profit for 19X2			40,800

210

(b) **Discontinuing drill bits (1)**   £   £
   Increase in contribution:

Drill bits (–6,000) × (–£2)	12,000	
Saw blades 1,000 × £8	8,000	
Lathe bits 1,000 × £10	10,000	30,000

   Increase in administration expenses   2,200

   Increase in profit   27,800
   Profit for 19X1   27,000

   Profit for 19X2   54,800

(c) **Discontinuing drill bits (2)**   £
   Increase in contribution: Drill bits (–6,000) × (–£2)   12,000
   Increase in administration expenses   2,200

   Increase in profit   9,800
   Profit for 19X1   27,000

   Profit for 19X2   36,800

(d) **Switching production (1)**   £   £
   Increase in contribution:

Drill bits (–6,000) × (–£2)	12,000	
Lathe bits 5,000 × £10	50,000	62,000

   Increase in administration expenses   2,200

   Increase in profit   59,800
   Profit for 19X1   27,000

   Profit for 19X2   86,800

(e) **Switching production (2)**   £   £
   Increase in contribution:

Drill bits (–6,000) × (–£2)	12,000	
Extra lathe bits 5,000 × £4	20,000	
Present lathe bits 5,000 × (–£6)	(30,000)	2,000

   Increase in administration expenses   2,200

   Decrease in profit   (200)
   Profit for 19X1   27,000

   Profit for 19X2   26,800

7 Report for the managing director

(a) *Outline of strategy which will maximise the company's profitability*

It is not possible to produce sufficient units to meet maximum predicted
sales because at stage 2, 11,750 hours would be necessary whereas only
10,850 hours are available (Appendix 1).

The greatest total profit will be obtained by concentrating on the products that yield the highest amount of contribution per stage 2 labour hour (the limiting factor of production). Appendix 2 shows that production should first be concentrated on chairs, using 2,750 stage 2 hours. Next, 3,750 stage 2 hours can be used to produce tables, leaving a balance of 4,350 hours available for the manufacture of benches.

(b) *Profit forecast*

Product	Stage 2 hours	Contribution per hour £	Total contribution £
Chairs	2,750	15	41,250
Tables	3,750	10	37,500
Benches	4,350	5	21,750
	10,850		100,500

Appendix 1		Benches	Tables	Chairs
Maximum sales		1,750	1,500	2,750
Stage 2 hours per unit		3	$2\frac{1}{2}$	1
Maximum required		5,250	3,750	2,750
Total required	11,750			
Total available	10,850			

Appendix 2	Benches		Tables		Chairs	
	£	£	£	£	£	£
Selling price		60		71		45
Variable costs:						
Materials: timber	10		12		2	
metal	3		4		7	
fabric	—		—		6	
Packing:	2	15	2	18	1	16
Labour: Stage 1	2		1		1	
Stage 2	12		10		4	
Stage 3	1	15	3	14	2	7
Variable overheads		15		14		7
		45		46		30
Contribution		15		25		15
Contributed per stage 2 labour hour		5		10		15

(a)   (i)   Potential profitability of leaflet printing

	A £	B £	C £	Total £
Selling price	100	220	450	
Variable costs	40	70	130	
Contribution (per 1,000)	60	150	320	

1 Minimum order: 30,000

	A	B	C	Total
Contribution	1,800	4,500	9,600	
Specific fixed costs	2,400	4,000	9,500	
Direct profit	(600)	500	100	nil
Less: Indirect fixed costs				(4,000)
Loss				(4,000)

2 Maximum order: 60,000

	A	B	C	Total
Contribution	3,600	9,000	19,200	
Specific fixed costs	2,400	4,000	9,500	
Direct profit	1,200	5,000	9,700	15,900
Less: Indirect fixed costs				(4,000)
Profit				11,900

Comments

1 If the minimum printing order were placed for each type of leaflet, the business would sustain a loss of £4,000.

2 Leaflet A covers its own fixed costs at a level of 40,000. If orders for Leaflet A are below this level, it is not worthwhile fulfilling them.

Leaflets B and C break even (before deducting indirect fixed costs) at levels below the minimum order, so that they will always make a positive contribution towards general fixed costs.

3 In order for the business as a whole to break even, orders for either Leaflet B or Leaflet C would have to be above the minimum level.

Assuming orders for Leaflets A and C are at the minimum level, the loss of £4,000 would be eliminated by selling an extra 26,667 of Leaflet B.

Similarly, an extra 12,500 of Leaflet C combined with minimum orders for Leaflets A and B would result in neither profit nor loss.

213

(ii)

	£	£
Leaflet A: Contribution 50 × £60	3,000	
Leaflet B: Contribution 50 × £150	7,500	
	———	
		10,500
Less: Fixed costs: A	2,400	
B	4,000	
C	9,500	
Indirect	4,000	
	———	
		19,900
		———
		9,400
Add: Required profit		1,800
		———
Contribution from Leaflet C		11,200
		———

Hence quantity of Leaflet C is

$$\frac{£11,200}{320} \times 1,000 = \qquad\qquad 35,000$$

(b) Paper is now a scarce resource. The optimal way of utilising the remaining 170 packs is to rank the leaflets in order of contribution per pack of paper.

	A	B	C
	£	£	£
Contribution per 1,000 leaflets	60	150	320
Packs required per 1,000	2	6	16
Contribution per pack	30	25	20
Ranking	1	2	3

Advice: Use the paper to make the remaining 10,000 of Leaflet A. This will claim 20 packs. Next, make the remaining 10,000 of Leaflet B using 60 packs. The remaining 90 packs will produce 5,625 of Leaflet C.

(c) If a resource is used for a particular purpose, the cost to the business is the cost of the best alternative foregone (i.e., its opportunity cost). There are three possible costs in this situation:

(i) Replacement cost
Ten more packs could be bought in to replace the ones wasted.
(ii) Lost contribution
Sales are not met due to the shortage of paper.
(iii) Nil
Sales have reached maximum before the loss and there is no other use for the paper.

In general, the original cost is a sunk cost and therefore irrelevant.

9

(a)

	Porlock Pine £	Oare Evergreen £	Brendon Beauty £	Countisbury Dwarf £	Total £
Sales revenue, per acre	400	400	540	700	
Variable costs, per acre	180	220	250	350	
Contribution, per acre	220	180	290	350	
Acres occupied	25	25	25	25	
Total contribution	5,500	4,500	7,250	8,750	26,000
Fixed costs					(15,000)
Profit					11,000

(b)

	Porlock Pine	Oare Evergreen	Brendon Beauty	Countisbury Dwarf	Total
Arranged sales	600	400	360	—	
Acres required	6	5	4	—	
Acres available for Countisbury Dwarf				85	
Contribution per acre	220	180	290	350	
Total contribution	1,320	900	1,160	29,750	33,130
Fixed costs					(15,000)
Profit					18,130

Comment

Once 15 acres have been set aside to meet arranged sales of the three trees with the lowest contribution per acre, the remaining 85 acres may be used to grow the tree with the highest contribution per acre.

(c) If arrangements are cancelled: 100 acres available for Countisbury Dwarf.

	£
Half-price sales	500
Acres required	5
Contribution per acre	nil
Full-price sales:	
Acres available	95
Contribution per acre	350
Total contribution	33,250
Fixed costs	(15,000)
Profit	18,250

Profit is increased by £120. The proposal is therefore worthwhile.

16 Break-even charts and cost-volume-profit analysis

Exercises in cost-volume-profit analysis were included in Chapter 15. The questions in the present chapter bring in the special concept of the profit 'break-even points'.

The break-even point can, of course, be calculated without drawing a chart; and such calculations are called for in four of the questions (Nos. 3, 4, 5 and 8).

The remaining questions require you to draw either a break-even chart (including cost lines) or the simpler 'profit-volume' chart. The concept of the 'margin of safety', between the break-even point and the available sales volume, is also introduced.

STUDY REQUIREMENTS

Break-even analysis, profit-volume ratios, margin of safety, profit graphs.

QUESTIONS

1   Shown below is a typical cost-volume-profit chart:

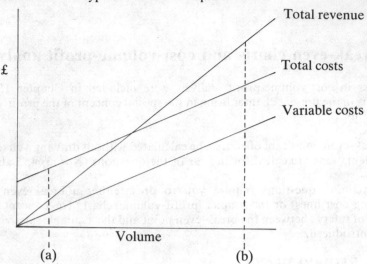

You are required to:

(a)   explain to a colleague who is not an accountant the reasons for the change in result on the above cost-volume-profit chart from a loss at point (a) to a profit at point (b);   *(3 marks)*

(b)   identify and critically examine the underlying assumptions of the above type of cost-volume-profit analysis and consider whether such analyses are useful to the management of an organisation.

(14 marks)
(Total 17 marks)

2

(a)   MC Ltd manufactures one product only, and for the last accounting period has produced the simplified profit and loss statement shown below:

Profit and loss statement

	£	£
Sales		300,000
Costs:		
Direct materials	60,000	
Direct wages	40,000	
Prime cost	100,000	
Variable production overhead	10,000	
Fixed production overhead	40,000	
Fixed administration overhead	60,000	
Variable selling overhead	40,000	
Fixed selling overhead	20,000	(270,000)
Net profit		30,000

You are required to construct a profit-volume graph from which you should state the break-even point and the margin of safety.

(b) Based on the above, draw separate profit-volume graphs to indicate the effect on profit of each of the following:

    (i)   an increase in fixed costs;
    (ii) a decrease in variable cost;
    (iii) an increase in sales price;
    (iv) a decrease in sales volume.   *(25 marks)*

3

(a) Dobing Ltd make pipes of one type only. The budgets for 19X2 are as follows:

	units	£
Sales	27,500	550,000

Costs	Variable £	Fixed £
Direct materials	110,000	—
Direct labour	82,500	140,000
Overhead: production	55,000	—
administration	—	102,000
	247,500	242,000

You are required to calculate:

    (i)   the contribution per unit;
    (ii) the contribution margin ratio;
    (iii) the break-even point in both units and sales;
    (iv) the margin of safety ratio.

(b) Dobing Ltd is considering the acquisition of a new machine. This will add £48,000 to fixed production overhead but will halve labour costs. All other factors remain the same.

    (i)   What is the new break-even point in both units and sales?
    (ii) What level of sales is required to make the acquisition of the machine worthwhile?   *(20 marks)*

4   Maria runs a wine club. She buys six different types of wine in cases of 12 each and sells the wine in cases of six, each case containing one bottle of each type.

Purchase cost per case of 12:	£
Valpolicella	18.00
Bardolino	18.00
Liebfraumilch	18.60
Niersteiner	21.00
Bereich Bernkastel	20.40
Piesporter	24.00

	£
Selling price per case of 6	12.00
Variable distribution costs per case	0.50
Annual fixed expenses:	
Storage	2,000
Wages	1,000

Consider each question independently:

(a) What is the annual break-even point in sales revenue and in unit sales?

(b) If 3,800 cases were sold in the year, what would Maria's profit be?

(c) Maria thinks that by spending £200 per month on advertising, she can achieve annual sales of 5,000 cases. What would her profit be under this scheme?

(d) The wages are paid to an assistant, Barbara, who sells the wine. Barbara offers to forgo her salary in exchange for a 25p commission for every case sold. If Maria accepts Barbara's offer, what would be the annual break-even point in sales revenue and in unit sales?

(e) Maria's target profit is £6,000. How many cases must be sold to achieve this figure

    (i) if Barbara receives her £1,000 salary?
    (ii) if Barbara is paid by commission?

(f) What level of sales produces a profit figure which is the same whether Barbara is paid by salary or by commission?

(20 marks)

5 Norroy Pipes Ltd sells quality hand-made pipes, and has experienced a steady growth in sales for the past five years. However, increased competition has led Mr Trent, the chairman, to believe that an aggressive advertising campaign will be necessary next year to maintain the company's present growth.

To prepare for next year's advertising campaign, the company's accountant has prepared and presented Mr Trent with the following data for the current year 19X2:

	£
Variable costs (per pipe)	
Direct labour	8.00
Direct materials	3.25
Variable overhead	2.50
Total variable costs	13.75

Fixed costs	£
Manufacturing	25,000
Selling	40,000
Administrative	70,000
Total fixed costs	135,000
Selling price per pipe	25.00
Expected sales, 19X2 (20,000 units)	500,000

Mr Trent has set the sales target for 19X3 at a level of £550,000 (or 22,000 pipes).

You are required to calculate the following:

(a) What is the projected net income for 19X2?

(b) What is the break-even point in units for 19X2?

(c) Mr Trent believes an additional selling expense of £11,250 for advertising in 19X3, with all other costs remaining constant, will be necessary to attain the sales target. What will be the net income for 19X3 if the additional £11,250 is spent?

(d) What will be the break-even point in terms of units for 19X3 if the additional £11,250 is spent for advertising?

(e) If the additional £11,250 is spent for advertising in 19X3, what is the required sales level in terms of units to equal 19X2's net income?

(f) At a sales level of 22,000 units, what maximum amount can be spent on advertising if a net income of £100,000 is desired?

(20 marks)

6 The Garter group of companies is opening up a new works to produce Bluemantle which will sell for £10 per unit. Preliminary market research shows that demand will be less than 100,000 units per year, but it is not as yet clear how much less.

The group has the choice of buying one of two machines, each of which has a capacity of 100,000 units per year. Machine A would have fixed costs of £300,000 per year and would yield a profit of £300,000 per year if sales were 100,000 units. Machine B has a fixed cost per year of £160,000 and would yield a profit of £240,000 per year with sales of 100,000 units. Variable costs behave linearly for both machines.

You are required:

(a) To find the break-even point for each machine.
(b) To find the range of sales for which one machine is more profitable than the other.
(c) To produce a single profit-volume graph showing these features.

(15 marks)

(a) Eastham Ltd manufactures one product only and has the following budgeted data for 19X2:

Sales	£30 per unit
Variable costs	£10 per unit
Fixed costs	£400,000

You are required to draw a break-even chart using the above data. State the break-even point.

(b) Draw three separate break-even charts incorporating the effect of each of the following on the above data:

(i) Fixed costs increase by £100,000 for every 10,000 units made.

(ii) Quantity discounts are available, which affect variable costs as follows:

Units	Cost per extra unit
0 to 10,000	£10
10,001 to 20,000	£8
20,001 upwards	£6

(iii) The selling price of £30 can only be maintained if sales are limited to 28,000. If sales are to exceed this figure, a price of £25 must be adopted.

(c) Draw one break-even chart, showing the combined effects of (b) (i), (ii) and (iii) (up to 35,000 units). State the break-even point.

(30 marks)

8 You have just been appointed as chief accountant to Brainteasers Ltd, a company which manufactures and sells puzzles. You are given the following details for the year ended 1 April 19X1.

	£ thousands
Sales	A
Direct materials	800
Direct labour	B
Variable manufacturing overhead	200
Fixed manufacturing overhead	C
Variable selling expenses	120
Variable administrative expenses	D
Fixed selling and administrative expenses	200
Contribution	E
Gross profit	F
Net profit	400
Break-even point in sales revenue	2,000

No stock is carried, and there are no other costs apart from those listed above. The gross profit margin is 30% and the contribution margin ratio is 40%.

You are required to find the amounts represented by the letters A to F on the above list.

(25 marks)

ANSWERS

1

(a) The selling price exceeds the variable costs incurred. For instance, if the selling price is £5 and variable costs are £3, a contribution of £2 is made by each unit.

The contribution from sales firstly covers any fixed costs and secondly generates profits. If fixed costs are, say, £4,000, sales of 2,000 units will cover them.

At point (a) sales volume is insufficient to pay for all the fixed costs resulting in a loss. At point (b) the volume of sales is sufficient to generate a profit.

(b) **The underlying assumptions of cost-volume-profit analysis**

   (i) **Constant selling price**
   All units may be sold at the same price. This assumption is artificial in that volume is usually increased by dropping the price.

   (ii) **Constant fixed costs**
   Fixed costs remain the same in total for all levels of activity. In practice, fixed costs go up in 'steps' as activity increases.

   (iii) **Constant variable costs per unit**
   This assumption is also too simplistic since quantity discounts are often available as activity increases.

   (iv) **Common activity base**
   Since both costs and revenues are being measured on the same graph, activity must represent both production and sales. In other words, stock levels do not change. This assumption is perhaps unrealistic, especially in the short term.

   (v) **Constant product mix**
   A cost-volume-profit graph may be drawn for either a single-product firm, or for a firm which sells its several products in the same ratio. Thus changes in the mix of products cannot be analysed.

   (vi) **Fixed and variable costs**
   All costs may be identified as either fixed, variable or semi-variable. Semi-variable costs in turn may be split into their fixed and variable components.

   This raises two problems. Firstly, the splitting of semi-variable costs relies on such techniques as regression analysis. Secondly, many costs may be either fixed or variable, depending on the particular circumstances.

Use of cost-volume-profit analysis

Although the above assumptions mean that such analysis is invariably of limited use, cost-volume-profit graphs do still provide useful information to the management of an organisation.

They are well suited as a budgeting tool, in that a simple chart gives a general view before more detailed planning is attempted.

Furthermore, the basic graph may be altered by building in changes in selling price, changes in fixed costs and changes in variable costs.

Finally, most organisations operate within a fairly narrow and well-defined range of activity. It may be the case that the simplifying assumptions do not invalidate the analysis.

2

(a)

	£ thousands	£ thousands
Sales		300
Variable costs:		
Prime costs	100	
Production overhead	10	
Selling overhead	40	
		(150)
Contribution		150
Fixed costs:		
Production overhead	40	
Selling overhead	20	
Administration	60	
		(120)
Profit		30

The profit-volume graph shows that the break-even point is £240,000 and the margin of safety is £60,000.

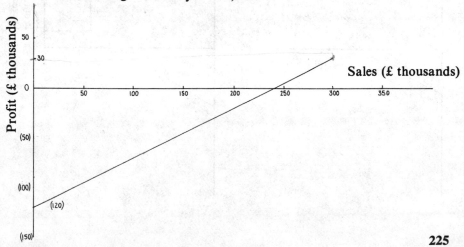

(b) The required graphs are shown below.

Key: ——————— Original contribution line
     — — — —   Revised contribution line

(i) An increase in fixed cost   (ii) A decrease in variable cost

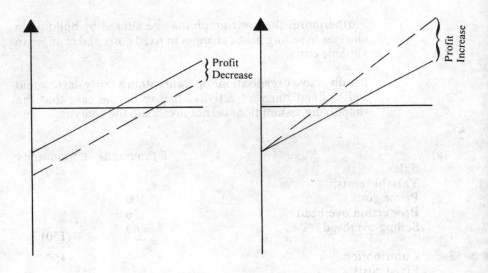

(iii) An increase in sales price   (iv) A decrease in sales volume

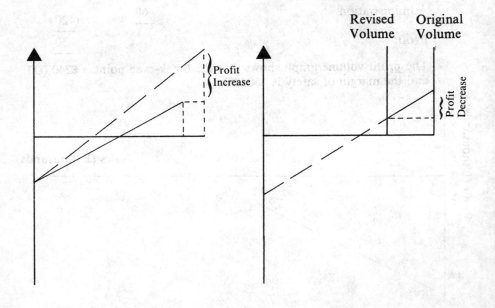

3

(a)
(i)

	£
Sales	550,000
Less: Variable costs	(247,500)
Contribution	302,500

$$\text{Contribution per unit} = \frac{£302,500}{27,500} = £11$$

(ii) $\text{Contribution margin ratio} = \dfrac{£302,500}{£550,000} = 55\%$

(iii) Break-even point:

    (a) Units: $\dfrac{\text{fixed costs}}{\text{contribution per unit}} = \dfrac{£242,000}{£11} = 22,000$

    (b) Sales: break-even units × selling price
        $= 22,000 × £20 = £440,000$

(iv) $\text{Margin of safety ratio} = \dfrac{\text{budgeted sales} - \text{break-even sales}}{\text{budgeted sales}}$

$$= \frac{£550,000 - £440,000}{£550,000} = 20\%$$

(b) (i) New fixed costs: £242,000 + £48,000 = £290,000

Contribution per unit	Originally		Now	
Sales	20		20	
Materials	4		4	
Labour	3		1.5	
Overhead	2	(9)	2	(7.5)
		11		12.5

Break-even point

    (a) Units: $\dfrac{£290,000}{£12.5} = 23,200$

    (b) Sales: 23,200 × £20 = £464,000

(ii) The extra fixed costs of £48,000 have to be recovered by the extra contribution of £1.50 per unit. This will be achieved at a level of sales of £48,000/£1.5 = 32,000 units.

Comment

Many students will consider (b)(ii) to mean that the profit must be the same as before, in which case the following calculation will be done:

	£
Original contribution	302,500
Add extra fixed costs	48,000
Required contribution	350,500

Contribution per unit: £12.5

$$\text{Worthwhile level of sales} = \frac{£350,500}{£12.5} = 28,040 \text{ units}$$

This interpretation is not correct, because at this level of sales the profit without the machine is higher than with the machine, and so the acquisition would not be worthwhile at 28,040 units.

4

		£	£
Selling price per case			12.00
Variable costs per case sold:			
Purchase cost: Valpolicella		1.50	
Bardolino		1.50	
Liebfraumilch		1.55	
Niersteiner		1.75	
Bereich Bernkastel		1.70	
Piesporter		2.00	
		10.00	
Distribution		0.50	(10.50)
Contribution per case			1.50

(a) Break-even point
  (i) Unit sales:

$$\frac{\text{fixed costs}}{\text{contribution per case}} = \frac{£3,000}{£1.50} = 2,000 \text{ cases}$$

  (ii) Sales revenue:

$$\frac{\text{fixed costs}}{\text{contribution margin ratio}} = \frac{£3,000}{12\frac{1}{2}\%} = £24,000$$

	£
(b) Total contribution: 3,800 × £1.50	5,700
Less: fixed expenses	(3,000)
Profit	2,700

(c) Total contribution: 5,000 × £1.50	7,500
Less: fixed expenses £3,000 + £2,400	(5,400)
	2,100

(d) (i) Unit sales:

$$\frac{\text{fixed costs}}{\text{contribution per case}} = \frac{£2,000}{£1.25} = 1,600 \text{ cases}$$

  (ii) Sales revenue:

$$\frac{\text{fixed costs}}{\text{contribution margin ratio}} = \frac{£2,000}{10.4167\%} = £19,200$$

(e)

	(i) Salary scheme £	(ii) Commission scheme £
Fixed costs	3,000	2,000
Profit	6,000	6,000
Required contribution	9,000	8,000
Contribution per case	£1.50	£1.25
Required sales	6,000 cases	6,400 cases

(f) Let x be the number of cases for which the profit is the same under both schemes.

  (i)   salary scheme: profit = £1.50x – £3,000
  (ii) commission scheme: profit = £1.25x – £2,000

The profits under both schemes are equal when

$$1.50x - 3,000 = 1.25x - 2,000$$
$$0.25x = 1,000$$
$$x = 4,000$$

Hence both schemes produce the same profit (£3,000) if 4,000 cases are sold.

5

	£
Selling price per unit	25.00
Variable costs per unit	(13.75)
Contribution per unit	11.25

(a) **Net income for 19X2**

	£
Contribution £11.25 × 20,000	225,000
Less: Fixed costs	(135,000)
	90,000

(b) **Break-even point for 19X2**

At break-even, contribution = fixed costs = £135,000
contribution per unit = £11.25

Hence break-even point in units $= \dfrac{£135,000}{£11.25} = 12,000$ units

(c) **Net income for 19X3**

	£	£
Contribution £11.25 × 22,000		247,500
Less: Fixed costs: other	135,000	
advertising	11,250	(146,250)
		101,250

(d) **Break-even point for 19X3**

$$\frac{\text{required contribution}}{\text{contribution per unit}} = \frac{£146,250}{£11.25} = 13,000 \text{ units}$$

(e) **Required sales level for 19X3 to generate £90,000 net income**

	£
Required income	90,000
Add: Fixed costs	146,250
Required contribution	236,250

$$\text{Required sales level} = \frac{£236,250}{£11.25} = 21,000 \text{ units}$$

(f) **Maximum available for advertising**

	£	£
Contribution £11.25 × 22,000		247,500
Less: accounted for: other fixed costs	135,000	
target income	100,000	(235,000)
Available for advertising		12,500

6

(a) **Break-even point**

	Machine A	Machine B
	£	£
Fixed costs	300,000	160,000
Profit at 100,000 units	300,000	240,000
Contribution at 100,000 units	600,000	400,000
Contribution per unit	6	4
Break-even point:	units	units
fixed costs	£300,000	£160,000
contribution per unit	£6	£4
Break-even point	50,000	40,000

(b) **Range of sales**   **More profitable machine**

Range of sales	More profitable machine
0 to 70,000 units	B
70,000 units upwards	A

Reasoning

When sales are nil, machine B is more 'profitable' because it makes a loss of £160,000 compared to £300,000. For every unit sold, machine A makes an extra contribution of £6 – £4 = £2. The extra 'profit' of £140,000 for machine B at nil sales is reduced by £2 per unit sold, and so a point of indifference is reached at 70,000 units, beyond which machine A is more profitable.

Comment

Perhaps the neatest way to answer parts (a) and (b) is to approach part (c) first.

(c) The required graph is shown opposite.

230

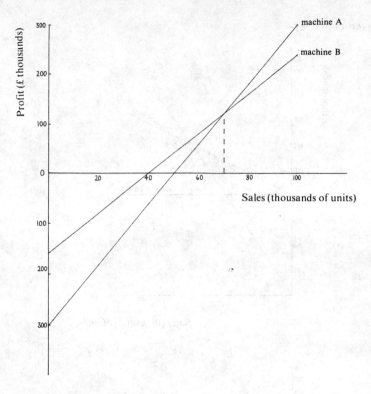

Profit (£ thousands) / Sales (thousands of units)

machine A
machine B

7 Calculation of break-even points

Chart (a)

$$\frac{\text{fixed costs}}{\text{contribution per unit}} = \frac{£400,000}{£20} = 20,000$$

Chart (c)
From the chart, it can be seen that the break-even point is between 20,000 and 30,000.

	£
Contribution from first 10,000 units (£30–£10) × 10,000	200,000
Contribution from second 10,000 units (£30–£8) × 10,000	220,000
Contribution from first 20,000 units	420,000
Total fixed costs between 20,000 and 30,000 units	600,000
Required contribution	180,000
Contribution per unit from next 8,000 units (£30–£6)	24

$$\text{Extra units required} = \frac{18,000}{24} = 7,500$$

Hence, units to break even:	
	10,000
	10,000
	7,500
	27,500

231

Break-even chart (a)

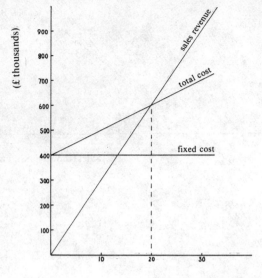

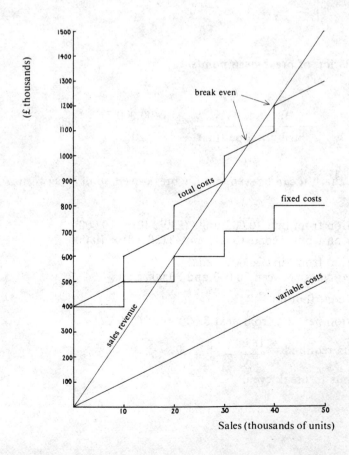

Break-even chart b(ii)

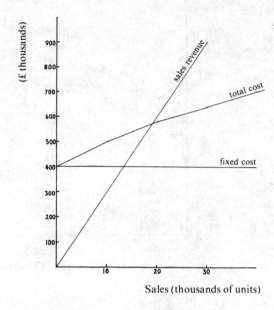

Sales (thousands of units)

Break-even chart (b)(iii)

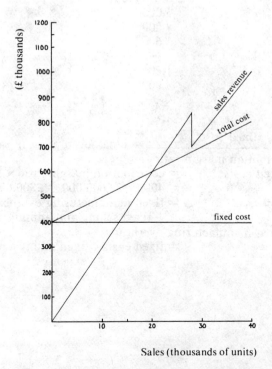

Sales (thousands of units)

Break-even chart (c)

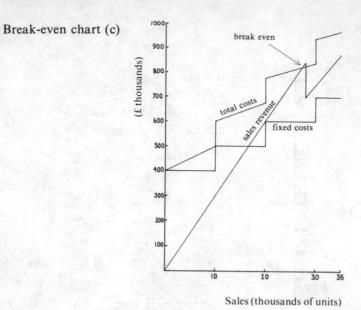

Sales (thousands of units)

8

	£ thousands
A	3,000
B	500
C	600
D	180
E	1,200
F	900

Workings

1   $\dfrac{\text{fixed costs}}{\text{contribution margin ratio}}$ = break-even point in sales revenue

   i.e. fixed costs = contribution margin ratio × break-even point
   = 40% × £2,000,000 = £800,000

2   fixed costs = fixed manufacturing overhead
      + fixed selling and administration expenses

   i.e. fixed manufacturing overhead
      = fixed costs – fixed selling and administration
        expenses

234

$$= £800,000 - £200,000$$
$$= £600,000 = C$$
$$= \text{fixed costs} + \text{net profit}$$

3 contribution
$$= £800,000 + £400,000$$
$$= £1,200,000 = E$$

4 contribution margin ratio $= \dfrac{\text{contribution}}{\text{sales}}$

$$\text{sales} = \dfrac{\text{contribution}}{\text{contribution margin ratio}} = \dfrac{£1,200,000}{40\%} =$$

$$£3,000,000 = A$$

5 gross profit margin $= \dfrac{\text{gross profit}}{\text{sales}}$

i.e. gross profit
$$= \text{gross profit margin} \times \text{sales}$$
$$= 30\% \times £3,000,000$$
$$= £900,000 = F$$

6 sales – manufacturing costs = gross profit
i.e. manufacturing costs
$$= \text{sales} - \text{gross profit}$$
$$= £3,000,000 - £900,000$$
$$= £2,100,000$$

7 manufacturing costs $= \text{direct materials} + \text{direct labour}$
$$+ \text{variable manufacturing overhead}$$
$$+ \text{fixed manufacturing overhead}$$

i.e. direct labour $= \text{manufacturing costs} - \text{direct materials} -$
$$\text{manufacturing overhead}$$
$$= £2,100,000 - £800,000 - £200,000 - £600,000$$
$$= £500,000 = B$$

8 gross profit – selling and administrative expenses = net profit
i.e. selling and administrative expenses $= \text{gross profit} - \text{net profit}$
$$= £900,000 - £400,000$$
$$= £500,000$$

9 selling and administrative expenses $= \text{variable selling expenses}$
$$+ \text{variable administrative expenses} + \text{fixed selling and administrative expenses}$$

i.e. variable administrative expenses $= £500,000 - £120,000 - £200,000$
$$= £180,000 = D$$

Note

All the details may now be shown using two statements:

(i) **Profit statements for the year ended 1 April 19X1**

	£ thousands	£ thousands
Sales		3,000
Less: Cost of sales		
Direct materials	800	
Direct labour	500	
Variable manufacturing overhead	200	
Fixed manufacturing overhead	600	
		(2,100)
Gross profit		900
Less: Variable selling expenses	120	
Variable administrative expenses	180	
Fixed selling and administrative		
expenses	200	
		(500)
Net profit		400

(ii) **Contribution statement for the year ended 1 April 19X1**

	£ thousands	£ thousands
Sales		3,000
Less: Variable costs		
Direct materials	800	
Direct labour	500	
Manufacturing overhead	200	
Selling expenses	120	
Administrative expenses	180	
		(1,800)
Contribution		1,200
Less: Fixed costs		
Manufacturing overhead	600	
Selling and administrative expenses	200	
		(800)
Net profit		400

17 Comparison of marginal and absorption costing

In Chapters 15 and 16 the questions were concerned with the use of contribution calculations for the purpose of decision-making.

The questions in the present chapter deal with marginal costing as an accounting system. Questions 1 to 6 each require alternative profit statements using respectively a marginal costing basis and a full absorption costing basis. Question 7 tests your understanding of marginal costing by requiring you to construct a profit statement from incomplete data segregating fixed from variable costs.

Five of the questions have a narrative content calling for either the relative advantages and disadvantages of the two systems or an explanation of differences in the profit figures derived from them. These essays provide an important test of your understanding; and you should check your own answers carefully against the model answers provided.

STUDY REQUIREMENTS

Theory and practice of marginal costing and absorption costing.

QUESTIONS

1 At a recent conference on cost control in a period of reduction in demand, your managing director was impressed by the remarks of one of the speakers who advocated a marginal costing system of management reporting.

The managing director has now asked you to compare the present absorption costing system with an alternative marginal costing system. You are required:

(a) To tabulate the merits of:

   (i) a marginal costing system; and
   (ii) an absorption costing system.

(b) To prepare for presentation to your board of directors two statements showing the budgeted results for the year in:

   (i) an absorption costing form;
   (ii) a marginal costing form;

   paying particular attention to the layout of your presentation, which should be based on the data shown below.

(c) To present ratios with each statement which will show the relative profitability of each product and comment briefly on these ratios.

The company produces two products; the standard cost data for one of each are as follows:

	Product	
	A	B
Direct materials:		
Units required	20	5
Price per unit	£0.50	£1.00
Direct labour:		
Hours allowed	5	10
Rate per hour	£2.00	£1.50

Budgeted data for the year are as follows:		
Direct labour hours	55,000	
Production overhead	£220,000	
	A	B
Sales	£375,000	£300,000
Profit as a percentage of selling price	20%	10%

Overhead absorption:
Production overhead is absorbed by a direct labour hour rate.
Administration overhead is absorbed on a basis of 20% of production cost.
Selling and distribution overhead is absorbed on a basis of 30% of production cost.

For the purpose of this presentation it has been decided that in order to facilitate the preparation of the marginal cost statement, it can be assumed that, using the overhead absorption cost per unit as a base, 20% of the production overhead can be regarded as variable, and $33^1/_3$% of the selling and distribution overhead can be regarded as variable.

(30 marks)

2   The following information has been extracted from the books of the My Heir Company by its proprietor concerning a new product that he put into production at the commencement of the period just completed.

Sales	10,000 units sold at £5 each
Production	15,000 units which were produced at the following cost:

	£
Direct materials	15,000
Direct labour	30,000
Variable expenses	6,000
Fixed expenses	12,000

The proprietor of the company has two sons, both of whom are studying accountancy, but at different colleges. He sends each of them a copy of the figures and asks them to produce a statement showing their calculation of the company's profit for the period and the value of its closing stock.

One of the sons, having just been taught full-cost product costing, prepares a statement following that method. The other, who has just learned all about period costing, produces his statement on that basis.

When the father receives the two statements he finds that they provide different profits and stock valuations. Therefore he returns a copy of both statements to each of his sons, asking them to make a check and to find out which one has made a mistake.

Required:

(a)   Formulate the two statements, presenting them in tabular form, showing the different ways that the sons were likely to have produced their statements. *(8 marks)*

(b)   Explain why these two methods gave different results. In your discussion, use data from the two statements to illustrate your answer as appropriate and briefly provide the arguments for and against these different approaches. *(12 marks)*
(Total 20 marks)

3   Hedge manufactures video recorders and has produced a budget for the quarter ended 31 March 19X4 as follows:

	£	£
Sales: 100 units at £500 per unit		50,000
Production cost of 120 units:		
Material	12,000	
Labour	24,000	
Variable overhead	6,000	
Fixed overhead	6,000	
	48,000	
Less: Closing stock 20 × £400	(8,000)	
		(40,000)
Profit		10,000

There was no opening stock on 1 January 19X4.

He budgets for production, sales and stock for the next three quarters of the year as follows (the sales price, variable costs per unit and fixed costs being the same as for quarter 1):

	Quarter 2 (units)	Quarter 3 (units)	Quarter 4 (units)
Opening stock	20	30	30
Production	120	120	120
Sales	110	120	130
Closing stock	30	30	20

You are required:

(a)   To produce a schedule showing the cost of production per unit and the contribution/profit per unit using marginal costing and total absorption costing.

(b)   To produce budgeted profit and loss accounts for the first four quarters of the year using marginal costing and total absorption costing.

(c)   To explain the difference in the budgeted profit figures for quarters 1 and 2 as calculated on the two different bases.

(20 marks)

4   Shown below is an extract from next year's budget for a company manufacturing two products in two production departments.

	Product A (units)	Product B (units)
Sales	11,500	15,750
Opening stock	1,000	2,000
Closing stock (at end of budget year)	1,500	1,250

	£ per unit	£ per unit
Selling price	140	80
Prime costs:		
Materials	14	26
Labour — Production Department 1	20	8
Production Department 2	18	12

Hourly wage rates for direct operatives are budgeted at £4 per hour in Production Department 1 and £3 per hour in Production Department 2. It should be assumed that all prime costs are variable.

Budgeted annual overheads:	Production Dept 1 £	Production Dept 2 £
Fixed overheads	315,000	613,800
Variable overheads	67,500	145,200
	382,500	759,000

The company operates a full absorption costing system and each production department charges its budgeted overhead to products by means of a departmental direct labour hour absorption rate.

Production and overheads are budgeted to occur evenly throughout the year. However, monthly sales do vary and the budgeted sales for the first month are, Product A 1,200 units and Product B 2,300 units.

The total cost per unit of the opening stocks is Product A £98 per unit and Product B £75 per unit. These stock values are based upon the costs in the current period and are *not* the budgeted unit costs for next year.

Required:

(a) Calculate the budgeted profit for the first month of next year for the above company. Any necessary assumptions should be clearly indicated. *(14 marks)*

(b) Calculate the effect on the above budgeted profit if in the first month, the actual results are as predicted except that actual production of Product B is 50 units higher than the budget. *(4 marks)*

(c) The accountant of the above company is considering changing from a full absorption costing system to a marginal costing system in which each month's fixed overheads will be written off immediately they are incurred.

Describe the effect of the above proposal on the first month's budgeted profit and explain the reason for that effect. Calculations are not required and you should assume that the opening stock values would be reduced to marginal cost *before* the first month's budgeted profit is calculated. *(4 marks)*

(Total 22 marks)

241

5 The Morris Company has the following data for 19X1 and 19X2:

	£
Basic production data at standard cost	
Direct materials	1.30
Direct labour	1.50
Variable overhead	0.20
Fixed overhead	
(£150,000 ÷ 150,000 units of normal volume)	1.00
Total standard factory cost	4.00
Selling price per unit	5.00

Other expenses:	
Fixed selling and administration	£65,000
Sales commission	5% of sales value

Output and sales in units	19X1	19X2
Opening stock	—	30,000
Production	170,000	140,000
Sales	140,000	160,000
Closing stock	30,000	10,000

You are required:

(a) To formulate a profit statement for each of the two years 19X1 and 19X2 under:
   (i) absorption costing;
   (ii) marginal costing. *(20 marks)*
(b) To prepare a reconciliation of the differences in net profit reported under the two systems. *(5 marks)*
   (Total 25 marks)

6 A budget is to be drafted on the basis of the following:

Direct material	£10 per unit
Direct labour	£5 per unit
Variable expenses	£8 per unit
Fixed costs	£27,000
Budgeted output 9,000 units	=90% capacity
Sales price	£30 per unit

Capacity can be increased to 120% without any increase in fixed costs.

The directors wish to see the financial effect of three levels of capacity utilisation, namely, 90% (as budgeted), 65% and 110%.

You are required:

(a) To prepare two statements, each one in comparative columnar form covering the three levels of utilisation:

    (i)   on a marginal costing basis, and

    (ii)   on a full absorption costing basis

bringing out clearly in your statements the different treatments of profit and overheads on the two different bases.

(b)   To state briefly the advantages and disadvantages of the use of the marginal costing basis for management accounting.

(25 marks)

7   The figures shown below are all that could be salvaged after a recent fire in the management accounting department of Fireprone Limited. Fireprone manufactures a single product, has no work-in-progress and allocates all the actual costs of manufacture to its product. It is known that the unit closing stock valuation in 19X5 was the same as in 19X4. Stock is valued at actual manufacturing cost on a FIFO basis.

	19X5	19X6
Selling price per unit	£10.00	£10.00
Variable manufacturing costs, per unit produced	£4.50	£4.00
Variable selling costs per unit sold	£1.25	?
Quantity sold	100,000	?
Quantity produced	105,000	130,000
Contribution margin per unit based upon the production and selling costs of the year in question	?	?
Total contribution margin earned on sales	?	£585,000
Fixed costs, manufacturing	£105,000	£117,000
Fixed costs, other	£155,000	?
Operating profit, before interest and taxation	?	£292,500
Total interest charges	£70,000	?
Opening finished stock quantity	?	?
Closing finished stock quantity	20,000	20,000
Taxation at 52% on operating profit less total interest charges	?	£110,500
Profit after taxation	?	?

You are required to prepare manufacturing, trading and profit and loss accounts for management for both years detailed to the extent that the available information permits.

(15 marks)

ANSWERS

1

(a) Merits of:

A marginal costing system	**An absorption costing system**
Avoids the problem of a unit fixed cost and under/over absorption.	Avoids the difficulty of classifying costs into fixed and variable.
Avoids any arbitrary apportionment of fixed costs between different products.	Ensures that all costs will be recovered in the long run.
Leads to contribution analysis, break-even charts and cost-volume-profit analysis, all of which are useful for short-term decision-making.	Leads to stable price-setting.
Recognises that profit is generated by sales, not by production.	Is common practice.
Values stock on a prudent basis.	Values stock so that costs are matched with revenues more accurately. Furthermore, the comparison with net realisable value safeguards prudence.
Is easy to understand and operate.	

(b) (i) **Budgeted results for the year in an absorption costing form**

	Product A	Product B	Total
Units	5,000	3,000	8,000
	£ thousands	£ thousands	£ thousands
Sales	375	300	675
Direct materials	50	15	65
Direct labour	50	45	95
Production overhead	100	120	220
Production cost	200	180	380
Administration	40	36	76
Selling	60	54	114
Total cost	300	270	570
Profit	75	30	105

(ii)   **Budgeted results for the year in a marginal costing form**

	Product A	Product B	Total
Units	5,000	3,000	8,000
	£	£	£
	thousands	thousands	thousands
Sales	375	300	675
Variable costs:			
Direct materials	50	15	65
Direct labour	50	45	95
Production overhead	20	24	44
Selling	20	18	38
	140	102	242
Contribution	235	198	433
Fixed costs:			
Production overhead			176
Administration			76
Selling			76
Profit			105

Appendix

Calculation of selling prices

	A		B	
		£		£
Direct materials	20 × £0.50	10	5 × £1.00	5
Direct labour	5 × £2.00	10	10 × £1.50	15
Production overhead $\dfrac{£220,000}{55,000} = £4$ per hour	5 × £4	20	10 × £4	40
Production cost		40		60
Administration	20%	8	20%	12
Selling	30%	12	30%	18
		60		90
Profit	$\dfrac{20}{80} \times 60$	15	$\dfrac{10}{90} \times 90$	10
		75		100

Calculation of sales in units

Revenue ÷ selling price £375,000/£75 5,000 £300,000/£100 3,000

(c)

	A	B
Profit as a percentage of sales	20%	10%
Contribution as a percentage of sales	62.67%	66%

Absorption costing indicates that product A is twice as profitable as product B, whereas marginal costing shows product B to generate a slightly higher contribution. The difference may be found in the treatment of fixed costs. Absorption costing attempts to recover all overheads over the product on a predetermined basis, which may be arbitrary, whereas marginal costing treats fixed costs as company-wide and not individual product expenses.

It may be concluded that the ratios highlighted under marginal costing give a better picture, and are more useful for decision-making about the two products.

2

(a)

	Full-cost product costing		Period costing	
	£	£	£	£
Sales		50,000		50,000
Direct materials	15,000		15,000	
Direct labour	30,000		30,000	
Variable expenses	6,000		6,000	
Fixed expenses	12,000		—	
	63,000		51,000	
Less: Closing stock				
($1/_3$ × £63,000)	(21,000)		($1/_3$ × £51,000)	
			(17,000)	(34,000)
		(42,000)	Contribution	16,000
			Fixed	
			expenses	(12,000)
Profit		8,000	Profit	4,000

(b) There were no errors in either of the statements. The different results follow from the different concepts used. One approach is based on the proposition that fixed overhead should be absorbed into the product cost, with the effect of producing a higher recorded profit (in the example above, £8,000) and residual stock valuation (£21,000) than when the more conservative approach is taken of allocating all fixed overheads incurred in the period to that period, when a lower profit (£4,000) and residual stock valuation (£17,000) will be computed. Nevertheless the performance of the organisation remains the same, it is only the accounting principles which have been applied that differ! In the full-cost approach, absorbing fixed overheads into product costs carries some of them forward in the residual stock values — hence the difference. However, over the complete life of the product total profits will be shown the same by both methods.

Some of the arguments for and against each method, stated in tabular form, are as follows:

	Fixed overhead absorbed by product	Fixed overhead expensed by period
Classification of fixed and variable overheads may be difficult and sometimes somewhat arbitrary.	Since classification is unnecessary, such problems do not arise.	Difficulty with semi-fixed/semi-variable costs.
Stock valuation.	Include full production costs on the argument that these have been necessarily incurred.	Include variable costs only — which accords with the argument that the additional cost of the stock is limited to its variable cost.
Profit.	Higher if stock holdings increase to accord with operations during period.	The prudence principle results in lower stock valuations.
Use of costs for pricing purposes.	Will have full costs as the pricing floor.	If fixed overheads are not included in production costs prices quoted might be too low.
Recovery of fixed overheads.	Problem of determining activity level for the absorption of fixed overhead, use of normal activity with recovery variances being treated as period expenses.	Activity problem does not arise as fixed overhead is expensed as a period expense.
Fixed costs may not be controllable at product or department level.	Allocation may cause danger of trying to control the uncontrollable.	Only controllable costs are included in product costs at cost centre level.
Overhead costs and productivity change from period to period.	Prices based on product cost will be more volatile.	Pricing variability is closely related to variable costs.
Other techniques.	Fits in well with standard absorption costing.	Fits in well with flexible budgeting.
Contribution.	Has to be calculated separately to ensure good decisions.	Already computed to help in decision making.

3

(a)

	Marginal costing	Absorption costing
	£	£
Cost of production per unit		
Material	100	100
Labour	200	200
Variable overhead	50	50
	350	
Fixed overhead		50
		400
Selling price per unit	500	500
Contribution/Profit per unit	150	100

(b)

	Quarters ending			
	31 March	30 June	30 September	31 December
	£	£	£	£
Absorption costing				
Sales	50,000	55,000	60,000	65,000
Opening stock	—	8,000	12,000	12,000
Cost of production	48,000	48,000	48,000	48,000
Closing stock	(8,000)	(12,000)	(12,000)	(8,000)
	40,000	44,000	48,000	52,000
Under (over) absorption of fixed overhead	—	—	—	—
Profit	10,000	11,000	12,000	13,000
Marginal costing				
Sales	50,000	55,000	60,000	65,000
Opening stock	—	7,000	10,500	10,500
Cost of production	42,000	42,000	42,000	42,000
Closing stock	(7,000)	(10,500)	(10,500)	(7,000)
	35,000	38,500	42,000	45,500
Contribution	15,000	16,500	18,000	19,500
Fixed overhead	6,000	6,000	6,000	6,000
Profit	9,000	10,500	12,000	13,500

(c) Quarter 1

	£
Profit per absorption costing	10,000
Profit per marginal costing	9,000
	1,000

Difference in stock valuation: 20 units at £50 = £1,000

Quarter 2	£
Profit per absorption costing	11,000
Profit per marginal costing	10,500
	500

Difference in stock valuation 10 units at £50 = £500

4

(a) Budgeted profit for the first month of next year

	Product A		Product B	
		£		£
Sales	1,200 × £140.00	168,000	2,300 × £80.00	184,000
Cost of sales:				
from stock	1,000 × £98.00	98,000	2,000 × £75.00	150,000
from production	200 × £107.75	21,550	300 × £77.50	23,250
Profit		48,450		10,750

Assumption: Stock is sold on a FIFO basis

Workings

Production budget	Product A (units)	Product B (units)
Sales	11,500	15,750
Add: Stock increase	500	(750)
	12,000	15,000

Labour hours budget	Dept 1	Dept 2
Product A: $\dfrac{12,000 \times £20}{£4}$	60,000	
$\dfrac{12,000 \times £18}{£3}$		72,000
Product B: $\dfrac{15,000 \times £8}{£4}$	30,000	
$\dfrac{15,000 \times £12}{£3}$		60,000
	90,000	132,000

Overhead absorption rates (per hour)	Dept 1 £	Dept 2 £
Fixed $\dfrac{£315,000}{90,000}$	3.50	
$\dfrac{£613,800}{132,000}$		4.65
Variable $\dfrac{£67,500}{90,000}$	0.75	
$\dfrac{£145,200}{132,000}$		1.10
	4.25	5.75

Production costs (per unit)	Product A £	Product B £
Materials	14.00	26.00
Labour — Dept 1	20.00	8.00
Dept 2	18.00	12.00
	52.00	46.00
Overhead — Dept 1 5 hrs × £4.25	21.25	
2 hrs × £4.25		8.50
Dept 2 6 hrs × £5.75	34.50	
4 hrs × £5.75		23.00
	107.75	77.50

(b) If actual production of Product B exceeds budgeted production by 50 units, fixed overhead will be over-absorbed, resulting in an increase in profits, as follows:

	£
Dept 1: 50 units × 2 hours × £3.50	350
Dept 2: 50 units × 4 hours × £4.65	930
Increase in budgeted profit	1,280

(c) If the company changes to a marginal costing system, fixed costs will not be considered as part of the product cost per unit. Instead, one month's worth of fixed costs will be charged against the monthly contribution.

Ignoring any changes in fixed costs from the previous year, this will have the effect of *increasing* profits. The first month's sales will exceed one-twelfth of annual sales and since absorption costing charges overheads in proportion to sales, a lower charge for overheads will arise under marginal costing.

If stocks increase over the budget period, absorption costing will show a greater profit; if stocks decrease, marginal costing will show the greater profit.

Comment

This question tests both the ability to calculate overhead recovery rates and the understanding of the two costing systems, absorption and marginal.

5

(a) (i) **Profit statement under absorption costing**

	19X1 thousands of units	19X1 £ thousands	19X2 thousands of units	19X2 £ thousands
Sales at £5	140	700	160	800
Opening stock at £4	—	—	30	120
Cost of production at £4	170	680	140	560
	170	680	170	680
Closing stock at £4	(30)	(120)	(10)	(40)
	140	560	160	640
Under/(over) absorption of fixed overhead at £1		(20)		10
Cost of goods sold		540		650
Gross profit		160		150
Less: Selling and administration		(65)		(65)
Commission		(35)		(40)
Net profit		60		45

(ii) Profit statement under marginal costing

	19X1 thousands of units	19X1 £ thousands	19X2 thousands of units	19X2 £ thousands
Sales at £5	140	700	160	800
Opening stock at £3	—	—	30	90
Variable cost of production at £3	170	510	140	420
	170	510	170	510
Closing stock at £3	30	90	10	30
Variable cost of goods sold	140	420	160	480
Manufacturing contribution		280		320
Variable sales commission		(35)		(40)
Contribution		245		280
Fixed costs:				
Factory overhead		(150)		(150)
Selling and administration		(65)		(65)
Net profit		30		65

(b) Reconciliation of profit figures

	19X1 £ thousands	19X2 £ thousands	Total £ thousands
Absorption	60	45	105
Marginal	30	65	95
	30	(20)	10
Increase in closing stock (units)	30,000	(20,000)	10,000
Difference in stock valuation	30,000 × £1 = £30,000	(−20,000) × £1 = −£20,000	10,000 × £1 = £10,000

6

(a) (i) Marginal presentation

		65%		90%		110%
Capacity utilisation			6,500		9,000		11,000
Sales units							
	£000s	£000s	£000s	£000s	£000s	£000s
Sales (£30 per unit)		195.0		270.0		330.0
Variable costs:						
Materials (£10 per unit)	65.0		90.0		110.0	
Labour (£5 per unit)	32.5		45.0		55.0	
Expenses (£8 per unit)	52.0	(149.5)	72.0	(207.0)	88.0	(253.0)
Contribution (£7 per unit)		45.5		63.0		77.0
Fixed costs		(27.0)		(27.0)		(27.0)
Profit		18.5		36.0		50.0

(ii) Absorption presentation

	£000s	£000s	£000s	£000s	£000s	£000s
Sales		195.0		270.0		330.0
Cost of sales:						
Materials	65.0		90.0		110.0	
Labour	32.5		45.0		55.0	
Variable expenses	52.0		72.0		88.0	
Fixed overhead absorbed £3 per unit)	19.5	(169.0)	27.0	(234.0)	33.0	(286.0)
		26.0		36.0		44.0
Fixed costs over/ (under) absorbed		(7.5)		—		6.0
Profit		18.5		36.0		50.0

(b) Advantages of using marginal costing

(i) When sales do not match production, the inclusion of fixed overhead in stock valuation tends to distort recorded profits from one period to another. For example, using the figures above, if production was constant at 9,000 units per period and sales for three successive periods were 6,500, 9,000 and 11,000 units, the absorption costing approach would record the following:

	Period 1		Period 2		Period 3	
Sales (units)	6,500		9,000		11,000	
	£	£	£	£	£	£
	thousands	thousands	thousands	thousands	thousands	thousands
Sales	195.0		270.0		330.0	
Cost of sales:						
Opening stock	—		65.0		65.0	
Production (£26 per unit per part (a))	234.0		234.0		234.0	
Closing stock	(65.0)	169.0	(65.0)	234.0	(13.0)	286.0
Profit		26.0		36.0		44.0

Thus, when a proportion of fixed overhead is carried forward in stock valuation the real effect of selling below or above the level of production capacity tends to be obscured as fixed overhead (which mainly accrues in relation to time) incurred in one period is reflected in cost of sales for a subsequent period.

(ii) The arbitrary apportionment of fixed costs complicates any attempt to measure relative profitability of different products or different sections of the business.

(iii) The separation of overhead into its fixed and variable constituents, which is a fundamental requirement of marginal costing, assists planning and control by:

(1) enabling break-even analysis techniques to be used for profit planning;
(2) providing data for establishing flexible budgets to control expenditure;
(3) clarifying the cost information on which to base non-routine decisions such as decisions to discontinue product lines, to make or buy component parts or temporarily to suspend activities.

Disadvantages of marginal costing

The disadvantages of marginal costing, from the management accounting viewpoint, relate mainly to misuse rather than to any theoretical drawbacks, for example:

(i) The relationship between costs and volume is usually based on short-term considerations. Any attempt to base a long-term decision on marginal costs requires a reappraisal of the basis of any short-term analysis which may have been carried out.
(ii) The separation of semi-variable costs into their fixed and variable elements is an arbitrary exercise which may be subject to inaccuracy and fluctuation at different levels of output. Con-

sequently, the basic cost information used in decision-making may contain a substantial degree of error.

(iii) Great care must be exercised when selling prices are based on marginal costs as prices should in the long term reflect a recovery of the utilisation of resources represented by fixed costs and a return on capital employed, appropriate to the item being sold, as well as covering the variable costs of manufacture.

Since marginal costing is the basis for several decision-making techniques, it should be borne in mind that whatever strategy is suggested by marginal cost analysis, whether this relates to pricing, investment, disinvestment, operating decisions or any other aspect of business, proper consideration of factors other than cost is frequently of greater importance than the cost analysis. For example, for the individual firm the determination of price is more a function of demand than of the cost of supply and therefore prices should be set with prime regard to the factors influencing demand, including competitors' prices. Similarly, a decision on whether to make in or buy out should not be taken without first of all exploring all non-accounting aspects of the problem such as continuity of supply and reliability of supplier.

7

	19X5		19X6	
	thousands of units	£ thousands	thousands of units	£ thousands
Sales at £10	100	1,000	130	1,300
Opening stock at £5.50	15	82.5	20	110
Cost of production:	105		130	
Variable		472.5		520
Fixed		105		117
		660		747
Closing stock at £5.50	(20)	(110)	(20)	(98)
	100	550	130	649
Gross profit		450		651
Less: Variable selling costs		(125)		(185)
Other fixed costs		(155)		(173.5)
Operating profit		170		292.5
Less: Interest charges		(70)		(80)
Profit before taxation		100		212.5
Less: Taxation		(52)		(110.5)
Profit after taxation		48		102

Comments

This question is a good test of understanding; working backwards to discover missing figures is more difficult than the more orthodox question.

Fireprone absorbs costs on an actual rather than a predetermined basis, so there is no under- or over-absorption of fixed overheads.

For 19X5 unit closing stock valuation is:

	£	£
Variable		4.50
Fixed	105,000	1.00
	105,000	5.50

This figure can be applied to opening stock, and so the gross profit figure is established.

For 19X6 quantities of opening stock, production and closing stock are given, so sales quantity can be computed.

Unit closing stock valuation is:

	£	£	
Variable		4.00	
Fixed	117,000	0.90	
	130,000	4.90	(FIFO basis)

Variable selling costs can be discovered as follows:

	thousands of units	£ thousands	£ thousands
Sales	130		1,300
Variable production costs	20 × £4.50	90	
	110 × £4	440	(530)
Manufacturing contribution			770
Total contribution			(585)
Variable selling costs			185

'Other fixed costs' is then a balancing figure.

18 Joint products and by-products

Question 2 asks for an explanation of the difference between joint products and by-products. The accounting treatment of by-products involves merely a credit to the appropriate process account for any sales proceeds and will normally be included in your examination only as a minor feature in a question about process costing.

There are two important features of joint product costing for examination purposes, and they are usually both covered in the same question:

(a) The apportionment of pre-separation costs. Various bases are available; and the question will usually tell you which one to apply. Note the brief discussion of this problem in the answer to question 2(b).

(b) The identification of post-separation costs and revenues for the purpose of deciding whether further processing will improve total profits.

STUDY REQUIREMENTS

Problems of common costs, joint products and by-products.

QUESTIONS

1   FPI Ltd is in the food processing industry and in one of its processes, three joint products are manufactured. Traditionally, the company has apportioned work incurred up to the joint products' separation point on the basis of weight of output of the product.

You have recently been appointed cost accountant, and have been investigating process costs and accounting procedures.

You are required to prepare statements for management to show:

(a) the profit or loss of each product as ascertained using the weight basis of apportioning pre-separation-point costs;
(b) the optimal contribution which could be obtained from the manufacture of these products.

The following process data for October are given:

Costs incurred up to separation point £96,000

	Product A	Product B	Product C
	£	£	£
Costs incurred after separation point	20,000	12,000	8,000
Selling price per tonne:			
Completed product	500	800	600
Estimated, if sold at separation point	250	700	450
	tonnes	tonnes	tonnes
Output	100	60	80

The cost of any unused capacity after the separation point should be ignored.

(25 marks)

2

(a) Explain briefly the distinction between joint products and by-products.

(b) Discuss briefly the problems involved in calculating the cost of manufacture of joint products with particular reference to the apportionment of pre-separation-point costs.

A common method of apportioning these pre-separation-point costs is by physical measurement; outline two other methods.

(c) In a process line of the JP Manufacturing Company Limited, three joint products are produced. For the month of October the following data were available:

	Product		
	X	**Y**	**Z**
Sales price per kilogram	£5	£10	£20
Post-separation-point costs	£10,000	£5,000	£15,000
Output in kilograms	2,500	1,000	1,500

Pre-separation-point costs amounted to £20,000.

The joint products are manufactured in one common process, after which they are separated and may undergo further individual processing. The pre-separation-point costs are apportioned to joint products according to weight.

You are required:

(i) to prepare a statement showing the estimated profit or loss for each product and in total;

(ii) as an alternative to the costing system used in (i) above, to present a statement which will determine the maximum profit from the production of these joint products.

The sales value of each product at separation point is as follows:
X: £3   Y: £4   Z: £6

(30 marks)

3   From a joint process, Slowleftarm Ltd manufactures four products, known as Peel, Rhodes, Blythe and Verity. Unfortunately, the cost accountant, Lock, has thrown away some details of the process, and the information that remains is as follows:

	Peels	**Rhodeses**	**Blythes**	**Verities**	**Total**
Units produced	1,000	2,000	3,000	4,000	10,000
	£	£	£	£	£
Joint costs	A	B	1,000	1,250	3,500
Sales value at separation	2,000	C	4,000	D	E
Sales value if processed further	5,000	4,000	F	8,000	G
Additional costs of further processing	H	1,400	1,400	I	7,000
Net sales value if processed further	3,800	2,600	J	K	16,000
Gain or loss from further processing	L	M	N	O	P

You are required to calculate the fifteen missing amounts designated by the letters A to P in the above total, and to state which products should be sold at separation instead of being processed further.

Joint costs are allocated in proportion to sales value at separation.

(10 marks)

4 A company manufactures two types of industrial sealant by passing materials through two consecutive processes. The results of operating the two processes during the previous month are shown below:

Process 1	£	kg
Cost incurred:		
Materials 7,000 kilograms at £0.50 per kg	3,500	
Labour and overheads	4,340	
Output:		
Transferred to Process 2		6,430
Defective production		570

Process 2	£	kg
Cost incurred:		
Labour and overheads	12,129	
Output:		
Type E sealant		2,000
Type F sealant		4,000
By-product		430

It is considered normal for 10% of the total output from Process 1 to be defective and all defective output is sold as scrap at £0.40 per kg. Losses are not expected in Process 2.

There was no work-in-process at the beginning or end of the month and no opening stocks of sealants.

Sales of the month's output from Process 2 were:
Type E sealant	1,100 kg
Type F sealant	3,200 kg
By-product	430 kg

The remainder of the output from Process 2 was in stock at the end of the month.

The selling prices of the products are, Type E sealant £7 per kg and Type F sealant £2.50 per kg. No additional costs are incurred on either of the two main products after the second process. The by-product is sold for £1.80 per kg after being sterilized, at a cost of £0.30 per kg, in a subsequent process. The operating costs of Process 2 are reduced by the net income receivable from sales of the by-product.

You are required:

(a) to calculate, for the previous month, the cost of the output transferred from Process 1 into Process 2 and the net cost or saving arising from any abnormal losses or gains in process 1;   *(6 marks)*

(b) to calculate the value of the closing stock of each sealant and the profit earned by each sealant during the previous month using the following methods of apportioning costs to joint products:

    (i)   according to weight of output,
    (ii) according to market value of output;   *(12 marks)*

(c) to consider whether apportioning process costs to joint products is useful. Briefly illustrate with examples from your answer to (b) above.
                                                        (4 marks)
                                                   (Total 22 marks)

ANSWERS

1

(a) **Profit statement for October**

Product	Output tonnes	Selling price £	Sales revenue £	Pre-separation costs £	Post-separation costs £	Total costs £	Profit/ (loss) £
A	100	500	50,000	40,000	20,000	60,000	(10,000)
B	60	800	48,000	24,000	12,000	36,000	12,000
C	80	600	48,000	32,000	8,000	40,000	8,000
	240		146,000	96,000	40,000	136,000	10,000

It is assumed that the company sells no tonnes of output at separation, but processes further.

(b) **Optimal contribution**

(i) *Decision whether to sell at separation point*

	Sales revenue £	Post-separation costs £	Net revenue £	Estimated revenue at separation £	Decision
A	50,000	20,000	30,000	25,000	Process further
B	48,000	12,000	36,000	42,000	Sell at separation
C	48,000	8,000	40,000	36,000	Process further

(ii) *Optimal contribution statement*

	£
Revenue after separation point:	
Product A	30,000
Product B	42,000
Product C	40,000
	112,000
Costs before separation point	(96,000)
Profit	16,000

Note

'Contribution' means sales less marginal costs. The question gives no indication of the behaviour of any costs if input and, therefore, output are increased, and so the 'contribution' cannot be established. However, this plan maximises profit from the process.

2

(a) Joint products are products that arise simultaneously from the same process, each product having a significant sales value to merit classification as a main product. An example is oil refining, where diesel, petrol and paraffins are joint products.

By-products are products that arise incidentally in the production of the main product(s), and have a relatively small sales value in comparison. An example is a sawmill, where sawdust is a by-product.

The distinction between joint products and by-products is often a matter of judgment by management.

(b) Joint products incur costs before they can be separated. To establish the cost of each product, these joint costs have to be apportioned to the products on an acceptable basis. The difficulty is that any basis chosen is to a certain extent arbitrary because the cost has arisen before the products are distinguishable.

Two other methods of apportioning joint costs:

(i) According to sales value, which may be:
    (1) Market value at separation.
    (2) Market value after further processing.
    (3) Final market value less post-separation-point costs.

(ii) Weighted average method, in which all output is reduced to a common basis by technical estimation, which weights the different products.

(c) (i) *Statement of estimated profit or loss*

Product	Sales value £	Output kg	Joint costs £	Post-separation costs £	Total costs £	Profit/ (loss) £
X	12,500	2,500	10,000	10,000	20,000	(7,500)
Y	10,000	1,000	4,000	5,000	9,000	1,000
Z	30,000	1,500	6,000	15,000	21,000	9,000
Total	52,500	5,000	20,000	30,000	50,000	2,500

Decision whether to sell at separation point or to process further

	Sales value £	Post-separation costs £	Post-separation revenue £	Revenue at separation point if sold £
X	12,500	10,000	2,500	7,500
Y	10,000	5,000	5,000	4,000
Z	30,000	15,000	15,000	9,000

To maximise profits, X should be sold at separation point, Y and Z should be processed further.

Statement showing maximum profit under this scheme

		£	£
Revenue after separation	X	7,500	
(from above)	Y	5,000	
	Z	15,000	27,500
Less: Joint costs			(20,000)
Profit from production			7,500

Comment

A general question on joint products, which tests knowledge of four separate aspects of the subject at a basic level.

3 Ratio of joint costs to sales value at separation: 25% (from Blythes)

		£	
A	£2,000 × 25%	500	
D	£1,250 × 4	5,000	
E	£3,500 × 4	14,000	
C	£14,000 – (£2,000 + £4,000 + £5,000)	3,000	
B	£3,000 × 25%		
	or £3,500 – (£500 + £1,000 + £1,250)	750	
G	£16,000 + £7,000	23,000	
F	£23,000 – (£5,000 + £4,000 + £8,000)	6,000	
H	£5,000 – £3,800	1,200	
I	£7,000 – (£1,200 + £1,400 + £1,400)	3,000	
J	£6,000 – £1,400	4,600	
K	£8,000 – £3,000		
	or £16,000 – (£3,800 + £2,600 + £4,600)	5,000	
L	£3,800 – £2,000	1,800	gain
M	£2,600 – £3,000	(400)	loss
N	£4,600 – £4,000	600	gain
O	£5,000 – £5,000	nil	
P	£16,000 – £14,000		
	or 1,800 – £400 + £600 + nil	2,000	

Peels and Blythes should be processed further. Rhodeses should be sold at separation. Verities, based solely on the information provided, would generate the same contribution whether sold at separation or processed further, so the company would probably look to other factors such as demand for the unprocessed and processed products.

4

(a) **Cost of output transferred**

	kg	£
Cost of input:		
Materials	7,000	3,500
Labour and overheads	—	4,340
	7,000	7,840
Less: Normal loss	700	280
	6,300	7,560
Cost per kilogram		£1.20
Transferred to Process 2		
(6,430 kg at £1.20)		£7,716

	kg	£
Net saving from abnormal gain		
Abnormal gain at £1.20	130	156
Less: Scrap value £0.40	130	52
		104

(b) **Value of closing stocks**

	£
Joint cost — Process 2	
Cost of input	7,716
Labour and overheads	12,129
	19,845
Less : By-product net income (430 kg at £1.50)	645
	19,200

(i) **According to weight of output**

	Weight kg	Cost £	Unit cost £
Type E	2,000	6,400	3.20
Type F	4,000	12,800	3.20
	6,000	19,200	

Type E
Value of closing stocks   £3.20 × 900 kg   £2,880
                                                                   ‾‾‾‾‾‾
Profit   (£7 − £3.20) × 1,100 kg   £4,180
                                                                   ‾‾‾‾‾‾

Type F
Value of closing stocks   £3.20 × 800 kg   £2,560
                                                                   ‾‾‾‾‾‾
Profit   (£2.50 − £3.20) × 3,200 kg
Loss   (£2,240)
                                                                   ‾‾‾‾‾‾

(ii) **According to market value**

	Market value £	Cost £	Unit cost £
Type E	14,000	11,200	5.60
Type F	10,000	8,000	2.00
	24,000	19,200	

Type E
Value of closing stocks   £5.60 × 900 kg   £5,040
                                                                   ‾‾‾‾‾‾
Profit   (£7 − £5.60) × 1,100 kg   £1,540
                                                                   ‾‾‾‾‾‾

Type F
Value of closing stocks   £2.00 × 800 kg   £1,600
                                                                   ‾‾‾‾‾‾
Profit   (£2.50 − £2.00) × 3,200 kg   £1,600
                                                                   ‾‾‾‾‾‾

(c) For stock valuation purposes, cost includes all costs incurred in bringing items to their present location or condition. Hence it is necessary to apportion process costs.

However, the choice of method of apportionment is arbitrary and so apportionment is not useful for any other purposes. In fact, it can even lead to wrong decisions. For instance, under the weight of output method, Type F sealant is sold at a loss, implying that the final product is not worthwhile. Decisions should be taken ignoring any apportionment of joint costs since the process as a whole is profitable.

19 Advanced variance analysis

The four questions in this chapter introduce mix and yield variances, an idle time variance, the variable overhead efficiency variance, and also sales margin variances.

Note carefully the three-way analysis between material usage, mix and yield variances in the answer to question 1 and contrast it with the two-way (mix and yield) analysis in answer 2. The three-way analysis should always be made if there is sufficient data to do so. You may want to revise these concepts further.

STUDY REQUIREMENTS

    (a)   Sales variances in relation to budgetary control.
    (b)   Material and labour variances from standards.
    (c)   Mix and yield variances in process costing.
    (d)   Overhead variances.

QUESTIONS

1 Thomas Ltd manufactures a product known as Lykit. Each batch of seven kilograms of Lykit has the following standard production cost:

Input: Raw material		£
T	5 kilograms at £2 per kg	10
R	3 kilograms at £3 per kg	9
J	2 kilograms at £1 per kg	2
	10 kilograms	21

The expected loss of 3 kilograms has no value.

During the week ending 15 December, the following results were achieved:

Input:		£
T	1,500 kilograms at £2.20 per kg	3,300
R	1,800 kilograms at £2.90 per kg	5,220
J	700 kilograms at £1.10 per kg	770
	4,000 kilograms	9,290

Output:
3,010 kilograms of Lykit

You are required to calculate the following variances for materials:

   (i)   Total
  (ii)   Price
 (iii)   Usage
 (iv)   Mix
  (v)   Yield   *(15 marks)*

2 Martino Manufacturing's budget for 19X1 included a profit of £60,000 derived from the production and sale of 60,000 litres of DMS. The standard cost card for producing 8 litres of DMS is shown below:

	£
Materials: G: (4.5 litres at £5 per litre)	22.5
V: (4.5 litres at £3 per litre)	13.5
(1 litre normal loss)	
	36.0
Labour: (3 hours at £2 per hour)	6.0
Variable overhead (3 hours at £4 per hour)	12.0
	54.0
Fixed overhead (300% of labour cost)	18.0
	72.0
Profit (10% on selling price)	8.0
Selling price for 8 litres	80.0

The results for the year showed that 62,400 litres had been produced and sold for £620,000 at the following cost:

	£
Materials: G: (35,000 litres)	170,000
V: (32,500 litres)	98,000
Labour: (25,000 hours paid; 23,500 hours worked)	55,000
Variable overhead	100,000
Fixed overhead	130,000

You are required to produce an operating statement reconciling budgeted and actual profit.

(16 marks)

3 The AC/DC Company manufactures special electrical equipment. The management has established standard costs for many of its operations and uses a flexible budget. Overhead is applied on a basis of standard labour-hours. The rectifier assembly department operates at the following standard rates:

Standard costs
One multiplex rectifier TR-906
Materials:
4 sheets soft iron at £1.12 each
2 spools copper wire at £2.39 each
Direct-labour rate £2.50 per hour
Combined-overhead rate £2.10 per direct-labour hour

The flexible budget indicates that total overhead would amount to £4,489 and £4,989 at production levels of 500 and 600 units, respectively. The production budget for the past month called for 2,340 direct-labour hours, £2,925 variable-overhead costs, and £1,989 fixed-overhead costs. Only 550 rectifiers were produced, at the costs listed below:

Materials purchased:
3,000 sheets soft iron, £3,300
1,500 spools copper wire, £3,600

Materials used:
2,215 sheets soft iron
1,106 spools copper wire

Direct labour:
2,113 hours, £5,409.28

Overhead:
Variable costs, £2,769
Fixed costs, £2,110

Required:

(a) What is the standard time for assembling a rectifier?
(b) What is the standard unit cost?
(c) What was the material price variance during the past month?
(d) The material usage variance?
(e) The direct-labour price variance?
(f) The direct-labour efficiency variance?
(g) Variable-overhead spending variance?
(h) Variable-overhead efficiency variance?
(i) Fixed-overhead budget variance?
(j) Fixed-overhead volume variance?

Work to the nearest penny.

(20 marks)

4 Athos Ltd commences business on 1 January 19X1 and the management accountant produces a budget for the year ended 31 December 19X1.

	£
Sales (3,000 units at £200 per unit)	600,000
Standard cost of a unit:	
Materials (18 kg at £2 per kg)	36
Labour (6 hours at £2.50 per hour)	15
Variable overheads (6 hours at £4 per hour)	24
Fixed overheads (6 hours at £10 per hour)	60
Production (3,200 units)	135
Profit (3,000 units at £65)	195,000

Raw materials purchases would be 62,400 kg.

At the end of the year the financial accounts show a profit of £184,800 made up as follows:

	£	£
Sales (2,800 units)		588,000
Production (3,100 units)		
Materials purchased (62,000 kg at £2.20)	136,400	
Less: Closing stock (5,000 kg at £2.20)	(11,000)	
Cost of materials used	125,400	
Labour (20,000 hours paid, 19,000 hours worked)	48,000	
Variable overheads	71,500	
Fixed overheads	201,500	
Cost of 3,100 units	446,400	
Less: Closing stock of finished goods (3/31)	43,200	
Cost of goods sold		403,200
Actual profit		184,800

You are required:

(a) To produce revised profit and loss accounts with closing stock valued at:

    (i)   standard total absorption cost; and
    (ii) standard marginal cost. *(10 marks)*

(b) To produce an operating statement reconciling budgeted profit and actual profit shown in (a)(i). *(10 marks)*
(c) To reconcile the profit in (a)(i) and the profit given in the financial accounts. *(5 marks)*
(d) To produce a summarised operating statement reconciling budgeted contribution and the profit shown in (a)(ii). *(5 marks)*
(e) To reconcile the two profit figures in (a). *(4 marks)*

(Total 34 marks)

ANSWERS

1 (i) **Total variance**

	£
Actual cost of 3,010 kilograms output	9,290
Expected cost of actual output: $\dfrac{£21}{7} \times 3{,}010$	9,030
	260 A

(ii) **Price variance**

	Actual price £	Standard price £	Difference £	Actual usage kg	
T	2.20	2	0.20 A	1,500	300 A
R	2.90	3	0.10 F	1,800	180 F
J	1.10	1	0.10 A	700	70 A
					190 A

(iii) **Usage variance**

	Actual usage kg	Expected usage (for actual output) kg	Difference kg	Standard price £	
T	1,500	2,150	650 F	2	1,300 F
R	1,800	1,290	510 A	3	1,530 A
J	700	860	160 F	1	160 F
					70 A

(iv) **Mix variance**

	Actual mix Actual usage	Standard mix Actual usage	Difference	Standard price	
T	1,500	2,000	500 F	2	1,000 F
R	1,800	1,200	600 A	3	1,800 A
J	700	800	100 F	1	100 F
	4,000	4,000			700 A

(v) **Yield variance**   kg   £

    Actual yield   3,010

    Expected yield: $4,000 \times \dfrac{7}{10}$ 2,800

                                               210 F

    at £3 per kg   630 F

Comment

All five variances may be shown as follows:

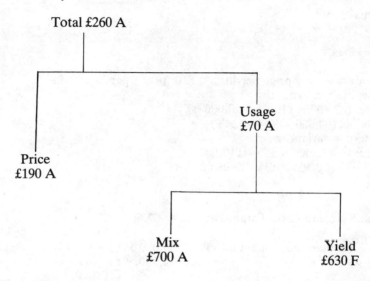

2 Operating statement for 19X1

	£	£
Budgeted profit		60,000
Sales margin variances		
Price (adverse)	(4,000)	
Volume (favourable)	2,400	
		(1,600)
		58,400

Cost variances	Favourable £	Adverse £	
Materials Price	4,500		
Mix		2,500	
Yield	10,800		
Labour Rate		5,000	
Efficiency		200	
Idle time		3,000	
Variable overhead Rate		6,000	
Efficiency		400	
Fixed overhead Expenditure	5,000		
Efficiency		600	
Capacity	6,000		
	26,300	17,700	8,600
Actual profit			67,000

Workings

Standard selling price per litre = £10; profit per litre = £1

	£
Sales margin variances:	
Price: $(62,400 \times £10) - £620,000$	4,000 (A)
Volume: $(60,000 - 62,400) \times £1$	2,400 (F)
Materials variances:	
Price: G: $(35,000 \times £5) - £170,000$	5,000 (F)
V: $(32,500 \times £3) - £ 98,000$	500 (A)
	4,500 (F)

Mix: Standard cost of standard mix = $67,500 \times \dfrac{£36}{9}$ 270,000

Standard cost of actual mix = $35,000 \times £5$ 175,000

         $32,500 \times £3$ 97,500

         272,500

Mix variance   2,500 (A)

Yield: 67,500 litres should produce   60,000 litres

        Actual yield   62,400 litres

        Difference   2,400 litres

        Yield variance = $2,400 \times \dfrac{£36}{8}$ = £10,800 (F)

Labour variances

Rate:	$(25,000 \times £2) - £55,000$	= £5,000 (A)
Efficiency:	$(\dfrac{62,400}{8} \times 3 - 23,500) \times £2$	= £200 (A)
Idle time:	$(25,000 - 23,500) \times £2$	= £3,000 (A)

Variable overhead variances

Rate: $(23,500 \times £4) - £100,000$ $=$ £6,000 (A)

Efficiency: $(\dfrac{62,400}{8} \times 3 - 23,500) \times £4$ $=$ £400 (A)

Fixed overhead variances

Expenditure: $(\dfrac{60,000}{8} \times £18) - £130,000$ $=$ £5,000 (F)

Efficiency: $(£200 \times 3)$ $=$ £600 (A)

Capacity: $(60,000 \times \dfrac{3}{8} - 23,500) \times £2 \times 3$ $=$ £6,000 (F)

Profit figures

Budget: $60,000 \times £1$ $=$ £60,000

Actual: $£620,000 - £553,000$ $=$ £67,000

3

(a) Total overhead:

		£
600	units	4,989
(500)	units	(4,489)
100		500

$$\text{Variable overhead rate} = \frac{£500}{100} = £5 \text{ per unit}$$

$$\text{Variable overhead hourly rate} = \frac{£2,925}{2,340 \text{ hours}} = £1.25 \text{ per hour}$$

$$\text{Standard time} = \frac{£5}{£1.25} = 4 \text{ hours}$$

(b)

			£	£
Materials	4 sheets × £1.12	=	4.48	
	2 spools × £2.39	=	4.78	
				9.26
Labour	(4 hours × £2.50)			10.00
Variable overhead	(4 hours × £1.25)			5.00
Fixed overhead	(4 hours × (£2.10 − £1.25))			3.40
Standard unit cost				27.66

(c)

			£
Sheets	3,000 × £0.02 (F)	=	60 F
Spools	1,500 × £0.01 (A)	=	15 A
Materials price variance			45 F

(d)	Sheets	$(550 \times 4) - 2,215 =$	$-15 \times £1.12$	$=$	£ 16.80 (A)
	Spools	$(550 \times 2) - 1,106 =$	$- 6 \times £2.39$	$=$	14.34 (A)
	Materials usage variance				31.14 (A)

(e) Direct labour rate variance
(2,113 hours × £2.50) – £5,409.28   =   £126.78 (A)

(f) Direct labour efficiency variance
(550 units × 4 hours) – 2,113 hours   = 87 hours (F) × £2.50
                                        = £217.50 (F)

(g) Variable overhead expenditure variance
(2,113 hours × £1.25) – £2,769   = £127.75 (A)

(h) Variable overhead efficiency variance
87 hours (F) × £1.25   = £108.75 (F)

(i) Fixed overhead budget variance
£2,110 – (2,340 hours × £0.85)   = £121 (A)

(j) Fixed overhead volume variance
2,340 hours – (550 × 4 hours)   = 140 hours (A) × £0.85
                                  = £119 (A)

Comment

Part (a) of this question requires the most thought, and parts (b) to (j) cannot be attempted until an answer to part (a) has been established.

The key to part (a) is the phrase 'flexible budget', which recognises the idea that as output increases, variable costs increase in proportion, but fixed costs remain unaltered. Thus the increase in costs from 500 to 600 units must be variable only, and the variable rate per unit can be calculated. This could have been calculated in the following way:

	£
Total overhead for 500 units	4,489
Fixed overhead at any level	(1,989)
Variable overhead for 500 units	2,500

Rate per unit £5.

The variable rate per hour can be calculated, and hence the number of hours.

If presented with a question such as this in an examination, a student must attempt all parts to gain the marks. If the student cannot answer part (a), then a figure for standard time should be put in to show the examiner that the student understands variance analysis.

In this example, a calculated guess is not difficult; 2,113 labour hours have been used to make 550 units, so 4 hours is a sensible estimate.

Material price variance has been recognised on purchase.

Fixed overhead budget variance is a term sometimes used for expenditure variance.

4

(a) **Revised profit and loss accounts**

(i) *Stock at standard total absorption cost*

	£ thousands	£ thousands
Sales		588.0
Cost of sales:		
Materials	136.4	
Less: Closing stock (5,000 kg at £2)	(10.0)	
	126.4	
Labour	48.0	
Variable overheads	71.5	
Fixed overheads	201.5	
Cost of producing 3,100 units	447.4	
Less: Closing stock (300 kg at £135)	(40.5)	
		406.9
Actual profit		181.1

(ii) *Stock at standard marginal cost*

	£ thousands	£ thousands
Sales		588.0
Cost of sales:		
Cost of producing 3,100 units (as above)	447.4	
Less: Closing stock (300 kg at £75)	(22.5)	
		424.9
Actual profit		163.1

(b) **Operating statement: total absorption costing**

	Favourable	Adverse	
	£ thousands	£ thousands	£ thousands
Budgeted profit			195.0
Sales margin variances			
Price	28		
Volume		13	
			15.0
		c/f	210.0

	Favourable	Adverse	
	£ thousands	£ thousands	£ thousands
			b/f 210.0

Cost variances

		Favourable	Adverse
Materials:	Price		12.4
	Usage		2.4
Labour:	Rate	2.0	
	Efficiency		1.0
	Idle time		2.5
Variable overheads:	Rate	4.5	
	Efficiency		1.6
		6.5	19.9
Fixed overheads:	Expenditure		9.5
	Efficiency		4.0
	Capacity		2.0
			35.4
			6.5

	28.9
Actual profit	181.1

(c) Reconciliation of profit figures

	£
Profit per financial accounts	184,800
Profit per operating statement	181,100
Difference	3,700

This difference arises as a result of the different stock valuations. In the first case stock is valued at actual cost, in the second at standard cost.

	£
Stock at actual cost (£43,200 + £11,000)	54,200
Stock at standard cost (£40,500 + £10,000)	50,500
Difference	3,700

If an operating statement were required reconciling budgeted profit with the figure shown in the financial accounts, then some of the cost variances shown in (b) would need to be capitalised (carried forward in the stock valuation) and only a proportion of the variances set against budgeted profit.

	£
Materials price variance carried forward in raw materials stock (5/62 of £12,400)	1,000
Total cost variances carried forward in finished goods (300/3,100 of (£28,900 – £1,000))	2,700
Total variances capitalised	3,700

(d) Operating statement: marginal costing

	£	£
Budgeted contribution		375.0
Sales margin variances		
Price (favourable)	28.0	
Volume (adverse)	(25.0)	
		3.0
		378.0
Cost variances		
Materials, labour, variable overheads (adverse)		(13.4)
Actual contribution		364.6
Fixed costs		
Budgeted overheads	192.0	
Expenditure variance (adverse)	9.5	
Actual overheads		(201.5)
Actual profit		163.1

(e) Reconciliation of profit figures

	£
Profit under total absorption costing	181,100
Profit under marginal costing	163,100
Difference	18,000

This difference is purely due to different stock valuations.

	£
Stock of finished goods at total absorption cost	40,500
Stock of finished goods at marginal cost	22,500
Difference: 300 units of fixed overhead cost (£60/unit) carried forward in stock under total absorption costing	18,000

Workings

Calculation of variances for total absorption costing

Sales		
Price: (2,800 units × £200) – £588,000	£28,000	F
Volume: (3,000 units – 2,800 units) × £65	£13,000	A

Materials		
Price: 62,000 kg × (£2 – £2.20)	£12,400	A
Usage: (3,100 units × 18 kg – 57,000 kg) × £2	£2,400	A

Labour
Rate: (20,000 hours × £2.50) – £48,000   £2,000 F
Idle time: (20,000 hours – 19,000 hours) × £2.50   £2,500 A
Efficiency: (3,100 units × 6 hours – 19,000 hours) × £2.50   £1,000 A

Variable overheads
Rate: (19,000 hours × £4) – £71,500   £4,500 F
Efficiency: (18,600 hours – 19,000 hours) × £4   £1,600 A

Fixed overheads
Expenditure: (£60 × 3,200) – £201,500   £9,500 A
Efficiency: (18,600 hours – 19,000 hours) × £10   £4,000 A
Capacity: (19,000 hours – 19,200 hours) × £10   £2,000 A

Calculation of variances for marginal costing

Sales volume: (3,000 units – 2,800 units) × £125   £25,000 A
Under marginal costing, there is only one fixed overhead variance:
£9,500 A expenditure variance.

20 Standard marginal costing

Under a marginal costing system, fixed costs are written off as they are incurred. There is no absorption of fixed overheads; and thus no absorption variances. Variable costs can be accounted for on the basis of either actual costs or standard costs with variance analysis. In the latter event, the system in use is sometimes referred to as 'standard marginal costing'. This chapter gives two examples of standard marginal costing.

STUDY REQUIREMENTS

(a) Standard costing and basic variance analysis, as for Chapter 14, excluding fixed overhead recovery variances.

(b) Marginal costing, as for Chapter 17.

QUESTIONS

1 LMJ Ltd makes china ornaments. The standard cost card shows:

Materials (100 g)	2.00
Wages (5 hours at £1)	5.00
Variable overheads	1.25
Standard marginal cost	8.25
Standard contribution	1.75
Standard selling price	£10.00

You obtain the following information for October 19X7:

Budget:	Sales	2,000 units	
	Fixed overheads	£3,000	
Actual:	Sales effected	2,200 units for	£23,600
	Production	2,500 units	
	Materials used	255 kg for	£5,300
	Wages paid	13,000 hours for	£13,400
	Variable overheads	12,600 hours for	£3,780
	Fixed overheads		£3,150

There was no opening or closing stock of material nor any opening stock of finished goods or work-in-progress. Variable overheads are absorbed on the basis of labour hours worked.

You are required to prepare, for the month of October 19X7:

(a) An operating statement along marginal costing lines.
(b) A reconciliation of the profit shown by your statement with that shown in the financial accounts.

(20 marks)

2 DJ Ltd publishes an annual edition of a sporting book known as 'The Skipper'. For the forthcoming edition the following budget has ben prepared:

	£
Materials	16,000
Labour	20,000
Variable overhead	10,000
Fixed overhead	15,000
Total costs	61,000
Sales revenue	80,000
Budgeted profit	19,000

Sales were expected to be 4,000 books. Each book uses 0.4 kg of material and two hours of labour. DJ Ltd operates a standard marginal costing system, absorbing variable overhead on the basis of labour hours.

At the end of the year it was discovered that, although actual production was 4,000 books as planned, actual sales fell 500 short of the budget. Actual costs turned out to be as follows:

	£
Materials (1,760 kg)	14,080
Labour (7,600 hours)	22,800
Variable overhead	11,400
Fixed overhead	14,720
	63,000

Sales Revenue amounted to £77,000.

There were no opening stocks of raw materials. However, during the year David, the managing director of DJ Ltd, took advantage of a liquidation sale to buy 2,000 kg of materials at £4 per kg. The entire closing stock of 200 kg of materials came from this special purchase.

It is the company's policy to value all stocks at standard cost.

You are required to prepare an operating statement and to comment on the closing stock valuation of raw materials. *(24 marks)*

ANSWERS

1   Operating statement October 19X7

	£	£	£
Budgeted contribution			3,500
Sales variances:			
Price		1,600 (F)	
Volume		350 (F)	
			1,950
			5,450
Marginal-cost variances:			
Materials: Price	200 (A)		
Usage	100 (A)		
Labour: Rate of pay	400 (A)		
Efficiency	100 (A)		
Idle time	400 (A)		
Variable: Expenditure	630 (A)		
Efficiency	25 (A)		
			(1,855)
Actual contribution			3,595
Less: Fixed overheads: Budget		3,000	
Expenditure variance		150 (A)	
			(3,150)
Net profit			445

Reconciliation of net profit

	£	£
Sales		23,600
Less: Cost of sales:		
Materials	5,300	
Labour	13,400	
Variables	3,780	
	22,480	
Less: Closing stock (300 at £8.25)	(2,475)	
		(20,005)
		3,595
Less: Fixed overheads		(3,150)
Net profit		445

Calculation of variances

			£	
Materials:	Price	(£5,300 – £5,100)	200	(A)
	Usage	(255 kg – 250 kg) at £20 per kg	100	(A)
Labour:	Rate of pay	(£13,400 – £13,000)	400	(A)
	Efficiency	(12,600 – 12,500) hours at £1	100	(A)
	Idle time	(13,000 – 12,600) hours at £1	400	(A)
Variable:	Expenditure	(£3,780 – £3,150)	630	(A)
	Efficiency	(12,600 – 12,500) hours at 25p	25	(A)
Fixed:	Expenditure	(£3,150 – £3,000)	150	(A)
Sales:	Price	(£23,600 – £22,000)	1,600	(F)
	Volume	(2,200 – 2,000) at £1.75	350	(F)

Comment

An operating statement under standard marginal costing has the following features:

(a) The starting point is budgeted contribution.
(b) The sales volume variance shows the effect on contribution of changing the sales turnover.
(c) All variable cost variances are set out before fixed costs are deducted.
(d) There is only one fixed overhead variance.

	£ F	£ A	£
Budgeted contribution			34,000
Sales variances			
Price	7,000		
Volume		4,250	2,750
			36,750
Cost variances			
Materials: Price	3,520		
Usage	400		
Labour: Rate		3,800	
Efficiency	1,000		
Variable overhead: Expenditure		1,900	
Efficiency	500		
	5,420	5,700	280
Actual contribution			36,470
Less: Fixed overhead:			
Budget		15,000	
Less: Favourable expenditure variance		280	
			14,720
Actual profit			21,750

Workings

Standard cost card

	Total cost (÷ 4,000) £		Unit cost £
Materials	16,000	0.4 kg at £10	4.00
Labour	20,000	2 hrs at £2.50	5.00
Variable overhead	10,000	2 hrs at £1.25	2.50
	46,000		11.50
Sales	80,000		20.00
Contribution	34,000		8.50

Actual contribution

	£	£
Sales		77,000
Less: Cost of sales		
Materials	14,080	
Less: closing stock (200 at £10)	2,000	
	12,080	
Labour	22,800	
Variable overhead	11,400	
	46,280	
Less: Closing stock (500 at £11.50)	5,750	
		40,530
		36,470

Calculations of variances

			£
Materials:	Price:	Actual cost	14,080
		Standard cost (1,760 at £10)	17,600
			3,520 F

			kg
	Usage:	Actual quantity used (1,760 − 200)	1,560
		Expected quantity for 4,000 books	1,600
			40
		at £10 per kg	£400 F

			£
Labour:	Rate:	Actual cost	22,800
		Standard cost (7,600 hrs at £2.50)	19,000
			3,800 A

			hrs
	Efficiency:	Actual hours	7,600
		Expected hours for 4,000 books	8,000
			400
		at £2.50 per hour	£1,000 F

			£
Variable overhead:	Expenditure:	Actual cost	11,400
		Expected cost	
		(7,600 hrs at £1.25)	9,500
			1,900 A
	Efficiency: 400 hours at £1.25		500 F

			£
Fixed overhead:	Expenditure:	Actual cost	14,720
		Expected cost	15,000
			280 F

			£
Sales:	Price:	Actual Revenue	77,000
		Expected Revenue (3,500 at £20)	70,000
			7,000 F

		Books
Volume:	Actual volume	3,500
	Budgeted volume	4,000
		500
	at £8.50 contribution	£4,250 A

Comment on the closing stock valuation of raw materials.

Since the special purchase represents the whole of the closing stock, it would be more appropriate to value the stock at the discounted purchase price of £4 rather than at standard cost of £10. This would have the effect of spreading the benefit of the cheap purchase over the related sales rather than crediting the entire benefit as a favourable price variance this time.

21 Costing and inflation

A condition of inflation is characterised by frequent increases in prices and wage rates, which can be difficult to forecast. These changes will create problems in, for example, budgeting, variance analysis and decision-making.

This chapter contains two questions taken from advanced-level examination papers.

Question 1 gives you an opportunity to identify in more detail the problems you can envisage and possible solutions to them. The answer necessarily includes a reference to 'inflation accounting', but it should be noted that as yet there is no comprehensive system of this kind in common use.

Question 2 provides a numerical example to illustrate some of the above problems.

STUDY REQUIREMENTS

(a) Your previous studies of cost accounting, budgetary control, standard costing and contribution analysis all provide material which can suggest possible problems and solutions.

(b) Any material on profit reporting under conditions of inflation will be helpful; for example the explanatory notes in SSAP 16, 'Current Cost Accounting'.

QUESTIONS

1 You have just been appointed cost accountant to a manufacturing company.

You are required to discuss:

(a) The problems in maintaining the company's costing system you would expect to face as a direct result of rapid inflation.
(b) The procedures you would endeavour to adopt in order to overcome those problems.
(c) The additional difficulties to those at (a) above you would expect if the system were a standard costing system.

(20 marks)

2 In the year ended 31 December 19X5 the actual costs, output, and sales of a company manufacturing a range of products were as follows:

	Product			
	A	B	C	D
Per unit:	£	£	£	£
Selling price	20	40	50	30
Variable costs:				
Direct materials	4	9	10	3
Direct wages	3	5	10	4
	units	units	units	units
Manufactured and sold	7,500	5,000	3,000	6,000

Variable overhead was incurred at a rate of 200% of direct wages.

Fixed overhead was £200,000 for the year.

The company's summarised budgeted results for the year ended 31 December 19X5 were:

	£
Sales	700,000
Variable cost of sales	455,000
Contribution	245,000
Fixed overhead	190,000
Budgeted profit	55,000

In preparing its budget for the year ending 31 December 19X6 the company has made the following allowances for inflation over the actual figures for 19X5:

(i) An increase in all selling prices of 10%; these increases are not expected to alter the quantities of each product sold, as compared with 19X5.
(ii) An increase in unit product costs of:

	%
Direct materials	10
Direct wages	20
Variable overhead	10

(iii) An increase of 2% in fixed overhead.

In addition to those allowances for inflation, the company proposes the following changes in its cost, sales volume, and selling price structure:

Product A   Increase the price by 10%, yielding a reduction of 5% in volume sold.

Product B   Use different direct materials which will reduce direct materials cost by £2 per unit and reduce volume sold by 4%.

Product C   (i) Incur advertising cost of £10,000 for the year which is expected to increase sales by 20%.
(ii) Buy a machine costing £8,000 which would reduce direct labour hours by 20% for the same grades of labour.

Product D   Reduce the selling price by 10%, giving an increase in sales volume of 15%.

Increase stocks held by an average of £40,000 over the whole year; this would be financed by bank overdraft at an interest rate of 12% per annum.

Increase the size of the delivery van fleet at an outlay of £9,000 and an increase in annual fixed costs of £2,000 (excluding depreciation).

The company calculates its depreciation on a straight-line basis with a standard life of five years for production equipment and three years for non-production equipment.

You are required:

 (a)   To show, in a format helpful to management, a summary statement of the budgeted and actual results for the year ended 31 December 19X5 with an analysis of the difference between the two profits.

 (b)   To compile a budgeted profit and loss account for the company for the year ending 31 December 19X6 after taking account of:

   (i)   allowances for inflation only;
   (ii) allowances for inflation and the additional changes proposed.

 (c)   To calculate (to the nearest £1,000) the separate break-even points for the actual results of the year ended 31 December 19X5 and budget for 1976 at (b) (ii) above.

 (d)   To comment very briefly on:

   (i)   the differences between the results of (b) (i) and (b) (ii) above;
   (ii) the implications for the company of the results of (c) above.

(35 marks)

ANSWERS

1

(a) The costing system provides information for a number of purposes, including the following:

    (i) The determination of costs and hence profit for an accounting period.

    (ii) The valuation of inventories.

    (iii) Planning, e.g. operating budgets.

    (iv) Control, e.g. comparison of results with budget.

    (v) Decision-making, e.g. setting prices based on cost.

Each of the above functions is impaired by rapid inflation:

    (i) Profits and balance sheets based on historic costs become meaningless. Profits, in general, are overstated, while asset values are too low.

    (ii) Inventories valued using FIFO or average price will result in holding gains as well as operating profit, with the danger of underpricing jobs.

    (iii) Inflation has to be built into budgets, which is difficult.

    (iv) Large unfavourable variances may result from budget over-spending.

    (v) Decisions based on out-of-date costs may be the wrong decisions.

(b) To overcome these problems, the following suggestions are made:

    (i) Accounts may be prepared using a form of inflation accounting, so that assets are stated at up-to-date values.

    (ii) Stocks may be valued at LIFO or replacement cost.

    (iii) Budgets may be prepared more frequently.

    (iv) An attempt may be made to reduce costs that are most prone to rapid inflation.

    (v) The flow of information may be speeded up so that decisions are based on current costs.

(c) A standard costing system would be subject to the following additional difficulties:

    (i) Standards have to be changed more frequently, a costly and time-consuming process.

    (ii) Unfavourable variances are the rule, rather than the exception. This results in two consequences:

        (1) The variance analysis is less useful as an explanation of what has happened.

        (2) There are motivational problems amongst those responsible for the variances.

(iii) Although unfavourable variances may arise frequently, it is possible to generate favourable variances by overestimating the rate of inflation.

2

(a) **Statement of results for the year ended 31 December 19X5**

	Budgeted results £	Actual results £	Budget variances £
Sales	700,000	680,000	20,000 A
Variable costs of sales	(455,000)	(427,500)	27,500 F
Contribution	245,000	252,500	7,500 F
Fixed overhead	(190,000)	(200,000)	10,000 A
Profit	55,000	52,500	2,500 F

(b) **Budgeted profit and loss accounts for the year ending 31 December 19X6**

	(i) Allowing for inflation only £	(ii) Allowing for inflation and additional changes £
Sales	748,000	786,555
Variable cost of sales	(480,400)	(477,675)
Contribution	267,600	308,880
Fixed overhead	(204,000)	(225,400)
Profit	63,600	83,480

(c) **Break-even points (assuming a constant product mix)**

Fixed costs	£200,000	£225,400
Contribution per unit	$\frac{£252,500}{21,500} = £11.74$	$\frac{£308,880}{22,425} = £13.77$
Break-even point in units	17,030	16,364

(d) (i) The higher contribution generated by b(ii) more than covers the rise in fixed costs, resulting in a higher profit. Appendix 3 gives details of the different products, and the changes suggested for products A, B and C all increase contribution. The changes suggested for product D do not increase its contribution, and result in higher extra stockholding and delivery costs.

(ii) The break-even point in 19X6 is lower, and the margin of safety is higher. This means that unit sales can fall by a higher percentage before a loss will be sustained.

Note

The rise in profit between b(i) and b(ii) does not take account of any gains that may arise through holding extra stocks in times of price increases.

Appendices

1 Details of actual results for year ended 31 December 19X5

		A		B		C		D	Total
Units		7,500		5,000		3,000		6,000	21,500
		£		£		£		£	
Selling price		20		40		50		30	
Revenue		150,000		200,000		150,000		180,000	680,000

Variable costs	Unit	Total	U	T	U	T	U	T
	£	£	£	£	£	£	£	£
Materials	4	30,000	9	45,000	10	30,000	3	18,000
Wages	3	22,500	5	25,000	10	30,000	4	24,000
Overhead	6	45,000	10	50,000	20	60,000	8	48,000
	13		24		40		15	
Total		97,500		120,000		120,000		90,000 427,500

2 Allowances for inflation

		A		B		C		D	Total
Selling price		22		44		55		33	
Sales revenue plus 10%		165,000		220,000		165,000		198,000	748,000
Variable costs:									
Materials plus 10%	4.4	33,000	9.9	49,500	11	33,000	3.3	19,800
Wages plus 20%	3.6	27,000	6.0	30,000	12	36,000	4.8	28,800
Overhead plus 10%	6.6	49,500	11.0	55,000	22	66,000	8.8	52,800
	14.6		26.9		45		16.9		
		109,500		134,500		135,000		101,400	480,400

3 Allowances for inflation plus proposed changes

	A	B	C	D	Total
Units	7,125	4,800	3,600	6,900	22,425
	£	£	£	£	
Selling price	24.2	44	55	29.7	
Sales revenue	172,425	211,200	198,000	204,930	786,555
Variable costs:	£	£	£	£	
Materials	4.4	7.9	11.0	3.3	
Wages	3.6	6.0	9.6	4.8	
Overhead	6.6	11.0	17.6	8.8	
	14.6	24.9	38.2	16.9	
Total	104,025	119,520	137,520	116,610	477,675

Fixed

Overhead £204,000 + £10,000 + $\dfrac{£8,000}{5}$ + (£40,000 × 12%) + $\dfrac{£9,000}{3}$ + £2,000   225,400

22 Performance measurement

Performance measurement, as illustrated in the two questions in this chapter and as it occurs in examination questions, is commonly based on ratio analysis.

In addition to accounting ratios, you should be able to suggest physical measures of performance such as the output of work for a given input of working time. In this connection you should refer back to the activity, capacity usage and efficiency measures used in variance analysis. You must also be prepared to envisage practical reasons for volume, price and cost changes, some of which may arise from your own working experience.

STUDY REQUIREMENTS

(a) Performance evaluation techniques.
(b) Profitability ratios and their derivatives.
(c) Past studies of variance analysis and of cost-volume-profit analysis.

QUESTIONS

1 AB Ltd manufactures two products, P and Q, which are normally made in a standard grade of material.

On some occasions AB Ltd receives orders for its products to be made in a much more expensive material, whilst on others customers place orders for the two products but require special material to be used that the customer provides as a free issue. Neither of these variations from the normal procedure alters the conversion cost of the products manufactured.

Data on the company's products are as follows:

	Product P	Product Q
Per unit of product:		
Direct materials, in metres	5	10
Direct labour, in man-hours	4	6
Selling price:	£	£
Using standard material	28	47
Using expensive material	68	127
Using free-issue material	18	27
Cost of material, per metre	£	
Standard	2	
Expensive	10	

Rate of pay for direct labour, £1 per hour

Variable overhead is 50% of direct wages

Fixed overhead is absorbed at a rate of £2 per man-hour

Budgeted man-hours per period are 4,400

For each of three successive periods, Nos 7, 8 and 9, AB Ltd's total output in numbers of each product was identical, but the proportions of each produced in standard material, expensive material, and free-issue material varied as shown below. Opening and closing stocks were the same for each period.

Number of units of product:	Period 7		Period 8		Period 9	
	P	Q	P	Q	P	Q
Made in:						
Standard material	300	300	200	100	250	100
Expensive material	100	50	300	250	50	50
Free-issue material	100	50	—	50	200	250
Total	500	400	500	400	500	400

AB Ltd prepares periodic accounts, and the managing director views with special interest the ratio of profit as a percentage of sales.

You are required:

   (a) To calculate the percentage of profit to sales for each of periods 7, 8 and 9.

   (b) To state whether or not you consider the ratio of profit to sales to be a satisfactory index of periodic performance for AB Ltd; explain very briefly your views.

   (c) State what other indices of profit performance (that can be drawn from the data available in this question) the managing director of AB Ltd could advantageously use. List their advantages over the percentage of profit to sales.

(20 marks)

2   You are advising a cheese wholesaler who sells four main products through a large number of depots. The accounting system is weak and the directors have in the past had little reliable information about depot profitability. You have assembled the data available for the last financial year about depot profitability for all depots which reveals a wide disparity in depot results. Data for three depots with good profitability, and three bad depots, together with other information which you have obtained, are set out below:

Comparative table of depot profitability for the year ended 31 December 19X1

	Depot					
	A	**B**	**C**	**D**	**E**	**F**
Sales in tonnes	58.5	22.6	18.0	46.6	37.9	52.7
			£ thousands			
Sales value	681.2	272.1	214.5	540.7	456.5	594.9
Gross margin on sales	29.0	11.7	9.2	24.2	19.6	25.0
Operating expenses	15.8	12.9	8.4	21.3	9.1	12.2
Transport costs	9.6	3.7	2.5	8.5	1.4	10.2
Charges for transport recovered (where shown separately on sales invoices)	(9.6)	(3.1)	—	(0.8)	(1.4)	(10.2)
Total costs (net of transport recoveries)	15.8	13.5	10.9	29.0	9.1	12.2
Profit/(Loss)	13.2	(1.8)	(1.7)	(4.8)	10.5	12.8

Sales are effected from depots by representatives to retail shops, multiples, hotels, restaurants and other large and small outlets. It is a weekly trade and representatives are notified each week the minimum prices at which they can sell large orders of each product. Due to varying local market conditions, varying sizes of sales orders and the infrequency of some orders, representatives have opportunities to obtain better than minimum prices and are expected so to do. Delivery charges are made for use of transport delivering from depots to

299

customers either separately or in the selling prices charged; these charges are standard according to the vehicle used and the size of order. No discounts are given. Sales invoices are issued weekly.

Because of the large number of depots, the company has been unable as a routine to account in the costing and financial books for the movement of stocks into and out of depots. For this reason, supplies are charged to depots according to the sales of each week at prices which are designed to give depots a standard gross margin for all products on the minimum selling prices set.

Each depot is the responsibility of a manager and its operations include selling by representatives, operation of the depot store, operation of a local transport fleet and an accounting and general office.

You are required:

(a) To specify, using the data given in the table, four indices or ratios which you would use to rank the performance of the six depots.

(b) To suggest four reasons for the seeming failure fully to recover transport costs in all cases.

(c) To specify three sales factors which you would consider critical in terms of weekly control of depot profitability by top management, giving your reasons.

(15 marks)

ANSWERS

1

	P			Q		
	Standard material	Expensive material	Special material	Standard material	Expensive material	Special material
	£	£	£	£	£	£
Selling price	28	68	18	47	127	27
Costs per unit:						
Material	10	50	—	20	100	—
Labour	4	4	4	6	6	6
Variable overhead	2	2	2	3	3	3
	16	56	6	29	109	9
Contribution per unit	12	12	12	18	18	18

(a) **Profit as a percentage of sales for periods 7, 8 and 9**

		Period 7		Period 8		Period 9
Contribution:	P	6,000		6,000		6,000
	Q	7,200		7,200		7,200
		13,200		13,200		13,200
Less: fixed costs: 4,400 × £2		(8,800)		(8,800)		(8,800)
Profit		4,400		4,400		4,400

Sales:	P	300 × £28	8,400	200 × £28	5,600	250 × £28	7,000
		100 × £68	6,800	300 × £68	20,400	50 × £68	3,400
		100 × £18	1,800	—	—	200 × £18	3,600
			17,000		26,000		14,000
	Q	300 × £47	14,100	100 × £47	4,700	100 × £47	4,700
		50 × £127	6,350	250 × £127	31,750	50 × £127	6,350
		50 × £27	1,350	50 × £27	1,350	250 × £27	6,750
			38,800		63,800		31,800
Profit to sales			11.34%		6.90%		13.84%

(b) The percentage of profit to sales is misleading. The selling price of each product fluctuates with the type of material used; the extra cost of expensive material (£40 and £80) is added on to selling price, while the products made from free-issue material are sold at standard selling price, less the usual cost of materials.

(c) A more sensible index of profit performance should exclude these material fluctuations. There are three possibilities from the data:

(i) *Profit as a percentage of sales less material costs*

This establishes a settled 'net' selling price of £18 for P and £27 for Q, regardless of the type of material. Net sales for all three periods, total £19,000 (500 × £18 + 400 × £27), giving the same percentage of 22.22%.

(ii) *Profit as a percentage of labour cost*

Labour cost is a constant input. For each quarter it totals £4,400 (500 × £64 + 400 × £6), giving a constant percentage of 100%.

(iii) *Profit as a percentage of conversion cost*

Conversion cost is the cost of converting raw materials into finished goods.

	P	**Q**	**Total**
Labour	4	6	
Variable overhead	2	3	
Fixed overhead	8	12	
	14	21	
Units	500	400	
	7,000	8,400	15,400

$$\frac{4,400}{15,400} = 28.57\%$$

Again, material fluctuations are eliminated.

2

(a) Four indices or ratios which would be used to rank the performance of the six depots are:

(i)   profit or loss as a percentage of sales value;
(ii) the percentage of gross margin to sales value;
(iii) operating expenses per tonne sold; and
(iv) the percentage of transport costs recovered.

Using the data for depot A given in the table:

(i)   Profit as a percentage of sales value $= \dfrac{13.2}{681.2} \times 100 = 1.9\%$

(ii) The percentage of gross margin to sales value $= \dfrac{29.0}{681.2} \times 100 = 4.3\%$

(iii) Operating expenses per tonne sold $\dfrac{£15.8}{58.5} = £0.27$

(iv) The percentage of transport costs recovered $= \dfrac{9.6}{9.6} \times 100 = 100\%$

(b) (i) In some cases transport charges to customers are included in the selling price, so that the recovery of these charges would not be apparent from the data available. The representatives may negotiate a price above the minimum for a product on the understanding that no separate charge for transport will be made. This fact may explain the apparent under-recovery of transport charges for depots B, C and D.

(ii) The transport charges are standard according to the vehicle used and the size of order. No account is taken of the distance involved except perhaps in the calculations underlying the standard charges. It appears, therefore, that the same charge will be made for a 3-tonne load on a 5-tonne van for a distance of one mile as for a distance of twenty miles. If average journey distances are greater than those envisaged when the standards were computed, transport costs will not be recouped.

(iii) The calculations of the standard charges for transport may not be correct. Variable operating expenses may have increased above the levels set when the standard was computed. The total mileage run during the period may be lower than was expected when the standards were computed so that the mileage is insufficient to recoup the fixed charges at the established rate. The incidence of accidents, the cost of repairs, and perhaps the hire of alternative transport equipment may exceed the budgeted level.

(iv) The pattern of journeys undertaken may be different from that envisaged when the standard charge was computed. It may be that the number of single journeys undertaken by the vehicles is greater than was expected. If the vehicles are routed with greater expertise, the number of empty return journeys will be reduced and the volume of unused capacity on vehicles for outward journeys will be diminished.

(c) Three sales factors considered critical in terms of weekly control of depot profitability by top management, together with reasons, are as follows:

(i) Volume of turnover. Since the company operates on low gross margins, a high turnover is essential if fixed costs are to be covered and a satisfactory rate of return on capital obtained.

(ii) Average product selling prices. Representatives have opportunities of obtaining orders at higher than minimum prices. In order to ensure that these opportunities are taken, it is essential that data be made available relating to average product selling prices as compared with the notified minima. Comparative information from other depots would help to raise standards.

(iii) Product mix. Variations in product gross margins on minimum prices will not be reflected in depot results because of the employment of a standard gross margin for charging all products to depots. Consideration of depot turnover and actual gross margin by products is therefore essential, so that each manager can concentrate sales effort on the most profitable products, and is aware of the profit significance of the various products sold.

23 Linear programming

In examinations in cost accounting, it is likely that you will be required to make use only of simple linear programming techniques, using a graphical solution.

The object will be the maximisation of profit or contribution or cash flow — the three aspects that are illustrated in the questions in this chapter.

STUDY REQUIREMENTS

(a) Operational research: linear programming.
(b) Contribution analysis.

QUESTIONS

1 Barton Ltd manufactures two sorts of ornamental monkeys known as the Joe and the Alex. The following production details are relevant:

	Joe	Alex
Per unit		
Contribution	£6	£5
Mixing department hours	3	4
Glazing department hours	2	1
Polishing department hours	4	3

Each department has a limited number of hours available for the forthcoming budget period, as follows:

	hours
Mixing	600
Glazing	250
Polishing	720

You are required:

(a) to formulate the linear programming problem for the above information;
(b) to solve the problem graphically;
(c) to state the optimal production plan and the associated contribution.

2 The Shamrock Rubber Company makes two products, elastic bands and pencil rubbers. One elastic band yields a contribution of 80p and requires 50 g of rubber and 4 labour hours; one pencil rubber yields a contribution of £1 and requires 100 g of rubber plus 2 labour hours. The company can obtain a daily supply of up to 2.5 kg of rubber and has a permanent labour force of 1 full-time and 1 part-time worker, who control the automatic machines to provide the equivalent of 110 labour hours per day. What production schedule would you formulate to yield as large a net cash flow as possible and what is this cash flow?

(15 marks)

3 Wisden Ltd can manufacture four products: bats, stumps, gloves and pads. Details for the products are:

	Bats £	Set of stumps £	Pair of gloves £	Pair of pads £
Selling price per unit	40	20	2	20
Variable costs per unit	32	15	1	9
Planing machine: hours per unit	1	3	—	—
Timber department labour: Hours per unit	5	2	—	—
Stitching department labour: Hours per unit	—	—	$1/_2$	6

Each month, the following resources are available:

Planing machine	6,000 hours
Timber department labour	10,500 hours
Stitching department labour	500 hours

You are required to determine the monthly production plan that would maximise profits.

(15 marks)

1

(a) Let x be the number of units of monkey Joe.
Let y be the number of units of monkey Alex.
Let C be the total contribution.

The objective function to be maximised, is:

$$C = 6x + 5y$$

The constraints are as follows:

Mixing time	$3x + 4y \leqslant 600$
Glazing time	$2x + y \leqslant 250$
Polishing time	$4x + 3y \leqslant 720$

To summarise, the linear programming problem is to maximise:

$$C = 6x + 5y$$
$$\text{subject to} \quad 3x + 4y \leqslant 600$$
$$2x + y \leqslant 250$$
$$4x + 3y \leqslant 720$$
$$\text{and} \quad x, y \geqslant 0$$

(b)

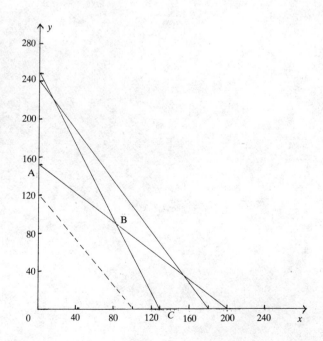

The graph is drawn by plotting the equations:

$3x + 4y = 600$ when $y = 0, x = 200$
                      when $x = 0, y = 150$
$2x + \ y = 250$ when $y = 0, x = 125$
                      when $x = 0, y = 250$
and
$4x + 3y = 720$ when $y = 0, x = 180$
                      when $x = 0, y = 240$

and by finding the slope of the objective function:

Let $C = 600 = 6x + 5y$

     when $y = 0, x = 100$
     when $x = 0, y = 120$

The polygon 0ABC is the feasible region. The point in the feasible region at which the objective function is furthest away from the origin is point B. This is therefore the optimal solution.

At point B:

     $3x + 4y = 600$; and
     $2x + \ y = 250$

This may be solved simultaneously: multiply the second equation by 4:

     $8x + 4y = 1{,}000$

and subtract the first from it:

     $5x = 400$
     $x = 80$

substituting this into the first equation:

     $240 + 4y = 600$
           $4y = 360$
             $y = \ 90$

The optimal plan is to manufacture 80 of monkey Joe and 90 of monkey Alex. The contribution from this plan will be (£6 × 80) + (£5 × 90) i.e., £930.

2 Let the company produce x elastic bands and y pencil rubbers daily, and let C equal the daily cash flow.

Constraints on this production are:

Quantity of rubber: $50x + 100y \leqslant 2{,}500$
$$\text{i.e. } x + 2y \leqslant 50$$
Labour hours: $4x + 2y \leqslant 110$
$$\text{i.e. } 2x + y \leqslant 55$$

Production cannot be negative.
$x \geqslant 0; \qquad y \geqslant 0$

Objective function maximise:
$C = 0.80x + y$

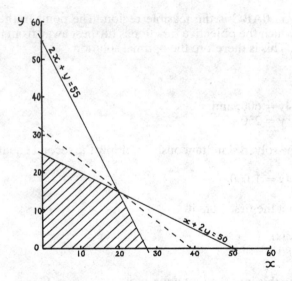

In the graph the shaded area is the feasible region. The broken line represents the objective function which meets the feasible region at the point of intersection of the lines $x + 2y = 50$ and $2x + y = 55$. To solve the two equations simultaneously multiply the first by 2.

$$2x + 4y = 100$$
and subtract the second from it.

$$
\begin{aligned}
2x + 4y &= 100 \\
2x + \ y &= 55 \\
3y &= 45 \\
y &= 15
\end{aligned}
$$

Substitute back in the first:
$$
\begin{aligned}
x + 2 \times 15 &= 50 \\
x &= 20
\end{aligned}
$$

310

So for maximum net cash flow the company should make 20 elastic bands and 15 pencil rubbers each day. With this production the net cash flow is

$$C = £0.8 \times 20 + £1 \times 15$$
$$= £31$$

3 Although at first glance this looks complicated (an objective function with four variables), the question may be reduced to a simple linear programming exercise by recognising that two of the products are governed by two of the constraints, while the other two are governed by one constraint only.

(a) **Bats and stumps**

Let c be the contribution, x be the number of bats, y be the number of sets of stumps.
Objective:
Maximise.............. $c = 8x + 5y$
Subject to: .... $x + 3y \leqslant 6{,}000$
$$5x + 2y \leqslant 10{,}500$$
$$x, y \geqslant 0$$

The graph gives the solution:
$$x = 1{,}500, \quad y = 1{,}500$$

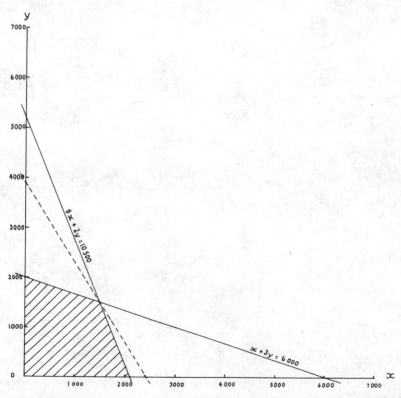

(b) **Gloves and pads**

	Gloves £	Pads £
Contribution per unit	1	11
Contribution per labour hour	2	1.83

Therefore all 500 hours should be used to make gloves.

Optimal production plan

Products	Numbers	Contribution £
Bats	1,500	12,000
Stumps	1,500	7,500
Gloves	1,000	1,000

Index

Page numbers in roman type refer to questions, and those in *italics* to answers.

Subcontractors, invoices related to sales
  invoices   127, *133*
Supervisory labour
  graph of expense   6, *9, 10*
  wages, accounting treatment   31, *36*

Total absorption costing   43
Trading accounts
  budgeted   140, 146-7, *151, 162*
  effect of differing methods of pricing issues
    15, *23-4*
  forecasts   141-2, *155*
  reconciling actual and budgeted profit
    170-1, *181-2, 183-4*
  with subcontracted contracts   128, *133-4*

Unit costs
  calculation   48-9, *61*
    for successive manufacturing processes
      85, *89-92*
  of second-quality products   49, *62-3*
  of units completed   86, *92*
  standard   270, *275*

Variance analysis   168-75, 268-71, *176-91,*
  272-80
Variances
  capacity   174, *191*
  fixed overhead capacity   170-1, *183-6*
  labour   168, 269-70., *176, 275-7, 287*
    rate and efficiency   170-1, *183-6*
  materials   168, *176*
    direct cost   168-9, *178-9*
    mix   268, *272-3*
    price   168-71, 268-87, *178-9, 182-6,*
      272-3, 275-7

Variances: materials — *continued*
  usage   168-9, 170, 268, *178-9, 182, 272-3*
  yield   268, *272-3*
  overhead   269-70, *275-7*
  production overheads, cost, expenditure
    and volume   168-9, *178-9*
  productivity   174, *191*
  sales   170, *182*
  wages, direct cost, rate and labour
    efficiency   168-9, *178-9*

Wages
  cost calculation from standard cost data
    173, *188*
  of operators, in different circumstances
    31, *39*
  variances, cost and rate   168-9, *178-9*
  see also Piecework rates; Premium bonus
    schemes
Waste
  definition   97, *103*
  process account and ash account
    98, *106-7*
  profitability of processing   98, *105*
Weighted average   15, *21, 22*
  cost of production and value of closing
    stock   15, *25*
Work-in-progress
  closing, calculation of value   84, *88, 89*
  control accounts   174, *191*
  related to job costing   119, *123*
  value, calculation for successive processes
    85, *90-1*

Yield, variance   268, *273*

317